Lecture Notes in Economics and Mathematical Systems

511

Springer
Berlin
Heidelberg
New York
Barcelona
Hong Kong
London
Milan
Paris
Tokyo

Mathias Külpmann

Stock Market Overreaction and Fundamental Valuation

Theory and Empirical Evidence

 Springer

332.63222
K96 ⅃

Author

Dr. Mathias Külpmann
Goldman, Sachs & Co. oHG
Investment Banking Division
Friedrich-Ebert-Anlage 49 / Messe Turm
60308 Frankfurt/Main, Germany

This monograph does not necessarily represent the views of Goldman Sachs, its author retains sole reponsibility for its content.

Cataloging-in-Publication data applied for

Die Deutsche Bibliothek - CIP-Einheitsaufnahme

Külpmann, Mathias:
Stock market overreaction and fundamental valuation : theory and empirical evidence / Mathias Külpmann. - Berlin ; Heidelberg ; New York ; Barcelona ; Hong Kong ; London ; Milan ; Paris ; Singapore ; Tokyo : Springer, 2002
  (Lecture notes in economics and mathematical systems ; 511)
  ISBN 3-540-42670-1

ISSN 0075-8450
ISBN 3-540-42670-1 Springer-Verlag Berlin Heidelberg New York

JK

Springer-Verlag Berlin Heidelberg New York
a member of BertelsmannSpringer Science+Business Media GmbH

http://www.springer.de

© Springer-Verlag Berlin Heidelberg 2002
Printed in Germany

The use of general descriptive names, registered names, trademarks, etc. in this publication does not imply, even in the absence of a specific statement, that such names are exempt from the relevant protective laws and regulations and therefore free for general use.

Typesetting: Camera ready by author
Cover design: *design & production*, Heidelberg

Printed on acid-free paper   SPIN: 10852784   55/3142/du   5 4 3 2 1 0

Acknowledgements

This monograph owes a lot to Günter Franke. I am very grateful to him for constant advice and encouragement. The discussions with him have been the salt of this inquiry.

Others have helped as well. I owe the initial idea for this monograph to my former colleague Bernd Meyer. Axel Adam-Müller, Markus Herrmann, Dieter Hess, and most recently Erik Lüders and Stamen Gortchev have commented on various versions of this monograph. Econometric advice has been provided by Winfried Pohlmeier and his team, most notably Frank Gerhard. At the chair of Günter Franke, Gisela Laniecki, Elvira Grübel, and a host of student research assistants have always been helpful in creating a productive atmosphere. For personal support I would like to thank my parents.

Cambridge/M.   Mathias Külpmann

Contents

Introduction

Discovery commences with the awareness of anomaly, i.e., with the recognition that nature has somehow violated the paradigm-induced expectations that govern normal science. (Thomas Kuhn)[1]

In his book on the *Structure of Scientific Revolutions,* Thomas Kuhn has described the scientific research process as follows. Research is conducted around a central paradigm in order to test the predictions of this theory. If more and more evidence arises which contradicts the existing paradigm a new paradigm has to be found which comprises an explanation for both the new phenomena which could not be explained by the old paradigm and the old phenomena which could be explained. The search for this new paradigm is at the heart of a scientific revolution.

A central paradigm in financial economics is that capital markets are efficient. A common definition of stock market efficiency is that stock prices reflect all available information at a certain point in time. Therefore, it should not be possible to predict future stock returns from past returns. A major motivation to investigate the time series pattern of returns has always been the notion that a significant dependence in stock returns could be exploited by technical trading. The question whether stock prices are predictable has a long tradition in financial economics dating back to studies of Louis Bachelier at the beginning of the century and, better known, the work of Alfred Cowles and Holbrook Working in the 1930ies. Eugene F. Fama summarized the more recent discussion in two landmark articles in 1970 and 1991. Until 1970 the literature indicated that no intertemporal dependence could be observed which Fama interpreted as evidence for capital market efficiency. By 1991, increasing evidence had been found which indicated some form of intertemporal dependence: to some extent stock returns seem to be predictable.

One of these findings of intertemporal dependence is due to DeBondt and Thaler (1985): the winner-loser effect. The winner-loser effect is a finding of intertemporal dependence in the cross section of stock returns: stocks which have outperformed the market (the "winner" firms) tend to underperform the market subsequently, stocks which have underperformed the market (the "loser" firms) outperform the market subsequently. This finding implies that past stock returns can be used to predict future stock returns. Current stock prices do not reflect all

---

[1] Kuhn (1970), pp. 52 f.

available information and hence market efficiency seems to be violated. The old paradigm of market efficiency is challenged.

The question arises whether a new paradigm is needed to explain the winner-loser effect. According to Kuhn (1970) three ways are available to react to an anomaly which cannot be explained by the ruling paradigm (p. 84). First, science "ultimately proves able to handle the crisis-provoking problem". Then no new paradigm is needed as the problem can be solved within the old paradigm. Second, even "radical new approaches" fail to explain the anomaly. Then it is left to a "future generation with more developed tools". The third possible reaction is that the crisis ends with "a new candidate for paradigm and with the ensuing battle over its acceptance".

First one has to reconsider the concept of market efficiency. Although at first sight the winner-loser effect seems to contradict market efficiency, closer inspection reveals the following. The winner-loser effect does not contradict market efficiency as long as the difference in returns between the winner and the loser portfolio is expected. To test whether this is the case it is necessary to specify a model according to which expectations are built. Therefore, a test whether the winner-loser effect occurs in an efficient capital market can only be pursued conditional on that an asset pricing model holds.

In a first step I investigate whether asset pricing models can explain the winner-loser effect. A standard assumption of these models is that investors behave rationally in the stock market. Starting point for any model of rational asset pricing is a no arbitrage condition. Starting from this no arbitrage condition a general asset pricing model can be derived. According to this model high expected returns are due to a high exposure to systematic risk. Small expected returns are due to a small exposure. For the winner-loser effect this implies that the difference in the performance between the winner and the loser portfolio is due to a difference in the exposure to systematic risk. If conditional on past performance the loser portfolio performs better than the winner portfolio, the loser portfolio must have a higher exposure to systematic risk.

In the general asset pricing model the exposure to systematic risk is measured by the covariance with the aggregate pricing function, which is also known as the *pricing kernel*. As it is not possible to observe this aggregate pricing function, it is not possible to test for the general asset pricing model directly. To be able to test for a model of rational asset pricing it is necessary to relate stock returns to aggregate variables which are observable. From the general asset pricing model the capital asset pricing model (CAPM) can be derived under further restrictive assumptions. In the CAPM the exposure to systematic risk is measured by the covariance with the market return. For the winner-loser effect this implies that the difference between the winner and the loser portfolio must be due to differences in the covariance with the market return. This is the first explanation of the winner-loser effect which I explore.

It turns out that within the CAPM only part of the winner-loser effect can be explained. Although I observe differences in the exposure to systematic risk for the winner and the loser portfolio these differences are not sufficient to explain the winner-loser effect. Therefore, the question arises whether a new paradigm is available which can explain the winner-loser effect better. An alternative explanation of the winner-loser effect is that the observed return reversals are due to irrational behaviour of market participants. This proposition has already been made by DeBondt and Thaler (1985). They interpreted their findings as evidence of an overreaction to news announcements. When positive news is incorporated into stock prices, investors become too optimistic. In the same way negative news induces investors to become too pessimistic. This causes persistence in short-term returns. After longer time horizons investors realize that they have been misled and readjust stock prices to their fundamental values. This causes long-term reversals in stock returns.

One possible way to explore the pattern of news announcements is to relate the pattern of stock returns to movements in fundamentals such as dividends and profits. The pattern of news announcements for the winner portfolio should be as follows. After a period of positive news investors become too optimistic. Afterwards investors are disappointed due to a series of unexpected negative news. If these news are reflected in profits, a period of increases in profits should be followed by a period of decreases. The reverse pattern should obtain for the loser portfolio. A period of negative news announcements is followed by a period of positive news announcements. A period of decreases in profits should be followed by a period of profit improvements. This is the second explanation which I pursue in this monograph.

The main finding of this monograph is that this pattern can indeed be observed. For the winner-loser effect the pattern of portfolio returns is parallelled by changes in fundamentals. These findings support the new paradigm of irrational behaviour of market participants. The days of the old paradigm of market efficiency seem to have passed. However, it turns out that this conclusion is not coercive.

The relationship between stock returns and fundamentals can also be interpreted in an alternative way. In a framework of rational asset pricing changes in fundamentals might also proxy for changes in the exposure to systematic risk. According to this interpretation an increase in profits for the loser portfolio indicates an increase in systematic risk. A decrease in profits for the winner portfolio indicates a decrease in systematic risk. This second interpretation seems to be at odds with the failure of the CAPM to explain the winner-loser effect. However, compared with the general asset pricing model, the CAPM relies on restrictive assumptions which might be violated. The CAPM might capture the exposure to systematic risk only imperfectly. In that case the winner-loser effect might still occur within the general asset pricing model.

The main finding of this monograph can be interpreted both from the point of view of the old paradigm and from the point of view of the new paradigm. Unfortunately, so far it is not possible to decide which of the interpretations is appropriate. The question, whether the old paradigm of efficient markets or the new paradigm of irrational behaviour of investors describes the behaviour of stock markets better, remains unresolved. The only way to answer this question is to find a way to test for the general asset pricing model directly. Otherwise, the results for the old paradigm always depend on the restrictive specification of the asset pricing model. As long as no possibility is available to test for the general asset pricing model directly, both the old and the new paradigm offer possible explanations of stock market behaviour. As neither the old nor the new paradigm is clearly superior to explain the winner-loser effect, we are left with the second possibility of the three possibilities which Thomas Kuhn has outlined how to react to an anomaly. A final explanation of the winner-loser effect has to be left to a "future generation with more developed tools" (Kuhn (1970), p. 84).

Outline
The analysis is presented in three parts. In the first part I present evidence for the winner-loser effect for German data. In the second part the main question of this monograph is pursued. I investigate whether the winner-loser effect occurs within a framework of rational asset pricing. In the third part I go one step further. I investigate whether long-term reversals in fundamentals are due to temporary problems of corporate control.

The first part presents evidence for long-term reversals in the cross section of stock returns. First, I review the literature on the winner-loser effect (chapter 1), then I present my own investigation (chapter 2).

Starting from the seminal paper of DeBondt and Thaler (1985) the winner-loser effect has been observed for many national stock markets. From an economic point of view the decisive question is whether the winner-loser effect occurs within a framework of rational asset pricing. Alternatively already DeBondt and Thaler (1985) claimed that the winner-loser effect is due to irrational behaviour of investors. Recently, more elaborate theories of irrational behaviour have been developed. I review this literature in chapter 1.

Chapter 2 presents my own investigation of the winner-loser effect for German data from 1968 to 1986. Starting point of my investigation is the research design which has been proposed by DeBondt and Thaler (1985). First, I investigate the winner-loser hypothesis of long-term reversals in the cross section of stock returns within the setting of DeBondt and Thaler. In addition, I present a complementary method of investigation. I investigate the probabilities by which loser stocks become winner stocks and vice versa. For both methods I obtain supportive evidence for the winner-loser effect.

In the second part of my investigation the main question is whether it is possible to explain the winner-loser effect within a framework of rational asset pricing. In chapter 3, I present the theoretical framework, chapters 4–6 present the results of my empirical analysis.

The theoretical framework is developed in chapter 3 in three steps. First, I investigate the winner-loser effect within a framework of rational asset pricing. I derive the general asset pricing model from a condition of no arbitrage and present the CAPM as a special case. In the general asset pricing model stock returns are related to an aggregate pricing variable. In the CAPM stock returns are related to the market return. Alternatively, stock returns can be related to fundamentals such as dividends and profits. I present two interpretations of this relationship. The first is that unexpected changes in fundamentals drive unexpected returns. According to this interpretation the winner-loser effect is due to a surprise effect: After a period of good performance of the winner stocks investors are surprised by their subsequent underperformance. After a period of poor performance of the loser stocks investors are surprised by their subsequent overperformance. The difference in returns between the winner and the loser portfolio is due to unexpected changes in the fundamental performance. This relationship is explored in the second part of chapter 3. In the last part of chapter 3 I present an alternative interpretation of the relationship between stock returns and fundamentals. I investigate this relationship in a framework of rational asset pricing. Expected changes in fundamentals are related to expected stock returns. It turns out that fundamentals might also proxy for the exposure to systematic risk.

Empirically, I relate the winner-loser effect to two sets of explanatory variables. In chapter 4, I investigate to which extent the CAPM is able to explain the winner-loser effect. The CAPM turns out to explain the winner-loser effect only imperfectly. Although I find differences in the CAPM-β across portfolios these differences are not sufficient to explain the winner-loser effect. In chapter 5, I relate stock returns to movements in fundamentals such as dividends and profits. The main finding in this section is that stock returns and changes in fundamentals move in parallel. For the winner portfolio I observe a period of increases in profits which is followed by a period of decreases. For the loser portfolio the reverse pattern can be observed. A period of decreases is followed by a period of increases. In chapter 6 I compare the explanatory power of fundamentals and the CAPM-β directly. For the cross section of stock returns the explanatory power of the CAPM can almost be neglected whereas fundamentals have significant explanatory power.

Unfortunately, these findings do not allow to decide whether the winner-loser effect occurs within a framework of rational asset pricing. Although the CAPM fails to explain the winner-loser effect this might be due to the restrictive assumptions of the CAPM. The winner-loser effect might still occur within the more general framework of rational asset pricing.

In the third part of the analysis I go one step further (chapter 7). If returns are driven by movements in fundamentals the question arises which is the reason for the observed reversals in fundamentals. My hypothesis is that long-term reversals in fundamentals are driven by temporary problems of corporate control. Periods of tight management control are followed by periods of loose control. Tight management control encourages management to show better performance. Afterwards it becomes difficult for the shareholders to encourage management to continue excellent performance as management will always point to its former merits. For the loser firms a period of poor management performance induces a tightening of management control. I investigate this hypothesis by means of accounting variables. The idea of the analysis is that problems of corporate control are due to an excessive free cash flow which is at the disposition of the management. The problem of an excessive free cash-flow is related to variables of financial decision making such as the debt-equity ratio and the payout ratio for dividends. This final chapter opens a new field of research which is at the intersection of asset pricing theory and the theory of corporate governance.

I The Winner-Loser Effect

Intertemporal dependence in stock returns has always been a subject of interest to financial economists. At the center of this investigation is a special finding of intertemporal dependence which is due to DeBondt and Thaler. They observed reversals over long horizons in the cross section of stock returns. Former overperforming stocks (the *winner* stocks) underperform the market subsequently and vice versa. This pattern is called the *winner-loser effect* and after the initial observation of DeBondt and Thaler (1985) it has been observed for many national stock markets.[2] This section first presents a review of the literature on the winner-loser effect (chapter 1). My own investigation for a German data set is presented in chapter 2.

---

[2] In this monograph I restrict my attention to this observation of reversals in the cross section of stock returns. Other types of reversals are observed by Poterba and Summers (1988), who report reversals in index returns, and Fama and French (1988), who report reversals for industry returns and size sorted portfolios.

1 Literature

This chapter first reviews the methodology and the main findings of the winner-loser effect in the literature. Second, I relate these findings to the concept of market efficiency. Then I review three types of explanations which have been proposed in the literature. Finally, I have a more detailed look at those papers which are most closely related to my own investigation.

1.1
Methodology

To investigate intertemporal dependence in stock returns DeBondt and Thaler used the following research methodology. The performance of the available stocks is observed during the *formation period*. After the formation period stocks are sorted according to their performance: portfolios of equal size are built such that the best stocks are in the first portfolio (the *winner portfolio*), the next best stocks are in the second portfolio and so forth. The worst performing stocks are sorted into the *loser portfolio*. After the formation period the performance of the stocks during the subsequent *test period* is observed by looking at the average return on each portfolio. The test period is chosen to be of equal length as the formation period.

If all information is reflected in current stock prices there should be no difference in the performance of winner and loser firms. Using data from the New York Stock Exchange for the period from January 1930 to December 1982, DeBondt and Thaler found evidence for short-term persistence and long-term reversals in stock returns. For a short formation period and a subsequent short test period the loser portfolio performed worse than the winner portfolio. For a long formation period and a subsequent long test period the loser portfolio performed better than the winner portfolio. For their sample DeBondt and Thaler found substantial differences in returns. For an investment horizon of 3 years the winner portfolio outperformed the loser portfolio by 24.6%, for 5 years by 31.9%. In addition DeBondt and Thaler also investigated shorter investment horizons. For one year the winner portfolio outperformed the loser portfolio by 7.6%.

Following DeBondt and Thaler the winner-loser effect has also been investigated for other stock markets and for other investment horizons. The results have been similar. For the German stock market Stock (1990), Schiereck and Weber (1995) and the most extensive study, Meyer (1994), have found evidence for significant long-term reversals. Stock (1990) investigates only the most liquid 41 stocks of the German stock market, Schiereck and Weber (1995) as well as Meyer (1994) rely on broad samples from the German stock market. All studies find a similar pattern of short-term momentum for 1 year and reversals for investment horizons which are larger than two years. Similar findings have been found for Belgium (Vermaelen and Verstringe (1986)), Spain (Alonso and Rubio (1990)), and Switzerland (Dressendörfer (1998)).[3]

At first sight the winner-loser effect contradicts market efficiency. Past returns can be used to predict future returns. Before I have a closer look at the investigations which are most closely related to my own investigation I first have a closer look at the concept of market efficiency. Then I turn to the explanations of the winner-loser effect which have been advanced in the literature.

1.2
Market Efficiency

The winner-loser effect is a special form of intertemporal dependence in stock returns. Intertemporal dependence in stock returns does imply that past information can be used to draw inference on future returns. The interesting question from an economic point of view is whether this implies an inefficiency of the capital market. In the theoretical discussion it first seemed possible to link intertemporal dependence in stock returns to problems of capital market efficiency directly. Samuelson (1965) showed that under the assumption of risk neutrality stock prices have to follow a martingale.[4] From an empirical perspective Fama (1970) introduced the concept of market efficiency and related it to Samuelson's finding. His basic idea was that if capital markets are efficient, all the information in some information set Φ is "fully reflected" in security prices. Following a distinction due to Roberts (1967), Fama (1970) distinguished between different information sets. If the information set consists of past prices, this implies *weak* form market efficiency. The question whether a broader information set can be used to predict stock returns is the subject of more general concepts of market efficiency. For the *semi-strong* form of market efficiency the information set also includes other information which is publicly available. In addition insider information is included for the *strong* form of market efficiency. In the sense of Fama (1970) the winner-loser effect rejects weak form market efficiency. Fama linked his idea of market efficiency to Samuelson's insight that stock prices should follow a

---

[3] Shorter investment horizons have been investigated by Jegadeesh (1990) and Jegadeesh and Titman (1993). For a data set from the US they found that daily, weekly, and monthly returns show negative autocorrelation. For an investment horizon of 3 to 12 months they report positive autocorrelation (Jegadeesh and Titman (1993), Bernard and Thomas (1990)). Schiereck and Weber (1995) obtain the same finding for the German stock market.

[4] Strictly speaking, forward prices follow a martingale. Under the assumption of risk neutrality stock prices have to be discounted by the risk-free rate and hence follow a submartingale. For a more detailed exposition cf. Chapter 3 of this monograph.

martingale. Hence, market efficiency and intertemporal dependence seemed to be linked directly.

However, as it turned out afterwards both insights were flawed. For the theoretical insight of Samuelson the assumption of risk neutrality turned out to be crucial (LeRoy (1973)). Fama's formal statement of market efficiency suffered from a tautology (LeRoy (1989), p. 1593). In Fama's definition not returns themselves had to follow a fair game but the variable $y_{t+1} = p_{t+1} - E(p_{t+1} \mid \Phi_t)$. However, this follows already from the law of iterated expectations and has to be true by definition. In his book '*Foundations of Finance*' Fama (1976) presented a new definition which explicitly includes the notion of rational expectations. His definition has two components: (1) all relevant information should be reflected in security prices, (2) the capital market should act as if it had rational expectations. Rational expectations imply that expectations become true on average. To test for rational expectations, it is necessary to specify a model according to which expectations are built.

Although this was already a major step forward in the understanding of market efficiency, the full insight into the relationship between market efficiency and the martingale model was only to be achieved in the ensuing theoretical discussion. It turned out that asset prices do not need to follow a martingale under the true probabilities, but under a newly defined probability measure which is a result of the asset pricing model. This insight was most clearly stated by Harrison and Kreps (1979): Under the condition of no-arbitrage a probability measure has to exist under which prices follow a martingale. This probability measure is called the equivalent martingale measure.[5] To test for market efficiency two possibilities are available. One can derive the equivalent martingale measure and test for the martingale property or one can test for the asset pricing model directly. In both cases one faces the problem of joint hypotheses: market efficiency and asset pricing theory can only be tested together. Therefore, Fama (1991) concluded that "it is a disappointing fact that, because of the joint-hypothesis problem, precise inferences about the degree of market efficiency are likely to remain impossible." (p. 1576)

1.3
The Winner-Loser Effect: Explanations

Three approaches have been pursued in the literature to explain the winner-loser effect. The first approach is a purely empirical one. Dependent on the investment horizon the pattern of intertemporal dependence has been related to different explanatory variables. For short-term horizons the pattern in stock returns has been related to the bid-ask spread[6] and lead-lag effects across stocks. For long-term

---

[5] A famous application of this change of measure was developed earlier by Black and Scholes (1973). To price options they transformed the fundamental stochastic differential equation such that it excluded the stochastic part. This implied a newly defined probability measure under which stock prices had to follow a martingale.

[6] As this monograph is mainly concerned with long-term dependence I do not review this literature here. The main arguments can be found in Roll (1984).

reversals it has been related to the size effect and other market anomalies. The question of capital market efficiency is addressed directly in the second and third approach. The second approach tries to reconcile the observed pattern in stock returns with standard asset pricing theory. The third approach resorts to irrational behaviour of a part of the market participants.

I start with the *empirical* explanations. Long-term reversals in stock returns have been related to capital market anomalies. *Anomalies* in stock returns are features of the time-series behaviour of stock returns which are not in line with capital market theory. Well-known in the literature are seasonal anomalies: turn-of-the-week, turn-of-the-month and turn-of-the-year effect. Because of the long run character of the winner-loser effect, only the turn-of-the-year effect may be relevant. However, as the winner-loser effect is concerned with cross-sectional features it cannot be explained by a pure time-series phenomenon as the turn-of-the-year effect. Still an interaction between the turn-of-the-year effect and the winner-loser effect has been observed: Half of the return of an arbitrage portfolio based on the winner-loser effect is obtained in January (Meyer (1994), p. 93). Another anomaly to which the winner-loser effect has been related is the *size effect*. The size effect, which first has been investigated by Banz (1981) and has been reported by many studies since, states that companies with a small size in general show a better performance than companies with a larger size. Size has also been found to be a significant factor in models of multi-factor explanations (Fama and French (1996)). The evidence for size as an explanatory factor for long-term reversals is mixed. Zarowin (1989) has claimed that the winner-loser effect coincides with the size effect. Also Schiereck and Weber (1995) cannot exclude that the size effect drives the winner-loser effect (p. 22). However, Meyer (1994) does not find any evidence for a larger fraction of small firms in the loser portfolio. Meyer (1994) and Chopra, Lakonishok, and Ritter (1992) report a different type of interaction between the size effect and the winner-loser effect. They observe that long-term reversals are more exacerbated for smaller firms than for large firms. In addition a theoretical argument can be made why size cannot offer a complete explanation of long-term reversals. From a theoretical point of view Meyer (1994) (p. 94) has pointed out that even if the size effect were able to explain part of the excess return during the test period it is not clear how the reverse behaviour during the formation period arises. Even if there is some evidence for an interaction between the size effect and the winner-loser effect during the test period, for the formation period the implications of the winner-loser effect go into the wrong direction. Hence, although the majority of studies finds an interaction between the size effect and negative long-term autocorrelation in stock returns, the size effect is not likely to be the driving force behind long run reversals in stock returns.

More fundamentally, relating the winner-loser effect to other market anomalies suffers from a methodological problem. Anomalies characterize that part of the return distribution that we do not understand. By relating the winner-loser effect to other market anomalies we do not really obtain an explanation of the observed behaviour, but connect our fields of ignorance.

One further empirical explanation which has been advanced in the literature for the observed pattern in stock returns are lead-lag effects across stocks. For short-term horizons of one week, Lo and MacKinlay (1990) report weak negative autocorrelation for portfolios whereas index returns show strong positive auto-correlation. The positive autocorrelation in index returns must then be driven by positive correlation across portfolios, which add up to the market portfolio. If the intertemporal covariance matrix for portfolio returns is denoted by $\Omega(k) = E\left[\left(R_{t-k} - \mu \right)\left(R_t - \mu \right)' \right]$ the first-order autocorrelation can be denoted by

$$\frac{Cov\left[R_{m,t-1}, R_{m,t} \right]}{Var\left[R_{m,t} \right]} = \frac{\iota'\Omega(1)\iota}{\iota'\Omega(0)\iota} = \frac{tr\left(\Omega(1) \right)}{\iota'\Omega(0)\iota} + \frac{\iota'\Omega(1)\iota - tr\left(\Omega(1) \right)}{\iota'\Omega(0)\iota}$$

where R_m denotes the return on an equally weighted market index, tr the trace of the matrix, and ι a unit vector (Campbell, Lo, and MacKinlay (1997), p. 74). The trace of a matrix is the sum of its elements along its main diagonal. Therefore, it captures autocorrelations of portfolio returns whereas the term on the right hand side captures the cross-autocorrelations. Negative autocorrelation in portfolio re-turns and positive autocorrelation in index returns then implies that the cross-autocorrelations have to be positive and their sum has to be larger than the absolute sum of the negative autocorrelations in portfolio returns. Negative auto-correlation implies *lead-lag* effects in portfolios. Campbell, Lo, and MacKinlay (1997) report that returns in large stocks lead returns in small stocks.[7]

The most straightforward way how to explain the intertemporal pattern in stock returns is to relate it to a model of intertemporal asset pricing. We can distinguish between theoretical approaches and their empirical implementation. From *in-tertemporal asset pricing models* it is well known that in efficient capital markets asset prices do not have to follow a random walk (LeRoy (1973), Lucas (1978)). Moreover it has been shown that this property can only be expected under quite restrictive assumptions (Franke (1984), Bick (1990), Stapleton and Subrah-manyam (1990)). However, until now an appropriate model for the explanation of the observed pattern of autocorrelations of asset returns has not been developed. Assuming constant absolute risk aversion and an autoregressive process for aggre-gate income, LeRoy (1973) has derived a mean reverting process for market re-turns. This model can be used for an explanation of the time series behaviour of aggregate returns. A fully specified model for the case of several tradable assets, which derives the pricing process of single assets from the underlying cash-flow

---

[7] Although this is an important factor for the explanation of index returns, this effect is not likely to play a big role for the explanation of the winner-loser effect. For the winner-loser effect I do not discuss the properties of index returns. I am only concerned with the cross-section of stock returns. Starting point for my investigation are portfolio returns which I do not disaggregate further. Disaggregation of performance related portfolios might not be economically meaning-ful. An alternative decomposition into industry portfolios is more promising. Industry compo-nents are likely to play an important role for the transmission between individual stock returns and the business cycle. However, in a preliminary analysis I have extracted industry compo-nents from my portfolios which did not show much explanatory power.

processes, has been developed by Stapleton and Subrahmanyam (1978). Unfortunately, this multi-period CAPM relies on restrictive assumptions and because of its complicated structure an empirical investigation is still missing.

Instead of a full intertemporal specification, in the *empirical literature* it has been tested whether a sequence of one period asset pricing models is able to explain the observed pattern in stock returns. In any rational asset pricing model expected returns should compensate for the exposure to systematic risk. The idea of the 'change in risk' hypothesis is that the exposure to systematic risk varies over time: For the loser portfolio a period of low exposure is followed by a period of high exposure. The winner portfolio shows the reversed pattern. One problem in testing the 'change in risk' hypothesis is that one has to specify an asset pricing model in order to estimate exposure to systematic risk. Therefore, a test of the 'change in risk' hypothesis is always a joint hypothesis test including the underlying asset pricing model. In a model which is based on the idea of no arbitrage, systematic risk is measured by the covariance between the return and the pricing kernel, $\text{cov}(R_i, \phi)$. Empirically, ϕ is not observable and therefore, one has to rely on more restrictive asset pricing models. The empirical literature on the winner-loser effect has used the CAPM as a reference model, in which systematic risk is captured by $\text{cov}(R_i, R_M)$. An alternative model which could be used to capture the exposure to systematic risk is the arbitrage pricing theory (APT) where the exposure to systematic risk is measured by the covariance with respect to various risk factors, F_j, $\text{cov}(R_i, R_{F(j)})$. The 'change in risk' hypothesis has been put forward most forcefully by Chan (1988). The evidence for this claim has been mixed. DeBondt and Thaler (1987) could not find any evidence for a difference in risk across portfolios. Although some of the earlier studies reported supportive evidence (Chan (1988) and Ball and Kothari (1989)), later studies did not support these results (Alonso and Rubio (1990), Chopra, Lakonishok, and Ritter (1992)). Meyer (1994) reports different results for different period lengths.

Lacking a clear-cut explanation in the framework of standard capital market theory an *alternative to* the postulate of *rational behaviour* has already been introduced by DeBondt and Thaler (1985). In psychological experiments Kahnemann and Tversky (1982) found out that people tend to overreact to unexpected news, thereby violating Bayes' law. Based on these findings DeBondt and Thaler (1985) proposed the following explanation of the winner-loser effect. Investors overstate the importance of current unexpected news: Stock prices move more than is justified by movements in fundamentals. After a while investors realize that stock prices are out of line with fundamentals, asset prices are again adjusted to fundamentals. As a consequence a positive excess return is followed by a negative excess return and vice versa. This explanation is in conflict with the postulate of rational economic behaviour. An asset allocation strategy which is in line with fundamentals for the entire period clearly dominates the strategy described above. It is not clear why economic agents should not prefer this strategy.

Recently, more sophisticated models of irrational behaviour of market participants have been proposed in the literature. In Barberis, Shleifer, and Vishny (1998) people suffer from the following misconception. People believe that corporate earnings switch between two states. In the first state earnings show mean reversion, in the second they show momentum. However, the true process for corporate earnings is a random walk. In a model of Bayesian updating people use the information in every period to update their prior beliefs. If an increase in earnings is followed by another increase in earnings the investor enhances the probability to be in the 'momentum' state of the economy. In a series of simulations Barberis et al. show that the model can create the observed pattern in returns. A different model is proposed by Daniel, Hirshleifer, and Subrahmanyam (1998). Their model relies on investor overconfidence and biased self-attribution. An investor is defined to be overconfident, "if he overestimates the precision of his private information signal." (p. 1841) Biased self-attribution leads the investor to increase his confidence if he receives supportive public evidence, but leads him to accept contradictory public evidence only reluctantly. However, as more and more public information becomes available eventually the stock price drops back to its fundamental value.

Whereas these models are based on a representative investor framework, the following two models rely on heterogeneous investors. DeLong, Shleifer, Summers, and Waldmann (1990) (DSSW) distinguish between three types of investors. Passive investors and informed rational speculators pursue rational trading strategies. The element of irrationality comes into the model due to positive feedback rules. The idea of DSSW is that informed rational speculators push the prices of stocks beyond the values which are justified by fundamentals. The positive feedback traders are likely to enter the market after a trend has been initiated by the informed rational speculators. By this strategy the informed rational speculators try to exploit the positive feedback traders. Of course, this model only works at the cost that the positive feedback traders make permanent losses. Hong and Stein (1997) develop a similar model where investors rely on different amounts of information. *Newswatchers* rely only on fundamentals, *momentum traders* rely only on price information. As in the work of DSSW price movements are initiated by investors who rely on fundamental information. However, Hong and Stein assume that newswatchers underreact to new information. In a second step momentum traders induce price momentum and a subsequent overshooting. In their model neither group of investors makes permanent losses.

Although at least some of the models presented seem to present a plausible explanation, models which rely on irrational behaviour of market participants all suffer from a serious draw-back. As a convincing concept of bounded rationality is still missing, the models relying on psychological explanations suffer from the problem of ad-hoc assumptions. The inherent problem of models of irrational behaviour is that they do not restrict the set of admissible observations. Almost any possible observation can be explained by means of irrational behaviour. This is a problem from a methodological point of view. A theory which potentially explains everything is likely to explain nothing (Sutton (1990)).

1.4
A More Detailed Look at the Literature

Before I turn to the results of my own investigation I have a closer look at five studies of the winner-loser effect which are closely related to my own investigation. Starting point for any investigation of the winner-loser effect are the two seminal papers by DeBondt and Thaler in the *Journal of Finance* from 1985 and 1987. The first paper reports the discovery of the winner-loser effect. The second is concerned with an explanation of this observation. Afterwards I turn to the three studies for the German stock market. The first paper which concentrates on a small sample is due to Stock (1990). More encompassing studies have been pursued by Meyer (1994) and Schiereck and Weber (1995).

In the previous section I have already shown that different explanations for the winner-loser effect have been provided in the literature. In the empirical literature the winner-loser effect has been related to three groups of explanatory variables. The first group refers to models of rational asset pricing. In particular it has been investigated whether the CAPM is able to explain the observed excess return. The second group refers to market anomalies. The seasonal pattern of the winner-loser effect has been explored and the winner-loser effect has been related to other explanatory variables such as the size of a company. The third group of variables refers to the hypothesis of irrational behaviour of market participants. All three types of explanatory variables are investigated by the subsequent papers. My own investigation focusses on the first and the third group of variables.

DeBondt and Thaler (1985)
For their investigation DeBondt and Thaler rely on monthly return data for common stocks from the New York Stock Exchange (NYSE) from 1926 to 1982 which they obtain from the CRSP data file. The number of firms which are included into the dataset increases over time from 347 to 1089. For period lengths of 1, 2, 3, and 5 years they investigate the performance of extreme portfolios. For 3 years the winner portfolio is defined by the 35 stocks which perform best during the formation period, the loser portfolio by 35 stocks which perform worst. For 5 years the number of stocks is increased to 50. The difference in returns between the winner and the loser portfolio is exploited by taking a long position in the loser portfolio and by taking a short position in the winner portfolio. This portfolio is called the winner-loser portfolio. The total return is obtained by adding up the excess returns on these two positions. Strictly speaking, this is not a return as this strategy does not require any capital. The return is calculated on the capital which is invested into the loser portfolio and which is financed by selling the winner portfolio.

For 3 years DeBondt and Thaler find an excess return of 24.6%, for 5 years of 31.9%. This long-term effect is called the winner-loser effect. In addition DeBondt and Thaler also investigate shorter investment horizons. For a two year period no significant results are obtained, whereas for a one year period they observe momentum: Former winner firms outperform former loser firms by 7.6% p.a. In addition the pattern of the winner-loser effect shows the following characteristic aspects. First, the winner-loser effect is asymmetric (p. 799). As compared to an equally weighted index most of the excess return is obtained for the loser portfolio. Second, DeBondt and Thaler observe a strong seasonality. Most of the return is obtained during January. In particular, the loser portfolio shows a strong overperformance during that month.

Two questions of methodology are already raised in this initial contribution. The first concerns the use of overlapping versus non-overlapping samples. The data can be pooled in two different ways. In the case that a non-overlapping sample is used the return periods which are investigated do not intersect. In the case of an overlapping sample the return periods do intersect. E.g., for a 5 year horizon in the overlapping case returns from 1968–1972 are pooled with returns from 1969–1973. In the non-overlapping case only returns from 1968–1972 are pooled with returns from 1973–1977. As DeBondt and Thaler rely on a sample period of more than 50 years the main results which they report are based on a non-overlapping sample. In addition they present graphical evidence for the case of overlapping data (p. 803). The qualitative results appear to be the same, although the overlapping results appear to be smoothed. "The effect of multiplying the number of applications is to remove part of the random noise." (p. 803)

The second methodological question in the analysis of the winner-loser effect is whether the excess return is adjusted for the exposure to systematic risk. The excess return is calculated as

$$\text{Excess Return} = R_i - E(R_i).$$

where the expected return $E(R_i)$ can be calculated in different ways. In the reference case which DeBondt and Thaler report in their paper the expected return is calculated as the average performance of the sample during the test period. A more accurate way how to determine the expected return from the point of view of economic theory is to use a model which accounts for the exposure to systematic risk.

Although they do not state their results explicitly DeBondt and Thaler (1985) refer to two models according to which they have also calculated excess returns, first the market model which relates stock returns to the return on the market in a linear way, and the CAPM. For the CAPM the following regression equation is investigated

$$R_i - R_f = \beta_i (R_M - R_f) + \varepsilon_i$$

where R_f denotes the risk-free rate and R_M denotes the market rate of return, ε is an error term. β_i captures the exposure to systematic risk. At the end of the formation period DeBondt and Thaler find that β_i for the loser firms is smaller than for the winner firms and hence the loser firms bear less systematic risk. The expected return on the loser portfolio is actually less than the expected return on the winner portfolio. This implies that their previous results which do not account for risk understate the winner-loser effect.

DeBondt and Thaler (1987)

Whereas the focus of the first paper from 1985 is on the description of the winner-loser effect, in their second paper DeBondt and Thaler investigate different possibilities how to explain the winner-loser effect. They relate returns to additional explanatory variables. In the first part of the paper they investigate the seasonal pattern and reinvestigate the exposure to systematic risk in a CAPM framework. In the second part, they relate the observed pattern to size and earnings per share.

A large part of the excess return is obtained during January. At first sight this seems to be a special observation of the *turn of the year* or *January effect*. However, this is not the case. According to the turn of the year effect during January an additional return is obtained on the entire market portfolio. If both winner and loser portfolios benefit from the turn of the year effect to the same extent, this should have no effect on the winner-loser effect. For the winner-loser effect this effect would disappear as a long position in the loser portfolio is financed by a short position in the winner portfolio. Therefore, the seasonal pattern of the winner-loser effect is an additional finding. The seasonal pattern is due to an additional return on the loser portfolio in January.

In addition, DeBondt and Thaler reinvestigate whether it is possible to explain the winner-loser effect within the CAPM. In their previous paper they estimated β only for the formation period. Investigating the difference in β during the test period they observe a difference between the winner and the loser portfolio of 0.22 which is too low to explain the observed excess return. DeBondt and Thaler weaken this evidence further as they estimate the β for an up market and for a down market separately. They report a positive β for the winner-loser portfolio in an up market and a negative β in a down market. This implies that the winner-loser portfolio should perform well both when the market is down and when the market is up. As such a portfolio is not particularly risky it remains unclear why it should earn an extra return.

In the second part of the paper DeBondt and Thaler relate the winner-loser effect to additional explanatory variables. They investigate differences across portfolios with respect to size, the market to book ratio and earnings yields. In addition they investigate the intertemporal development of earnings per share and other firm characteristics.

They do not find any particular pattern in terms of the size distribution. The average size of a company in any of the portfolios is approximately the same. However, they do find significant differences with respect to two other characteristics. At the end of the formation period loser firms show lower market to book ratios and lower earning yields. Therefore, DeBondt and Thaler conclude that "it seems more apt to characterize the winner-loser effect as an overvalued-undervalued effect" (p. 574). To corroborate this claim they also provide evidence for the intertemporal development of earnings per share. For the loser portfolio they observe a significant decrease during the formation period and an increase during the subsequent test period. For the winner portfolio they observe the reverse pattern. DeBondt and Thaler interpret these findings "to be consistent with the simple behavioural view that investors overreact to short-term (...) earnings movements." (p. 579)

They also report evidence for the development of the market value, total assets, and the market to book ratio, both during the formation and during the test period. For the loser firms they observe a steady increase in market value as well as in total assets. For the winner portfolio the opposite behaviour can be observed. Also the behaviour of the market to book ratio differs across portfolios. For the loser firms this ratio decreases during the formation period and increases afterwards. For the winner portfolio during both periods a steady increase can be observed. However, DeBondt and Thaler do not investigate the implications of these find- ings further. As this last part of their analysis is not led by hypotheses, it suffers from the problem of *data mining*. Any sample data set will show certain charac- teristics. However, as long as no hypothesis is pursued in the analysis these prop- erties remain economically meaningless.

The winner-loser effect has been reinvestigated for the German stock market in three studies. All three investigations are based on much smaller samples than the analysis of DeBondt and Thaler. All three investigations differ in emphasis and scope.

Stock (1990)

A study which focusses on the most liquid segment of the stock market is the in- vestigation by Stock (1990). His sample consists of 41 stocks from 1973–1989. This sample represents all stocks which were accepted for option trading in 1983. In 1981 about 75% of the trading volume were concentrated in these stocks. Stock investigates the hypothesis of long-term reversals for investment horizons of 1 to 5 years. For a horizon of 1 year Stock (1990) observes momentum. For a portfolio which buys the 5 best performing stocks and sells the 5 worst performing stocks he obtains a return of 5.82%. Increasing return reversals are obtained for periods of 3, 4, and 5 years. For these investment horizons a portfolio which buys the 5 worst performing and sells the 5 best performing stocks earns a return of 5.47%, 14.52% and 29.85% respectively. Except for the three year horizon these results are comparable to the results of DeBondt and Thaler. Stock's investigation is based on an overlapping sample. In addition he also presents evidence on a yearly base. The evidence is weaker than for the pooled sample, although in many cases it is still significant. For one year he still observes momentum in most cases, some of the results are significant. The same result is obtained for a contrarian strategy for 4 and 5 years where even more of the results are significant. In a contrarian strategy the purchase of a portfolio of former loser firms is financed by the short selling of a portfolio of former winner firms.

Stock presents nonparametric statistics. He reports the ranks of the extreme observations during the test period as compared to the formation period. Spearman rank correlation coefficients corroborate momentum for one year and reversals for more than three years. For more than three years the Spearman rank correlation coefficient becomes increasingly negative. In addition Stock provides an interesting method of investigation which uses the information both from short-term momentum and long-term reversals. All those stocks which are part of the winner and loser portfolio for the long term are eliminated which also appear in the winner and loser portfolios for the short term. This method of portfolio building increases the excess return of the winner-loser portfolio by 1 or 2 percentage points p.a.

More extensive studies of the winner-loser effect have been provided by Meyer (1994) and Schiereck and Weber (1995). They also provide some additional empirical evidence how to explain the winner-loser effect.

Meyer (1994)

The monograph by Meyer is by far the most extensive study. He investigates the hypothesis of long-term reversals for period lengths of 12, 24, 36, 60, 84, and 108 months. Meyer uses data from the Frankfurt stock exchange from 1961 to 1990. The average sample size depends on the time horizon. It differs between 159.4 stocks on average for a 12 month time horizon and 260.8 stocks for 108 months. Meyer compares portfolio returns to two indices: a value weighted performance index, the DAFOX, and an equally weighted index of the investigated sample, the GGI. In addition he varies the number of portfolios (2, 5, 10, 15, 20) to test in which way the results depend on how extreme the portfolios are.

For period lengths of 36, 60, 84, and 108 months Meyer observes reversals in the cross section of stock returns. In addition he finds that the more extreme the portfolios are, the larger the excess returns become. The largest excess return of 5,00% p.a. is obtained for a 5% quantile and a period of 60 months. Meyer investigates three additional questions.

First, Meyer investigates whether the CAPM explains the winner-loser effect (pp. 78–87). For his sample the CAPM cannot explain the winner-loser effect. The exposure of the winner-loser portfolio, which buys the loser portfolio and sells the winner portfolio short, sometimes increases from the formation to the test period (time horizons of 36 and 60 months) and sometimes it decreases (time horizons of 84 and 108 months).

In addition, Meyer (1994) investigates interactions with two other market anomalies: the January and the size effect. Similar to DeBondt and Thaler he observes a strong seasonality. Half of the returns on the winner-loser portfolio is obtained in January (p. 93). Zarowin (1989) claims that it is possible to explain the winner-loser effect by means of the size effect. According to the initial observation of Banz (1981), stocks with a smaller market capitalization earn a larger rate of return. Contrary to Zarowin, Meyer does not find any concentration of small stocks in the loser portfolio. Meyer reports a different type of interaction between the winner-loser effect and the size effect. He investigates whether the difference in returns between the winner and the loser stocks depends on size. Instead of investigating the difference between the entire winner and the entire loser portfolio he takes subportfolios according to size. He matches winner and loser firms of approximately the same size. As he reinvestigates the hypothesis of long-term reversals for these subportfolios, he observes a larger excess return for small firms.

Schiereck and Weber (1995)

The second extensive study of the winner-loser effect for the German stock market has been pursued by Schiereck and Weber (1995). The focus of their study is a bit different from the analysis of Meyer. They investigate periods of 3, 6, 12, and 60 months. Their investigation relies on data from the Frankfurt Stock exchange from 1961–1991. Contrary to Meyer their sample is based on the segment Amtlicher Handel alone. It comprises 206.67 firms on average for a one year horizon (Meyer: 260.80) and 185.36 firms for a five year horizon (Meyer: 202.85).

Also Schiereck and Weber observe short-term momentum and long-term reversals. For one year the return of the winner portfolio exceeds the return on the loser portfolio by 3.22% for portfolios of 40 stocks ($\approx$ 20% of their sample), by 7.88% for portfolios of 10 stocks ($\approx$ 5% of their sample). For a investment horizon of 5 years they observe a difference in returns between the loser and the winner portfolio of 3.11% p.a. for portfolios of 40 stocks, and a difference of 4.74% p.a. for portfolios of 10 stocks. These differences in returns are of approximately the same size as in Meyer (1994).

In addition Schiereck and Weber provide a more detailed analysis of short-term behaviour as they provide evidence for 3, 6, and 12 months. They observe almost always return momentum. They relate short-term momentum to differences in size and price across portfolios. Although Schiereck and Weber cannot find any significant difference in market capitalization across portfolios they find stocks in the loser portfolio to be cheaper in absolute terms. During the test period the price of an average winner stock is DM 435.61 as compared to DM 254.65 for the average loser stock. In addition they provide the following interesting observation. For winner stocks they observe an increase in dividends which on average is larger for winner firms than for loser firms (DM 0.72 for the winner firms as compared to DM 0.22 for the loser firms). For net profits relative to market value they obtain larger values for the winner firms than for the loser firms.

For long-term reversals Schiereck and Weber investigate the explanatory power of the CAPM. For the test period they find a difference in β of 0.17 between the winner and the loser portfolio. However, as they divide their sample period into two subperiods they observe that this result is entirely due to the first subperiod. The return on the winner-loser portfolio on the other hand occurs mainly in the second subperiod (p. 22). Therefore, the CAPM can only provide a partial explanation of the winner-loser effect at best. In addition Schiereck and Weber investigate size and price effects. With respect to size they find a significant difference between the market value of the winner portfolio of DM 1,524.8 Mio and

DM 495.2 Mio for the loser portfolio. In addition they find the price per share at the end of the formation period to be lower for the loser portfolio than for the winner portfolio (DM 483.70 to DM 151.56).

My investigation takes these investigations as a starting point. At the heart of my investigation is the question whether the winner-loser effect occurs within an efficient capital market. First, I provide a theoretical framework for the analysis of this question. So far such a framework is still missing. Empirically, I relate the winner-loser effect to two sets of explanatory variables, the CAPM β and changes in fundamentals such as dividends and profits. Starting from my theoretical framework I provide a new interpretation for the relationship between stock returns and additional explanatory variables.

1.5
Summary

Starting point for the investigation of this monograph is the observation of the winner-loser effect. For long-term horizons former winner stocks underperform the market subsequently, former loser stocks overperform it. This observation was first made by DeBondt and Thaler (1995) for the US market. As this observation has also been made for other stock markets the question arises whether it implies an inefficiency of the stock market. Stock prices have to follow a martingale in an economy with risk neutral investors. If investors show risk aversion this is no longer true. Although in a complete market a martingale measure can be found under which stock prices follow a martingale this does not hold under the true probabilities. Therefore, the question whether intertemporal dependence implies an inefficiency of the capital market can only be investigated conditional on an asset pricing model.

In the literature three approaches have been pursued to explain the winner-loser effect. First, the winner-loser effect has been related to additional explanatory variables. Long-term reversals in stock returns have been related to the size effect and to changes in risk. Although some interaction with the size effect has been observed in most studies it has not been sufficient to explain major parts of the observed excess return. Negative cross-autocorrelation has been found to play an important role for the explanation of intertemporal dependence in index returns. Second, the winner-loser effect has been related to asset pricing models. In an efficient capital market long-term reversals should be due to changes in the exposure to systematic risk. From the CAPM the evidence for changes is only week. Therefore, a convincing theory of the observed behaviour in stock returns is still missing. Alternative explanations have been proposed which do not rely on the assumption of rational investor behaviour.

2 Empirical Evidence for Germany

Starting point for my own analysis of intertemporal dependence in the German stock market is the winner-loser hypothesis of DeBondt and Thaler (1985). In this chapter I reinvestigate this hypothesis for the cross section of German stock returns from 1968 to 1986.

I investigate the winner-loser hypothesis of long-term reversals in stock returns in two different ways. First, I use the standard setting of DeBondt and Thaler which also has been used by other researchers to explore the winner-loser hypothesis. Stocks are sorted into portfolios according to their performance during a formation period. During a subsequent test period I compare the performance of the former winner portfolio with the performance of the former loser portfolio. In a second step I explore an alternative method of investigation. I calculate the probabilities by which stocks switch from one portfolio during the formation period to another portfolio during the test period. Both methods of investigation provide evidence in favour of the winner-loser hypothesis.

2.1
The Winner-Loser Hypothesis and the Dataset

2.1.1
Hypothesis

To test the winner-loser hypothesis I first use a setting which is due to DeBondt and Thaler (1985). Stocks are sorted according to their performance during a formation period and are grouped into portfolios. The 20% of all stocks which performed best during the formation period are sorted into the *winner* portfolio. The 20% of all stocks which performed worst during the formation period are sorted into the *loser* portfolio. The other stocks are sorted into the remaining three portfolios. If there is no information in past returns there should be no difference in performance between these portfolios. For most of the analysis the three middle portfolios are summarized into one middle portfolio. The winner-loser hypothesis can then be tested by means of a pairwise comparison.

In this section I investigate the following three hypotheses. First, I test whether the winner portfolio performs worse than the middle portfolio, $R_T^W < R_T^M$, where

R_T^W denotes the return on the winner portfolio during the test period and R_T^M denotes the return on the middle portfolio. If this is the case then a profitable trading strategy is available: A long position in the middle portfolio which is financed by a short position in the winner portfolio should earn a positive return on average. Second, I test in a similar way for a difference in the performance between the middle and the loser portfolio. If the winner-loser hypothesis holds then $R_T^M < R_T^L$, where R_T^L denotes the return on the loser portfolio. In that case again a profitable trading strategy is available which finances a portfolio of loser firms by a portfolio of middle firms. Third, I test for a difference in the performance between the two extreme portfolios directly. The performance of the winner portfolio is compared to the performance of the loser portfolio. According to the winner-loser hypothesis winner firms should perform worse than the loser firms: $R_T^W < R_T^L$. The trading strategy which exploits this difference in returns is known as a *contrarian* or *winner-loser* strategy. The purchase of the loser portfolio is financed by short selling of the winner portfolio. As this strategy is self-financing a return is not defined. Nevertheless, usually one refers to $R_T^L - R_T^W$ as the return on a contrarian strategy. The winner-loser hypotheses therefore can be summarized as follows.

Winner-Loser Hypothesis
Former winner firms perform worse than an average firm. Former loser firms perform better than an average firm.

$$R_T^W < R_T^M < R_T^L$$

In previous investigations it has been observed that the winner-loser hypothesis holds for period lengths of 36 months or longer (e.g., DeBondt and Thaler (1985), Meyer (1994)). For 24 months no significant results have been obtained. For shorter time horizons the reverse pattern has been observed. Former winner stocks outperform former loser stocks, $R_T^W > R_T^L$. The trading strategy which exploits this difference in returns is known as momentum strategy: The purchase of the winner portfolio is financed by short-selling of the loser portfolio. For a time horizon of 12 months I investigate whether a momentum strategy is profitable.

Short-term Momentum Hypothesis
Former winner firms perform better than an average firm. Former loser firms perform worse than an average firm.

$$R_T^W > R_T^M > R_T^L$$

If short-term persistence and long-term reversals can be observed, profitable trading strategies can be designed to exploit this pattern. The first obvious way to exploit this pattern is to invest into winner stocks in the short run and to invest into loser stocks in the long run. A more sophisticated strategy can be used to acquire the full difference in returns between the winner and the loser portfolio. Short-term persistence can be exploited by a *momentum* strategy which buys the winner portfolio and sells the loser portfolio. The reverse strategy is pursued to exploit long-term reversals. In a *contrarian* or *winner-loser* strategy the purchase of the loser portfolio is financed by short-selling of the winner portfolio. As these strategies are self-financing a return is not defined. Again, one refers to $R_T^W - R_T^L$ as the return of the strategy.

2.1.2
Dataset

For my investigation I use three sets of data. First, I use a broad sample of stock returns from the German stock market. I relate these returns to the risk free rate and the return on the market portfolio, which I need for the analysis of subsequent chapters. As the riskfree rate I use the monthly money market rate. As the market index I use the DAFOX, a value weighted index of the German stock market. Summary statistics for monthly returns are presented in table 1.

Table 1. Summary statistics for monthly returns: Money market and DAFOX

variable	mean	median	std.	skewness	kurt.
DAFOX	0.0079	0.0078	0.0418	0.1140	0.4010
riskfree rate	0.0055	0.0048	0.0023	0.7747	-0.3800

I obtain a monthly return on the market portfolio of 0.79% which is 24 basis points larger than the riskfree rate. A similar difference can be observed for the medians of the two distributions. The return on the market turns out to be substantially more volatile than the risk free rate (4.18% as compared to 0,23%). Both distributions show a slight positive skewness, the kurtosis is different in sign but of the same order of magnitude (0.40 for the DAFOX as compared to -0.38 for the risk free rate). These findings are in line with the summary statistics which are reported by Meyer (1999) (p. 118, table 6.2).

In this chapter my analysis is based on monthly return data from the Frankfurt stock exchange from 1968–1986. In later chapters I will relate the observed pattern in returns to accounting data. Return data were obtained from the *Karlsruher Kapitalmarktdatenbank (KKMD)*, accounting data from the *Jahresabschluß-datenbank Aachen*. The investigated sample is obtained from the matching of the two datasets. Corporations were included into the sample only if they were available from both data sources. To obtain a homogeneous dataset I restrict my attention to the period 1968–1986. During this period no major changes in German accounting rules have taken place. Banks and insurance companies are excluded from the sample as their balance sheet characteristics differ substantially from the balance sheets of industrial companies.

The following tables show for how many firms data is available from the KKMD (table 2) and from the Jahresabschlußdatenbank Aachen (table 3). The number of firms which is used in my investigation is considerably smaller. This is due to different reasons. The first reason is that bank and insurance companies are excluded from the sample. The second reason is the research design. Companies are only included into the sample if enough data is available both for the formation and the test period. Companies are only included into the sample if all monthly returns are available during the formation period and if data is available for at least the first month of the test period. Table 4 presents the results for the investment horizon of 5 years. From this table we can observe that only half of the Jahresabschlußdatenbank is used and only about 40% of the return data.

As I investigate only a fraction of the entire sample the question arises whether this fraction has the same properties as the entire sample. The following two tables 5 and 6 present summary statistics for monthly returns both for the entire sample from the KKMD and for the sample which I investigate. Table 5 presents summary statistics for the entire sample, table 6 presents a comparison of mean, median, and standard deviation on a yearly base.

Table 2. Number of firms available from the KKMD (stock return data)

year	#	year	#	year	#
1968	257	1975	418	1982	385
1969	257	1976	415	1983	387
1970	257	1977	408	1984	401
1971	252	1978	396	1985	409
1972	247	1979	392	1986	441
1973	240	1980	403		
1974	422	1981	385		

Table 3. Number of firms available from the Aachener Jahresabschlußdatenbank (accounting data)

year	#	year	#	year	#
1968	270	1975	281	1982	306
1969	271	1976	280	1983	310
1970	275	1977	285	1984	321
1971	275	1978	283	1985	326
1972	278	1979	285	1986	324
1973	279	1980	284		
1974	283	1981	300		

Table 4. Number of firms used in the sample

inv. horizon	#	inv. horizon	#
1968 – 1977	117	1973 – 1982	133
1969 – 1978	116	1974 – 1983	167
1970 – 1979	121	1975 – 1984	169
1971 – 1980	124	1976 – 1985	168
1972 – 1981	125	1977 – 1986	169

Table 5. Comparison between the total KKMD sample and the sample investigated: Summary Statistics for the Excess Return $(R_i - R_F)$

	mean	median	std.	skewness	kurt.
all	0.0028	0.0000	0.1419	−7.5153	319.9127
sample	0.0041	0.0000	0.1089	−10.3550	417.9081

The subsequent analysis is based on excess returns. Excess returns are calculated against the risk free rate, $R_i - R_f$. The most notable difference between the total KKMD sample and my sample is the mean. For the entire sample the mean of the monthly excess returns is 0.28% whereas for my sample it is 0.41%. The other summary statistics differ as well, but they are of the same order of magnitude. For the median I obtain a 0.00% return in both cases. The standard deviation of 14.19% is larger for the entire sample than for my subsample (10.89%). Both distributions are skewed to the left and show an excess kurtosis. For both skewness and kurtosis I obtain larger values for my sample, but both criteria are of the same order of magnitude.

Table 6 compares the two samples on a yearly base. The table is organized as follows. On the left hand side I present evidence for the entire sample from the KKMD, on the right hand side for the sample which I investigate. In the first row I present again the mean, median, and the standard deviation for the entire sample. The following rows present evidence on a yearly basis. Although there are differences between the two samples, these differences are small. Except for 1980 the sign of the mean excess return is always the same. Most of the time a large mean in one sample coincides with a large mean in the other one. The same holds with respect to the standard deviation.

By and large, the summary statistics for both samples are similar. Hence, the sample which I investigate can be taken to be representative for the entire cross section of stock returns.

Table 6. Comparison between the total KKMD sample and the sample investigated: Yearly Evidence for the Excess Return $(R_i - R_F)$

year	total			sample		
	mean	median	std. dev.	mean	median	std. dev.
Total	0.0028	0.0000	0.1419	0.0041	0.0000	0.1089
1968	0.0128	0.0035	0.0631	0.0122	0.0054	0.0577
1969	0.0239	0.0077	0.0958	0.0223	0.0091	0.0759
1970	-0.0190	-0.0124	0.0976	-0.0190	-0.0131	0.0907
1971	0.0051	0.0000	0.0895	0.0069	0.0000	0.0718
1972	0.0200	0.0101	0.0856	0.0177	0.0105	0.0935
1973	-0.0122	-0.0092	0.1389	-0.0155	-0.0104	0.1627
1974	-0.0421	0.0000	0.3490	-0.0311	-0.0093	0.2348
1975	0.0086	0.0000	0.1172	0.0144	0.0000	0.0813
1976	-0.0080	0.0000	0.1075	-0.0091	-0.0051	0.0569
1977	0.0114	0.0000	0.1089	0.0125	0.0066	0.0979
1978	0.0114	0.0000	0.1296	0.0091	0.0050	0.0842
1979	-0.0076	0.0000	0.0823	-0.0082	-0.0077	0.0769
1980	-0.0021	0.0000	0.1380	0.0005	0.0000	0.1322
1981	-0.0047	0.0000	0.0812	-0.0023	0.0000	0.0686
1982	0.0069	0.0000	0.1083	0.0097	0.0000	0.0663
1983	0.0179	0.0051	0.1273	0.0197	0.0121	0.0874
1984	0.0052	0.0000	0.1487	0.0020	0.0000	0.1371
1985	0.0237	0.0119	0.1341	0.0249	0.0127	0.0890
1986	0.0096	0.0000	0.1338	0.0078	0.0000	0.1127

The investigation is based on monthly returns which are continuously compounded,

$$R_{i,t} = \ln\left(\frac{S_{i,t}}{S_{i,t-1}}\right)$$

where $R_{i,t}$ denotes the return on a stock i, and $S_{i,t}$ the price of a stock in period t. The returns are adjusted for dividends, stock splits and other events which dilute the accurate measurement of returns.[8] Continuously compounded returns can be easily transformed into discrete returns

$$\hat{R}_{i,t} = e_{i,t}^R - 1 = \frac{S_{i,t} - S_{i,t-1}}{S_{i,t-1}}$$

where $\hat{R}_{i,t}$ denotes the return in discrete time. My investigation is based on continuously compounded returns as unlike discrete time returns they are additive in time

---

[8] The appropriate adjustment factors have been kindly provided by the *Karlsruher Kapitalmarkt Datenbank*. A detailed description how the adjustment factors are calculated is available in Sauer (1992).

$$R(t,t+2) = R(t,t+1) + R(t+1,t+2)$$

$$= \ln \frac{S_{t+1}}{S_t} + \ln \frac{S_{t+2}}{S_{t+1}} = \ln \frac{S_{t+2}}{S_t}$$

Portfolio returns are calculated by taking portfolio means

$$R_P = \frac{1}{N} \sum_{i=1}^{N} R_i \qquad (1)$$

Strictly speaking, this return is not exactly equal to the return on an equally weighted portfolio:

$$\hat{R}_P = \frac{1}{N} \sum_{i=1}^{N} \hat{R}_i$$

$$= \frac{1}{N} \sum_{i=1}^{N} (e^{R_i} - 1) \neq e^{\frac{1}{N} \sum_{i=1}^{N} R_i} - 1 = e^{R_P} - 1$$

The first row shows how the portfolio return is calculated in discrete time. The equivalent continuously compounded portfolio return solves $\ln(1 + \hat{R}_P)$. This is different from R_P as it is calculated in equation (1). The second row shows that this calculation leads to a different result. Nevertheless, following DeBondt and Thaler most of the literature uses equation (1) to calculate portfolio returns. To obtain comparable results to most of the literature, I also use R_P as portfolio returns.

2.2
The Standard Approach

For period lengths of 24 months or longer, I investigate the winner-loser hypothesis by three pairwise comparisons: I compare returns between the winner and the middle portfolio (WM), between the middle and the loser portfolio (ML), and between the winner and the loser portfolio (WL). Under H_0 the return on the winner and the middle portfolio are equal, $R_W = R_M$. The winner-loser hypothesis H_1 is that winner firms underperform the middle portfolio during the test period, $R_W < R_M$. Therefore, I test for H_0 by a one-tailed test. Similarly, H_0 for the middle/loser comparison is $R_M = R_L$, $H_1 : R_M < R_L$, for the winner/loser comparison H_0 is $R_W = R_L$, $H_1 : R_W < R_L$. For a time horizon of 12 months I test for short-term momentum and reverse the alternative hypotheses. I investigate these hypotheses for German stock returns from 1968 to 1986. A special feature of the way in which the data is analyzed is the use of overlapping samples. For longer time horizons the problem arises that only few non-overlapping samples exist for my sample of German stock returns from 1968 to 1986. For a time horizon of 60 months the first sample period dates from 1968 to 1977.

Hypotheses	H_0	H_1
Long-term Reversals (Winner-Loser Hyp.)	$R_W = R_M$ $R_M = R_L$ $R_W = R_L$	$R_W < R_M$ $R_M < R_L$ $R_W < R_L$
Short-term Momentum	$R_W = R_M$ $R_M = R_L$ $R_W = R_L$	$R_W > R_M$ $R_M > R_L$ $R_W > R_L$

As I test for the performance of stocks during the test period the next non-overlapping sample period dates from 1973 to 1982. For my dataset from 1968 to 1986 no more non-overlapping time period is available. The procedure which has been used in the literature to overcome this problem is to use overlapping samples. For an investment horizon of 60 months the ten sample periods 1968–1977, 1969–1978, .., 1977–1986 are pooled. From an econometric point of view the use of overlapping samples is a problem (Richardson and Smith (1991)). In a subsequent section I therefore also present evidence on a yearly basis. To avoid problems with seasonality only periods of full years are used; all samples begin in January.

2.2.1
Evidence for the Pooled Sample

Table 7 reports the results of my investigation. On the left hand side, it shows the cumulative mean returns of the equally weighted portfolios during the test period. For a one year formation period I obtain a return of 8.54% on the winner portfolio during the next year. This is larger than the return of 6.15% of the middle portfolio and much larger than the return of 5.30% on the loser portfolio. For an investment horizon of one year winner stocks tend to remain winner stocks. Loser stocks tend to remain loser stocks. For an investment horizon of 1 year a momentum strategy is successful. Buying the winner portfolio and short selling the loser portfolio results in a return of 3.24% (= 8.54% – 5.30%), which is reported in the ΔWL column.

On the right hand side, I test whether these differences are significant. I test for differences in returns by Wilcoxon rank sum statistics. The Wilcoxon rank sum statistic is a nonparametric statistic which tests for a shift in the distribution. It is a nonparametric alternative to a t-test which tests for differences in means if the underlying distribution is normal. For the comparison of the winner and the middle portfolio the Wilcoxon rank sum statistic is 1.564 which implies that the difference is significant at a level of 10%. More significant are the differences between the middle and the loser portfolio and the difference between the winner and the loser portfolio. The return on a 1 year momentum strategy earns a highly significant return of 3.24%. I turn to details of this test and the underlying assumption in a subsection below.

Table 7. Returns on the winner, the middle, and the loser portfolio during the test period for different period lengths.
For the test period it is tested whether the winner portfolio performs worse than the middle portfolio (WM), the middle portfolio worse than the loser portfolio (ML), and the winner portfolio worse than the loser portfolio (WL)

M.[c]	Mean			Diff.[a]	Wilc. rank sum stat., Level of Sign.[b]					
	Winner	Middle	Loser	ΔWL	WM		ML		WL	
12	0.0854	0.0615	0.0530	−0.0324	1.564	*	1.846	**	2.660	***
24	0.0954	0.1066	0.1204	0.0250	−0.191		−0.883		−0.775	
36	0.1369	0.1931	0.2244	0.0875	−3.034	***	−1.707	**	−3.618	***
48	0.1896	0.2974	0.3390	0.1494	−4.745	***	−2.269	**	−5.397	***
60	0.2856	0.4258	0.4986	0.2130	−5.561	***	−2.917	***	−6.237	***
72	0.3427	0.5473	0.6111	0.2684	−6.832	***	−2.820	***	−7.175	***
84	0.4609	0.6192	0.7285	0.2676	−5.278	***	−2.242	**	−5.571	***

[a] Difference between the return on the loser and the return on the winner portfolio
[b] Wilcoxon rank sum statistic for the comparison of the average return on different portfolios during the test period; WM denotes the comparison between winner and loser portfolio $(H_0 : R_W = R_M)$, ML denotes the comparison between middle and loser portfolio $(H_0 : R_M = R_L)$, WL denotes the comparison between winner and loser portfolio $(H_0 : R_W = R_L)$. For 12 months H_0 is tested against the hypothesis of short-term momentum, $R_W > R_M > R_L$. For longer time horizons H_0 is tested against the hypothesis of long-term reversals, $R_W < R_M < R_L$. The level of significance for a one-tailed test is shown by the following symbols, *** (**, *): H_0 can be rejected at a 1% (5%, 10%) significance level on the basis of the Wilcoxon rank sum statistic
[c] Months: Respective length of formation and test period in months

For a two year formation period the return on the winner portfolio is 9.54% during the next two years. Although the loser portfolio outperforms the winner portfolio, this difference is not significant. Significant evidence for reversals in stock returns is obtained for period lengths of three years and longer. For longer investment horizons the cumulative mean return on a winner-loser portfolio increases. From a return of 8.75% for a 36 months investment horizon the return increases in an almost linear way to 26.84% for a 72 months investment horizon. For an investment horizon of 84 months a slightly lower return of 26.76% can be observed. Not only the differences between the winner and the loser portfolio are significant. For all period lengths between 36 and 84 months the loser portfolio outperforms the middle portfolio and the middle portfolio itself outperforms the winner portfolio. Almost all of these differences between the winner and the loser portfolios are significant at a level of 1%. Only the differences between the middle and the loser portfolio are significant at a lower level for 36, 72, and 84 months.

To compare these results for different period lengths, table 8 presents the results on a yearly basis. A return of 72.85% in 7 years implies a yearly return of $1.7285^{(1/7)} - 1 = 8.13\%$. In addition, the right hand side of the table splits the total difference (WL) into the difference between the winner and the middle portfolio

(WM) and the difference between the middle and the loser portfolio (ML). In terms of returns $WL = WM + WL$ is equivalent to $R_L - R_W = (R_M - R_W)$ $+ (R_L - R_M)$. Also the shares of $(R_M - R_W)$ and $(R_L - R_M)$ are reported.

Table 8. Returns on the winner, the middle, and the loser portfolio during the test period for different period lengths, annualized data

M.[b]	Mean			Decomposition of the Winner-Loser Difference [a]				
	Winner	Middle	Loser	WL	WM		ML	
12	0.0854	0.0615	0.0530	−0.0324	−0.0238	73.65%	−0.0085	26.35%
24	0.0466	0.0520	0.0585	0.0119	0.0053	44.93%	0.0065	55.07%
36	0.0437	0.0606	0.0698	0.0261	0.0169	64.72%	0.0092	35.28%
48	0.0444	0.0672	0.0757	0.0313	0.0229	72.98%	0.0085	27.02%
60	0.0515	0.0735	0.0843	0.0327	0.0220	67.18%	0.0107	32.82%
72	0.0503	0.0755	0.0827	0.0324	0.0251	77.57%	0.0073	22.43%
84	0.0556	0.0713	0.0813	0.0257	0.0156	60.89%	0.0100	39.11%

[a] The total difference between the return on the winner and the loser portfolio (WL) is decomposed into the difference between the winner and middle (WM) and the difference between the middle and the loser portfolio (ML). In terms of returns $WL = WM + ML$ is equivalent to $R_L - R_W = (R_M - R_W) + (R_L - R_M)$. The shares are reported in terms of percentages
[b] Months: Respective length of formation and test period in months

For a one year investment horizon the return on the winner portfolio exceeds the return on the loser portfolio by 3.24%. This difference can be decomposed into $R_W - R_M = 2.38\%$ and $R_L - R_M = 0.85\%$. Hence, the difference is mainly due to the difference between the winner and the middle portfolio (almost 75%). The largest annual return on a contrarian strategy is obtained for an investment horizon of 5 years. The yearly return on the loser portfolio exceeds the return on the winner portfolio by 3.27%. Again this difference in returns is mainly due to the difference between the winner and the middle portfolio (67%). Similar results are obtained for investment horizons of 3, 4, 6, and 7 years. The overall picture which emerges is that the winner-loser effect is not symmetric, but that the winner portfolio is the driving force of the effect. Short-term persistence is driven by the persistence of the winner portfolio, long-term reversals are driven by reversals in the performance of the winner portfolio.

Figure 1 presents additional graphical evidence for the winner-loser effect for a formation period of 60 months. It shows the performance of the winner, the loser and the middle portfolios during the test period. It is interesting to note that the difference between winner and loser portfolio widens over the entire period. In addition stock returns show a strong seasonal pattern, in particular the winner portfolio. A widening of the spread between the winner and the loser portfolio during the first part of every year is followed by a partial shrinking during the second part. By and large, I find supportive evidence both for short-term persistence and long-term reversals. For a one year investment horizon I observe a return of 3.24% for a momentum strategy. In the short run former winner firms outperform former loser firms. Similar to previous findings in the literature I obtain the reverse pattern for longer investment horizons. In the long run contrarian strategies are successful. The largest yearly return of 3.27% on a contrarian strategy is earned for an investment horizon of 5 years. To some extent it seems possible to use past performance to predict future stock returns.

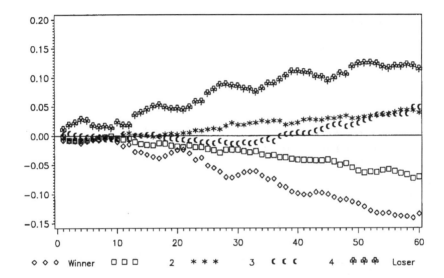

Figure 1. The winner-loser effect for cumulative portfolio returns during the test period for a period length of up to 60 months using data from the Frankfurt stock exchange (1968-1986). Stocks are sorted into portfolios according to their performance during the 60 months of the formation period. Portfolios are numbered from 1 (Winner) to 5 (Loser). The graph shows excess returns relative to the total sample mean

My findings are similar to the findings which have been reported in the literature. For the US market DeBondt and Thaler (1987) observe the same pattern of short-term momentum and long-term reversals. However, they obtain larger excess returns. For a one-year horizon they observe a return of 7.6% for a momentum strategy (my sample 3.24%). For long-term contrarian strategies they observe 24.6% for an investment horizon of 3 years, and 31.9% for 5 years (my sample 8.75% and 21.3% respectively). This effect might be due to the fact that DeBondt and Thaler rely on more extreme portfolios of winner and loser stocks. They investigate portfolios of approximately 10% of their sample whereas my portfolios comprise 20%. Also DeBondt and Thaler split the return of the winner-loser strategy into the difference $R_M - R_W$ and $R_L - R_M$. Contrary to my findings in their sample most of the return of a winner-loser strategy is due to the return on the loser portfolio.

My findings are also in line with the findings of the three investigations which have been pursued for the German stock market. For his sample of 41 German stocks from 1973 to 1989, Stock (1990) investigates the behaviour of the 5 best and the 5 worst stocks. For a one year investment horizon, he obtains a return of 5.82% on a momentum strategy. For 3, 4, and 5 years, he obtains excess returns of 5.47%, 14.52%, and 29.85%. These returns are mostly a bit larger than the returns which I obtain for my sample. Again, this might be due to the fact that my investigation is based on a less extreme part of the distribution.

For a sample from 1961-1990, Meyer (1994) observes short-term momentum for a 1 year time and a 2 year investment horizon. However, returns on a momentum strategy are not significant (p. 60). For longer investment horizons he also observes reversals. For a contrarian strategy which buys the 20% worst performing stocks and sells the 20% best performing stocks short he obtains a cumulative mean return of 5.07% for 3 years, 10.33% for 5 years and 18.75% for 7 years, all of which are significant (Meyer (1994) table 5.1, pp. 60f.). These returns are a bit smaller than my returns. However, Meyer obtains larger returns for more extreme portfolios. He observes the same asymmetry for his sample as I observe for my sample. The success of a contrarian strategy is mainly due to the underperformance of the winner portfolio.

The pattern of short-term persistence and long-term reversals is also observed by Schiereck and Weber (1995) for a similar sample from the German stock market from 1960-1991. For a portfolio of 40 winner and 40 loser stocks, which is approximately equivalent to 20% of their sample, they observe 3.49% return on a one year momentum strategy (p. 10) and 3.11% return per annum on a 5 year reversal strategy. In their investigation the return on the contrarian strategy is mainly due to the overperformance of the loser portfolio.

Taken together, these findings support the view that short-term persistence and long-term reversals are not a special property of my sample but a property of the cross section of stock returns. Although details of the results differ, the qualitative results are the same.

In the following, I address three methodological questions. First, I have tested the winner-loser hypothesis by Wilcoxon rank sum statistics. Alternative tests such as Spearman's rank correlation test have been proposed in the literature. Therefore, I first discuss the econometric methodology of the Wilcoxon rank sum test and of the available alternatives. Second, the evidence which has been presented so far is based on a pooled sample of overlapping observations. As it has already been mentioned above, the use of overlapping observations is a problem from an econometric point of view as these observations are not independent. To avoid this problem, I therefore also present evidence on a yearly basis. Third, the question can be raised whether the observation of long-term reversals might suffer from a survivorship bias. Stocks which performed poorly during the formation period might drop out of the sample during the subsequent test period. If only the surviving stocks are included into the sample this biases the performance of the loser portfolio upwards. This question is addressed in a third step.

2.2.2
Test Methodology

The winner-loser hypothesis can be pursued in two ways. The first is to test for independence in the performance during the formation and during the test period. The second approach is more related to problems of portfolio management. It tests for differences in the performance of former winner and former loser portfolios during the test period directly. This is the approach which is applied in this monograph.

For the first approach stocks are sorted according to their performance during the formation and during the test period. If the winner-loser hypothesis holds, low ranks during the formation period should lead to high ranks during the test period and vice versa. This hypothesis can be tested by means of the Spearman Rank Correlation Test. The idea of this test is as follows. Stocks are ranked according to their performance during the formation and during the test period. For every stock one obtains a matched pair of the two ranks. The rank correlation tests whether the ranks during the formation and during the test period are independent.

The rank correlation coefficient is defined as (cf. Lee (1993), p. 732)

$$\rho_s = 1 - \frac{6\sum_1^n d^2}{n(n^2 - 1)}$$

where d is the difference in ranks between the formation and the test period, n is the number of stocks in the sample. The winner-loser hypothesis implies that the correlation coefficient is negative. It should be possible to observe a lot of large differences in ranks, d.

Stock (1990) is an example for a study which investigates the winner-loser effect along these lines. For a sample of 41 of the most liquid German stocks he observes correlation coefficients which are significantly negative. For the Spearman Rank Correlation Coefficient he obtains a highly significant value of -0.50 for a three year horizon which increases monotonically with the investment horizon up to a level of -0.80 for a five year horizon.

In this monograph I pursue the second approach which is closer related to the perspective of a portfolio manager. For the portfolio manager not the reversals in rankings on an asset by asset level is interesting *per se*. For him the more important question is whether there is a difference in stock returns during the test period between former winner and former loser firms, which he can exploit. Of course, a negative correlation between the ranks during the formation and during the test period implies that such a difference exists. However, this question can also be investigated in a more direct way. This second approach tests for a difference in the location between the former winner and the former loser stocks during the test period.

The standard procedure to test for differences in the central moment of a distribution is to use t-statistics. However, this requires that the distribution from which the sample is drawn is a normal distribution. A non-parametric way to test for a difference in the location of two distributions is the Wilcoxon rank sum test.[9] A difference in the location of the distributions of X_1 to X_2 can be interpreted as

$$\text{prob}(X_1 > a) \geq \text{prob}(X_2 > a) \qquad \forall a$$

which means in terms of the distribution function

$$F_1(a) = \text{prob}(X_1 \leq a) \leq \text{prob}(X_2 \leq a) = F_2(a).$$

In this case, the probability of large values is larger for X_1 than for X_2.

The Wilcoxon rank sum test tests for X_1 and X_2 to be drawn from the same distribution function except for an additive treatment effect (Hollander and Wolfe (1973), p. 27):

$$F_1(a) = F_2(a - \Delta) < F_2(a)$$

If we test for the difference in the returns between the winner and the loser portfolio, this implies

$$F_{R_W}(a) = F_{R_L}(a - \Delta) < F_{R_L}(a)$$

which translates into

$$H_0 : \ \Delta \geq 0 \quad H_1 : \ \Delta < 0$$

The Wilcoxon rank sum test works as follows. Samples from the two distributions to be compared are pooled and sorted. Ranks are given for the relative performance of the assets: 1 for the worst, 2 . . . up to $N_1 + N_2$ for the best, where N_1 is the number of observations in the first sample and N_2 is the number of observations in the second sample. The test statistic is based on the sum of ranks for each sample. Under H_0:

$$\sum(\text{ranks of distribution 1}) \geq \sum(\text{ranks of distribution 2})$$

For the winner-loser effect

$$\sum(\text{ranks of the winner portfolio}) \geq \sum(\text{ranks of the loser portfolio})$$

---

[9] This test is also known as the Mann-Whitney U Test (cf. Lee (1993), p. 725).

The idea of this test is to compare the sum of the ranks for the two distributions and to test for a difference.[10] From a conceptual point of view both the Spearman Correlation Test and the Wilcoxon rank sum test are closely related as both of them rely on ranks of the pooled distributions (cf. Kendall (1962), Sections 3.12 and 13.9).

To test for the winner-loser effect, the main question from the point of view of portfolio management is whether there is a difference in the performance between the most extreme portfolios. The comparison of the returns on the winner and the loser portfolio is therefore at the heart of my analysis. Stocks from the former winner portfolio and the former loser portfolio are pooled and ranked according to their performance during the test period. Then the ranks are summed separately for the former winner and the former loser stocks. Under H_0 there is no difference in the performance of the former winner and the former loser stocks and the sum of ranks should be equal between the portfolios. In addition, I test for a difference in the performance of the winner and the middle portfolio, as well as between the middle and the loser portfolio. This analysis helps to reveal whether the winner-loser effect is driven by the overperformance of the loser stocks, or whether it is driven by the underperformance of the winner stocks.[11]

From a statistical point of view the question arises whether the assumptions of the Wilcoxon rank sum test are fulfilled. As in many statistical tests the crucial assumption is that random variables are assumed to be independent (cf. Hollander and Wolfe (1973), p. 27). As I draw my sample from the cross section of stock returns, this assumption is doubtful. Financial theory suggests that stock returns are driven by their exposure to a common pricing factor. The part of the return which is due to this exposure has to be subtracted before returns can be assumed to be independent.

At this point of my analysis I neglect the influence of the common pricing factor. From the point of view of financial theory the assumption of independence is violated. Unfortunately, this caveat also applies to the Spearman Rank Correlation Test, which also assumes independent random variables (cf. Hollander and Wolfe (1973), p. 185). However, empirically the explanatory power of the common pricing factor turns out to be quite low (cf. chapter 4 of this monograph).

---

[10] Critical values can be obtained from Büning and Trenkler (1978), p. 378 ff.

[11] In addition, one could also test for differences in the performance between the winner, the middle, and the loser portfolios simultaneously. This can be tested by the Kruskal-Wallis Test (cf. Lee (1993), pp. 729 ff.). The Kruskal-Wallis Test generalizes the procedure of the Wilcoxon Rank Sum Test: Returns during the test period from stocks in different portfolios are pooled and ranked. Under H_0 the returns in all portfolios are drawn from the same distribution. The Kruskal-Wallis Test then tests whether there is a difference in the location between any of the investigated portfolios. Although this is a natural extension of the pairwise comparison of the Wilcoxon Rank Sum Test, the additional information is not too helpful for the portfolio manager. From the Kruskal-Wallis Test he can only identify that there is a difference between the performance of any of the portfolios, but not between which of the portfolios. The essential information for the portfolio manager is obtained from the pairwise comparison. Therefore, my analysis is restricted to the Wilcoxon Rank Sum Test.

Therefore, the violation of the independence assumption turns out to be a theoretical caveat, rather than to be of empirical importance.

The Wilcoxon rank sum test tests for a shift in the location of two distributions. It should also be possible to observe this shift in a graphical presentation. Therefore, figure 2 presents additional graphical evidence for the return distributions of the winner, the loser, and the middle portfolio for different investment horizons.

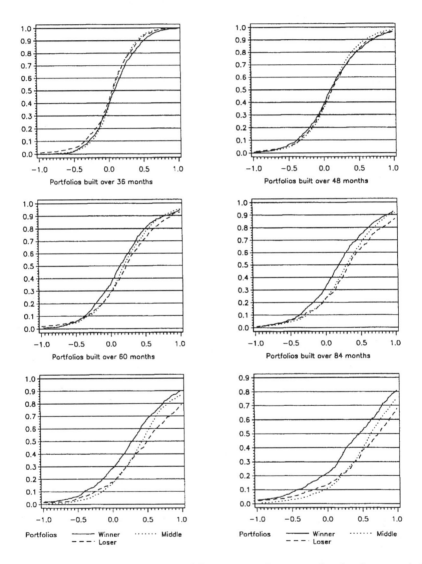

Figure 2. Distribution functions of portfolio returns on German stocks after the test period for different lengths of formation and test period (sample period 1968–1986)

For short investment horizons the distribution functions are quite close. For 12 months the distribution of the winner returns is below the distribution of the other returns for the major part of the distribution. This indicates that returns are larger than in the other portfolios. For 24 months no clear picture emerges. For longer investment horizons the winner portfolio is above the other distributions which indicates a poorer performance. The difference in the performance of the winner stocks and the other stocks widens for longer time horizons. For the difference in the performance of the middle and the loser portfolio the evidence is weaker. In most cases their distribution functions intersect. These findings add to the evidence that long-term reversals are mainly due to the underperformance of the winner portfolio.

2.2.3
Evidence on a Yearly Basis

The pooling of overlapping samples is a problem from a statistical point of view as the pooled samples are not independent (Richardson and Stock (1989)). Therefore, I also present evidence on a yearly basis.

Starting point is the evidence which has been presented for the pooled sample in table 7 for a time horizon of 60 months. For the pooled sample I have found a highly significant cumulative return for a contrarian strategy of 21.30%. Table 9 presents evidence for the same time horizon of 60 months on a yearly basis. It is structured in a similar way as table 7. On the left hand side I report the returns on the three different portfolios and on the right hand side the Wilcoxon rank sum statistics. In addition, the sample size is stated. The year on the left hand side of the table is the starting year of the formation period, the test period starts 5 years later. The table presents evidence for the sample periods which start in 1967 to 1984. For the pooled sample in table 7 the starting years 1968 to 1977 were used.

On a yearly basis, the evidence is weaker than for the pooled sample, but still consistent with the proposed winner-loser behaviour. Out of the ten periods from 1968 to 1977 we earn a return for a contrarian strategy in eight periods which is significant in five cases. The winner portfolio underperforms the middle portfolio in all but one case. Again five cases are significant. The loser portfolio outperforms the middle portfolio in only six cases, four of which are significant. These results corroborate the evidence that the winner-loser effect is more due to the performance of the winner portfolio than to the performance of the loser portfolio. More supportive evidence can be obtained from 1978–1984, years which are not included into the pooled analysis. In summary, the evidence for the pooled sample seems to overstate long-term reversals. Although the evidence on a yearly basis is weaker, still reversals in stock returns can be observed in most periods.

Table 9. Returns on the winner, the middle, and the loser portfolio during a 60 months test period, yearly evidence

Year	Mean			Wilc rank sum stat., Level of Significance[a]						#[b]
	Winner	Middle	Loser	WM		ML		WL		
1967	−0.1556	0.1332	0.2612	−1.677	**	−1.470	*	−2.109	**	115
1968	−0.0224	0.0550	0.2288	−1.722	**	−1.876	**	−2.746	***	117
1969	0.1767	0.3478	0.5668	−2.236	**	−2.299	**	−3.317	***	116
1970	0.2414	0.3800	0.4286	−0.681		−0.808		−1.165		121
1971	0.0694	0.2251	0.2939	−1.443	*	−0.622		−1.412		124
1972	0.1238	0.3119	0.1389	−1.353	*	0.995		−0.194		125
1973	0.1483	0.3018	0.1079	−0.882		2.601	†††	1.198		133
1974	0.3154	0.2939	0.0484	0.483		1.918	††	1.654	††	167
1975	0.3188	0.3571	0.3870	−0.431		−0.505		−0.731		169
1976	0.4477	0.6210	0.6942	−2.218	**	−0.914		−2.385	***	168
1977	0.5158	0.6951	0.9413	−1.182		−2.018	**	−2.591	***	169
1978	0.2889	0.4571	0.5617	−0.706		−1.375	*	−1.821	**	167
1979	0.3687	0.4449	0.5874	−0.812		−0.746		−0.632		167
1980	0.5461	0.7449	1.1076	−1.677	**	−2.051	**	−2.528	***	169
1981	0.1981	0.4799	0.7852	−2.526	***	−1.954	**	−3.193	***	175
1982	0.0037	0.4170	0.6142	−2.589	***	−1.983	**	−2.960	***	174
1983	0.2041	0.4920	0.6505	−2.661	***	−1.626	*	−2.901	***	170
1984	0.3755	0.4208	0.4463	−0.101		−0.491		−0.376		160

[a] Wilcoxon rank sum statistic for the comparison of the average return on different portfolios during the test period; WM denotes the comparison between winner and loser portfolio $(H_0 : R_W = R_M)$. ML denotes the comparison between middle and loser portfolio $(H_0 : R_M = R_L)$, WL denotes the comparison between winner and loser portfolio $(H_0 : R_W = R_L)$. H_0 is tested against the hypothesis of long-term reversals, $R_W < R_M < R_L$. The level of significance for a one-tailed test is shown by the following symbols, *** (**, *): H_0 can be rejected at a 1% (5%, 10%) significance level on the basis of the Wilcoxon rank sum statistic; ††† (††, †): H_0 can be rejected at a 1% (5%, 10%) significance level against the alternative hypothesis of long-term momentum, $R_W > R_M > R_L$
[b] Number of observations

2.2.4
Survivorship Bias

The third question which I investigate more closely is the possibility of a survivorship bias. A well-known problem from the literature on fund performance measurement is the possibility of a survivorship bias: Some funds might perform so badly that they merge into another fund or disappear. One has to be careful not to leave these disappearing funds out of the sample as this will bias the result (Ippolito (1989), p. 4). The analysis of the winner-loser effect might suffer from the same problem. If some of the corporations perform so badly that they finally go bankrupt, one has to be careful not to drop these stocks from the sample. If these stocks are taken out of the investigation, the remaining stocks show a better performance on average which biases the result. In the case of the winner-loser effect a survivorship bias might be suspected for stocks in the loser portfolio: After a poor performance during the formation period a corporation might be more likely to go bankrupt during the test period. If these corporations are omitted from the sample, the loser portfolio is likely to show a better performance due to a survivorship bias.

In the following the potential of a survivorship bias is analyzed for a period length of 60 months. So far for a stock to be included, data had to be available for every month during the formation period and in at least one month during the test period. As for the data set under investigation no insolvency is reported, the excess return at the moment when a corporation drops out of the market is set equal to zero. I analyze whether the reported results suffer from a survivorship bias in two ways. First, Table 10 shows at which point of time and from which portfolio assets drop out: Surprisingly, most companies drop out of the middle portfolio. 37 stocks drop out of the middle portfolio as compared to 14 for the extreme portfolios. Table 11 shows how this influences the return distribution. It reports portfolio returns for different cut-off dates. "Cut-off date" means that assets are excluded if data are available for no longer than the cut-off month. The first row reports the findings when all stocks are included which are traded at least in the first month of the test period. This is the same result which we have reported in table 7. The following row shows the result if all stocks are included which are traded during the first 12 months. For all cut-off dates the evidence of a winner-loser effect is almost equally supportive. Hence, our results are not likely to suffer from a survivorship bias.

2.3
Transition Matrix

So far my investigation has followed closely the setting of DeBondt and Thaler. I have reported the means of portfolio returns and have tested for the differences in the performance across portfolios. This section presents evidence for the winner-loser effect in a different setting. Again I sort stocks into portfolios according to both their performance during the formation and during the test period. I estimate transition probabilities: Given that a stock has been in the winner portfolio during the formation period I estimate the probability to find such a stock in any of the portfolios during the test period. The transition matrix reports the frequencies of stocks to switch from one portfolio during the formation period to another portfolio during the test period.

Table 12 reports results for a time horizon of 60 months when stocks are sorted into 5 portfolios. The table presents evidence in the following way. The element in row i and column j shows the frequency of a stock which has been in portfolio i during the formation period to appear in portfolio j during the test period. A stock which has been in the loser portfolio during the formation period has a probability of 26.35% to be in the winner portfolio during the test period.

Table 10. Number of shares which drop out during the test period

Portfolio	Month of Drop Out					Total Drop Out	Non Drop Out
	1–12	13–24	25–36	37–48	49–60		
winner	0	1	1	2	1	5	539
2	2	0	2	5	1	10	534
3	1	2	2	5	4	14	530
4	3	2	1	4	3	13	531
loser	0	2	1	4	2	9	535

Table 11. Returns on the winner, the middle, and the loser portfolio during the test period for different cut-off dates during the test period, length of period: 60 months

M.[c]	Mean			Wilc. rank sum stat., Level of Sign.[b]					
	Winner	Middle	Loser	WM		ML		WL	
1	0.2856	0.4258	0.4986	−5.560	***	2.917	***	−6.237	***
12	0.2856	0.4251	0.4986	−5.667	***	2.844	***	−6.237	***
24	0.2792	0.4251	0.5058	−5.629	***	2.910	***	−6.256	***
36	0.2806	0.4253	0.5064	−5.599	***	2.939	***	−6.259	***
48	0.2778	0.4335	0.5077	−5.599	***	3.086	***	−6.390	***
60	0.2778	0.4345	0.5114	−5.677	***	3.220	***	−6.567	***

[a] Wilcoxon rank sum statistic for the comparison of the average returon. different portfolios during the test period; WM denotes the comparison between winner and loser portfolio $(H_0 : R_W = R_M)$, ML denotes the comparison between middle and loser portfolio $(H_0 : R_M = R_L)$, WL denotes the comparison between winner and loser portfolio $(H_0 : R_W = R_L)$. H_0 is tested against the hypothesis of long-term reversals, $R_W < R_M < R_L$. The level of significance for a one-tailed test is shown by the following symbols, *** (**, *): H0 can be rejected at a 1% (5%, 10%) significance level on the basis of the Wilcoxon rank sum statistic
[b] "Cut-off" Month: Stocks are only included if they are traded during the formation period until the cut-off month

Table 12. Transition Matrix: probabilities of a transition from a portfolio in t (the formation period to a portfolio in t+1 (the test period) for a return period of 60 months

Portfolio in t	Portfolio in t+1 [a]				
	winner	2	3	4	loser
winner	0.180926	0.163471	0.182244	0.246250	0.227110
2	0.156086	0.213901	0.213257	0.271802	0.144954
3	0.221790	0.233783	0.238986	0.172134	0.133307
4	0.208911	0.215068	0.262522	0.184207	0.129292
loser	0.263563	0.223453	0.190056	0.148751	0.174176

[a] The element in row i and column j shows the frequency of a stock which has been in portfolio i to appear in portfolio j at the end of the next 5-year period

If past returns do not have any predictive power, all elements in the matrix should be equal to 20%. In the case of persistence in stock returns the elements on the declining diagonal should be larger than 20%, in the case of reversals the off-diagonal elements should be larger than 20%. In table 12 all elements on the increasing diagonal (SW to NE) are larger than 20%: 0.264, . . . , 0.227. In addition most of the elements near this diagonal are also larger than 20%. The largest values in a row are obtained for the transition probabilities $((1 \rightarrow 4), (2 \rightarrow 4), (3 \rightarrow 3), (4 \rightarrow 3),$ and $(5 \rightarrow 1)$. Hence, table 12 supports the view that there are reversals in stock returns. If a stock is in the winner portfolio during the formation period it has a higher probability to be in one of the poorer performing portfolios during the test period. The opposite is true of stocks in the loser portfolio.

In addition to this descriptive evidence we can try to draw statistical inference. Bundling stocks into portfolios puts a structure on our dataset which I exploit in a generalized linear model.[12] I test whether the attribution to a better performing portfolio during the formation period increases the probability to belong to a worse performing portfolio during the test period. I estimate the following logistic function

$$\log\left(\frac{\gamma_j(x)}{1-\gamma_j(x)}\right) = \theta_j + \beta_j x$$

where γ_j denotes the cumulative probability that given the parameter x the observation falls into one of the categories up to j, $\text{prob}(Y \le j \mid x)$.[13] In my investigation the variable to be explained is the probability that a stock falls into or below a portfolio j during the test period. As conditioning x variables I use the portfolio indices 1, 2, ..., 5 to which the stock is attributed during the formation period. To avoid linear dependence I use the first four portfolios as regressors which implies that I test for a difference in the performance of a stock in one of these portfolios as compared to the loser portfolio. β_j tests for differences in the performance during the test period if one conditions on a (formation period) portfolio j as compared to the loser portfolio. A positive value of the β_j implies a

---

[12] This structure is also known as "polytomous structure" (cf. McCullagh and Nelder (1989), chapter 5, p. 149ff.)

[13] This model belongs to the class of generalized linear models (cf. McCullagh and Nelder (1989)). A generalized linear model $Y = f(X)$ can be decomposed into three elements: (1) the distributional assumptions for the Y's , (2) the *linear* predictor $\eta = \beta^T x$ and (3) the link function which ties properties of the Y distribution to the linear predictor. This property may be the mean μ in the case of a normal distribution or the category probability $\pi(j)$ in the case of a polytomous distribution. In the case to be tested in the following the elements used are (1) a multinomial distribution with 5 classes, (2) a linear predictor and (3) a logistic function which fitted the data better than a *normit* and a *log-log* function. Although one could estimate the portfolio probabilities π_j directly in the case of polytomous data, cumulative response probabilities are likely to have better statistical properties (McCullagh and Nelder (1989), p. 151).

better performance of former portfolio j stocks during the test period as compared to the loser portfolio.

Table 13 presents the results: In the lower part the estimators for the β_j are reported. All of them have negative signs. Large and significant coefficients are obtained for β_1 and β_2 which capture the influence of the winner portfolio and the second portfolio. Negative coefficients imply that stocks which have been in the winner portfolio or in portfolio 2 are more likely to end up in one of the worse performing portfolios during the test period. The negative coefficients therefore imply reversals in stock returns. As only the coefficients for the winner and the second portfolio are significant this adds to our previous findings that the winner-loser effect is mainly due to the underperformance of the winner portfolio during the test period.

Table 13. Estimation Results for the Proportional Odds Model

parameter	estimate	std.dev.	P-value
θ_1	−1.2071	0.1010	0.0001
θ_2	−0.2214	0.0960	0.0211
θ_3	0.6353	0.0970	0.0001
θ_4	1.6254	0.1039	0.0001
β_1	−0.5989	0.1325	0.0001
β_2	−0.3691	0.1321	0.0052
β_3	−0.0093	0.1303	0.9434
β_4	−0.0829	0.1319	0.5296

To assess the model fit, the loglikelihood of 30.92 implies that the entire estimation is highly significant (p-value = 0.0001). In addition I use the following property to determine whether the linear specification is appropriate. The ratio of the odds of an observation to fall into or below a portfolio j is independent of the portfolio j. For this reason the model is also known as the proportional odds model (McCullagh and Nelder (1989), p. 153).

$$\frac{\gamma_j(x_1)/(1-\gamma_j(x_1))}{\gamma_j(x_2)/(1-\gamma_j(x_2))} = \exp(\beta_j(x_1-x_2))$$

The ratio of odds should be the same whether we look at the winner, one of the middle, or at the loser portfolio as the conditioning variable. The score statistic tests for this assumption. For the extended sample of data from 1967 to 1993 we cannot reject the proportional odds assumption (P-value of 0.1182). For the estimation period from 1968 to 1986 however I obtain a value for the score variable of 27.59 (P-value of 0.006 under the χ^2 distribution) which implies that we have to reject the proportional odds assumption. Hence, there seems to be some nonlinearity in the data. The proportional odds assumption might be too restrictive to fit the data.

Taken together, from the transition matrix as well as from testing a proportional odds model we obtain additional evidence for return reversals in the cross section of stock returns. Although the proposed linear structure might be too simple to fit the entire data set, it adds to the evidence for reversals in stock returns for longer time horizons.

2.4
Summary

Intertemporal dependence in stock returns has been reported by many researchers. This chapter adds to the evidence of short-term persistence and long-term reversals in the cross section of stock returns. For a one year time horizon I find a significant excess return of 3.24% p.a. for a momentum strategy. For time horizons of three years or longer I report excess returns for a contrarian strategy. The largest value of 3.27% p.a. is obtained for a time horizon of 5 years. At closer inspection long horizon reversals are mainly driven by the underperformance of the winner portfolio during the test period. This finding is corroborated by the cumulative distribution functions for the portfolio returns. The return distributions of the middle and the loser portfolio dominate the return distribution of the winner portfolio by first-order stochastic dominance. Evidence for return reversals for time horizons of 60 months is also found if we disaggregate the sample into non-overlapping yearly samples. Although the evidence for return reversals is weaker it is still significant on average. Long-term reversals could be driven by a survivorship bias if former loser firms drop out of the sample and are not included into the calculations. For my sample this effect cannot be observed. In a complementary section I have explored intertemporal dependence in stock returns in an alternative setting. Conditional on past performance we have determined the probabilities of stocks to be in the winner or the loser portfolio during the test period. The pattern of the estimated transition matrix also implies reversals in stock returns for a return period of 60 months. Although a proportional odds model proves to be too simple, it adds to the evidence that the results are mainly driven by an underperformance of the winner portfolio during the test period.

The main question which arises from these findings is whether the observed pattern occurs in an efficient capital market. If past returns can be used to predict future stock returns this might imply an inefficiency of the capital market. In the following section I first present a theoretical framework which shows how the winner-loser effect might occur in a framework of rational asset pricing. Empirically, I relate the winner-loser effect to two sets of explanatory variables, the CAPM β and fundamentals such as dividends and profits. I investigate which set of variables can explain the cross section of stock returns best. From a theoretical point of view I discuss how the relationship between stock returns and fundamentals can be interpreted. In the third section of this monograph I relate the winner-loser effect to an additional set of explanatory variables. I pursue the hypothesis that both winner and loser firms suffer from temporary problems of corporate control. For this investigation I use additional explanatory variables as the debt/equity ratio and the payout ratio. This will help to understand the forces which drive the winner-loser effect.

II Explaining the Winner-Loser Effect: CAPM versus Fundamentals

The aim of this monograph is to explain the surprising finding of the winner-loser effect. Prima facie, one would not have expected any particular pattern to emerge from conditioning on past information. From an economic point of view the decisive question is whether the observed pattern is due to rational asset pricing. Two interpretations are available for the observed reversals in stock returns. Either the observed pattern is in line with rational asset pricing. Then the observed differences between the returns on the loser and on the winner portfolio must be due to different exposures with respect to systematic risk. An alternative explanation is that the winner-loser effect comes as a surprise. Although no different return for the winner and the loser firms are expected, winner firms underperform loser firms systematically. This would contradict rational asset pricing. To explore this question I relate the observed pattern in stock returns to two sets of explanatory variables: the CAPM β and fundamentals such as dividends and profits.

The analysis in this section proceeds as follows. In chapter 3 I present the theoretical framework of my analysis. In chapters 4 to 6 I present the results of my empirical analysis. First, I investigate if the CAPM is able to explain the cross section of stock returns (chapter 4). Second, I relate the observed pattern in stock returns to movements in fundamentals (chapter 5). Third, I compare the explanatory power of the CAPM β and of fundamentals (chapter 6).

3 Explaining the Winner-Loser Effect: Theory

From a theoretical point of view the decisive question is whether it is possible to explain the winner-loser effect within a framework of rational asset pricing. In empirical asset pricing models stock returns are related to aggregate pricing variables. In the CAPM stock returns are related to the market rate of return. This is the first approach which I explore. The alternative approach which I pursue is that stock returns are related to fundamentals such as dividends and profits. From a theoretical point of view the question arises what this relationship implies. Two interpretations can be offered. The first is that unexpected movements in fundamentals lead to unexpected returns. Investors are surprised by movements in fundamentals. An unexpected increase in profits leads to a positive excess return, an unexpected loss to a negative excess return. I also offer a second interpretation. Expected movements in fundamentals lead to expected returns. In a framework of rational asset pricing I investigate whether expected returns might be driven by expected changes in fundamentals.

The structure of this section follows this line of reasoning. First, I present the framework of rational asset pricing. Starting from a no-arbitrage condition, I derive a general asset pricing model. Expected returns are determined by the covariance between returns and the aggregate pricing function. Under further restrictive assumptions the CAPM can be derived. In the CAPM expected returns are determined by the covariance of returns with the return on the market portfolio. I raise the question how long-term reversals might occur in such a framework of rational asset pricing.

An alternative approach to explain the winner-loser effect is to relate stock returns to movements in fundamentals of the individual companies. At first sight this is very different from standard asset pricing models. Rational asset pricing relates stock returns to aggregate quantities. If the characteristics of the individual companies play a role for the behaviour of expected stock returns, in general this contradicts the assumption of rational asset pricing. If the fundamental performance helps to explain the winner-loser effect, this might be a hint that the observed reversals in stock returns are unexpected. In this case unexpected changes in fundamentals help to explain unexpected returns. I present the theory which relates unexpected changes in fundamentals to unexpected returns.

In a third step I present an alternative interpretation of the relationship between stock returns and fundamentals during the test period. I develop a model which relates expected changes in fundamentals to expected returns. This delivers an alternative interpretation of the relationship between stock returns and fundamentals. At the same time it is a bridge between the accounting literature which focusses on unexpected returns, but uses idiosyncratic fundamental variables, and the literature in financial economics which focusses on expected returns which are related to aggregate quantities.

3.1
Rational Asset Pricing

In a market which is free of arbitrage asset prices are determined by

$$P_i = E(\phi X_i) \tag{2}$$

This equation is the *fundamental valuation equation*.[14] P_i is the price of the asset, X_i is the cash flow at the end of the period, and ϕ is the positively valued pricing kernel.[15]

The pricing kernel ϕ can be interpreted in different ways. In a complete market the pricing kernel can be related to Arrow Debreu prices. In a discrete-state setting the fundamental valuation equation can be rewritten as

$$P_i = \sum_s q_s \phi_s X_{i,s} \tag{3}$$

where q_s denotes the probability of state s, ϕ_s is the value of the pricing kernel in state s and $X_{i,s}$ is the final pay-out of asset i in state s. Arrow-Debreu prices are used to price assets in the following way

$$P_i = \sum_s \pi_s X_{i,s} \tag{4}$$

where π_s denote the Arrow Debreu prices for payouts in state s. From equations (3) and (4)

$$\phi_s = \frac{\pi_s}{q_s}$$

The pricing kernel are the Arrow Debreu prices per unit probability.[16]

---

[14] Ferson (1995) calls it the canonical asset pricing equation, p. 146.

[15] The existence of the pricing kernel is the result of the Minkowski Farkas Lemma (Kruschwitz (1995), p. 169.). Either the market is free of arbitrage. Then a pricing kernel ϕ with $\phi \geq 0$ exists such that equation (2) holds. Otherwise, it is possible to construct a portfolio which has a negative value at the beginning of the period, but cash flows which are greater than or equal to zero at the end of the period. Without short selling restrictions it is possible to make an arbitrage profit.

[16] Alternatively the pricing kernel ϕ can be characterized as stochastic discount factor (Ferson (1995), p. 146). Under certainty $P_i = \frac{1}{R} X_i$ where $\frac{1}{R}$ denotes the deterministic discount factor. The equivalent formulation under uncertainty is the fundamental valuation equation, $P_i = E(\phi X_i)$.

The pricing kernel can also be related to the concept of an equivalent martingale measure which is central in modern financial economics. Under the equivalent martingale measure the forward price of an asset is equal to its expected value at the end of the period. The forward price in a market which is free of arbitrage is $F_i = R_f P_i$. Multiplying equation (3) by the gross risk-free rate R_f yields

$$R_f P_i = \sum_s q_s \phi_s R_f X_{i,s} \quad \Leftrightarrow$$

$$F_i = \sum_s \hat{q}_s X_{i,s} = \hat{E}(X_i)$$

where $\hat{q}_s = q_s \phi_s R_f$. $\hat{q}_s$ are the equivalent martingale probabilities. The forward pricing kernel, $\phi_s R_f$, transforms the true probabilities q_s to the equivalent martingale probabilities $\hat{q}_s$.[17]

In an equilibrium pricing framework the pricing kernel can be related to properties of the utility function of the representative investor.[18] In a representative investor economy a representative investor faces the following decision problem. The investor can buy state contingent claims for every future state of the economy. He maximizes his expected utility subject to a budget constraint:

$$\max_{X_s} \quad \sum_s q_s u(X_s)$$

$$\text{s.t.} \quad \sum_s \pi_s X_s \leq W_0$$

where W_0 denotes the initial wealth and X_s are the cash flows which he receives in state s. The resulting first-order condition is

$$q_s u'(X_s) = \lambda \pi_s \tag{5}$$

where λ is the Lagrange multiplier. Summing over all states yields $\sum_s q_s u'(X_s) = \lambda \sum_s \pi_s$. $\sum_s \pi_s$ represents the price of a claim which pays a cash flow of one in every state of the world. Its current price must be equal to 1 discounted at the risk-free rate. Hence, $E(u'(X_s)) = \lambda R_f^{-1}$. Substituting this expression for λ in equation (5) yields

$$q_s \frac{u'(X_s)}{R_f E(u'(X_s))} = \pi_s = q_s \phi_s$$

and hence

$$\phi = \frac{1}{R_f} \frac{u'(X)}{E(u'(X))}. \tag{6}$$

---

[17] The derivative of one probability measure with respect to another is known as the Radon Nicodym derivative. The forward pricing function ϕR_f is the Radon-Nicodym derivative of $\hat{q}$ with respect to q (Neftci (1996), p. 288f.).

[18] cf. Franke and Hax (1999), p. 376.

The pricing kernel is the ratio of marginal utility to expected marginal utility which is discounted at the risk-free rate. Usually one assumes that $u''(X) < 0$, i.e. the representative investor is risk-averse. If the aggregate wealth of the economy is large then $u'(X)$ is low and hence the state prices per unit probability are low as well. The pricing kernel has large values in states of the economy when aggregate wealth is small.

From the fundamental valuation equation (2) we can derive a general asset pricing model in terms of returns.[19] In a one-period framework returns are determined as $R_i = X_i / P_i$. From the fundamental valuation equation

$$1 = E(\phi R_i) = \text{cov}(\phi, R_i) + E(\phi) E(R_i)$$

For a risk free asset $\text{cov}(\phi, R_i) = 0$. Therefore, $E(\phi) = R_f^{-1}$. As a result

$$E(R_i) - R_f = \frac{1 - \text{cov}(\phi, R_i)}{E(\phi)} - \frac{1}{E(\phi)} = -\frac{\text{cov}(\phi, R_i)}{E(\phi)} \qquad (7)$$

In the following I refer to this model as the *general asset pricing model*. The expected excess return, $E(R_i) - R_f$, is determined by the covariance, $\text{cov}(\phi / E(\phi), R_i)$. This covariance is called the *systematic* risk of the asset; systematic means that it captures the uncertainty of the return distribution as far as it relates to an economy-wide benchmark variable. As a consequence of equation (7) uncertainty which does not relate to ϕ has no influence on expected returns. From equation (6) I obtain the following interpretation of equation (7). A negative correlation of returns R_i with the pricing kernel implies a positive expected excess return. The correlation between the asset return and the pricing kernel is negative if a high return of the asset occurs in states of the world when marginal utility is low. Marginal utility is low if the aggregate wealth in that state is high as $u'' < 0$. As marginal utility is low, shareholders want to be compensated for holding these assets.

In a model of rational asset pricing stock returns are determined by equation (7). This is also the starting point for my analysis of the winner-loser effect. In a framework of rational asset pricing the differences in returns between the winner and the loser portfolio during the test period must be expected. Differences in expected returns must be due to differences in the exposure to systematic risk. During the test period the winner portfolio must have a lower exposure to systematic risk than the loser portfolio. To be able to implement equation (7) empirically it is necessary to specify the pricing kernel ϕ further. Two approaches are available (Ferson (1995), pp. 149 ff.). The first approach is consumption based asset pricing. The valuation problem is related to the consumption investment decision of a representative investor. The second approach is to use "beta models" in which stock returns are related to benchmark portfolios.

---

[19] Franke and Hax (1999), p. 378. For an alternative derivation see Duffie (1988), p. 94.

In an intertemporal consumption investment problem a representative investor maximizes his lifetime utility, V. He can keep his endowment until the next period and consume it afterwards or can sell part of his initial endowment and spend it for consumption. In every period the investor decides which part of his assets to hold and which part of the assets to sell and use for consumption. The optimality condition states that at the margin he should be indifferent between these two opportunities. The marginal utility of foregone consumption must be equal to the marginal utility of consumption which derives from investing and spending the money in the next period. For any asset this implies

$$P_t \frac{\partial V}{\partial C_t} = E\left[\left(P_{t+1} + D_{t+1} \right) \frac{\partial V}{\partial C_{t+1}} \right] \tag{8}$$

The left hand side shows the marginal utility which the investor receives from selling the asset and consuming in period t. The right hand side shows the expected marginal utility which the investor receives from keeping the asset until the next period and consuming in $t+1$. In a two period framework returns are defined as $\left(P_{t+1} + D_{t+1} \right) / P_t$. By comparison of equation (8) with the fundamental valuation equation this implies

$$\phi = \frac{\partial V / \partial C_{t+1}}{\partial V / \partial C_t}$$

This expression is known as the intertemporal marginal rate of substitution (IMRS). In an intertemporal general equilibrium framework this equation is equivalent to equation (6).

The most common approach to specify the IMRS is to use time-separable preferences. Then $\partial V / \partial C_t$ depends only on the marginal utility at time t. For additive preferences $V = \sum \beta^t u(C_t)$ where β denotes a time preference parameter and $u(C_t) = (C_t^{1-\alpha}) / (1-\alpha)$ one obtains

$$\phi = \beta \left(\frac{C_{t+1}}{C_t} \right)^{-\alpha}$$

This approach has been found to be insufficient. Direct testing has lead to a rejection of the model (cf. Hansen and Singleton (1982, 1984)). A reverse approach are calibration exercises. One uses standard models to generate return distributions from the observed pattern of aggregate consumption. However, for standard values for the coefficient of relative risk aversion α, the observed volatility of aggregate consumption was too low to be compatible with the fundamental valuation equation. Therefore more recent studies have resorted to models in which time preferences are nonseparable.[20]

---

[20] One possibility to obtain preferences which are nonseparable is to use recursive preferences which have been introduced by Kreps and Porteus (1978). For a recent application to German data see Meyer (1999).

The second approach how to implement the fundamental valuation equation is to use *beta pricing models*. In a *beta pricing model* all assets are priced relative to the pricing portfolio according to the following equation (Ferson (1995), p. 155):

$$E[R_i - R_{Pz}] = \beta_{iP} E[R_p - R_{Pz}], \qquad \forall i$$
$$\beta_{iP} = \frac{\text{cov}(R_i, R_p)}{\text{var}(R_p)} \tag{9}$$

where R_i denotes the return on the asset i, R_p is the return on the portfolio, and R_{Pz} is the return on a portfolio which is not correlated with R_p. If equation (9) holds for all assets in the pricing portfolio P, it can be shown that this portfolio is a minimum variance portfolio, i.e. it has the smallest variance of all portfolios with the same expected return (Roll (1977)).

The relationship between beta pricing models and the fundamental valuation equation can be seen as follows. From using equation (7) both for an individual asset and for a portfolio it follows

$$E(R_i) - R_f = \frac{\text{cov}(\phi, R_i)}{\text{cov}(\phi, R_p)} [E(R_p) - R_f] \tag{10}$$

The structure of equations (9) and (10) is similar. The excess return on a stock is determined by a risk premium $E(R_p) - R_f$ or $E(R_p) - E(R_{Pz})$ and a measure of the exposure with respect to systematic risk. Starting from equation (10) it can be shown that a beta pricing model holds for all portfolios whose returns maximize the squared correlation with ϕ (Ferson (1995), p. 155f.). A beta pricing model is tested by relating stock returns R_i to portfolio returns R_p. Starting from the fundamental valuation equation testing a beta pricing model therefore implies that a joint hypothesis is tested. It is tested whether the general asset pricing model holds and whether the portfolio maximizes the squared correlation with ϕ.

The most popular beta pricing model is the capital asset pricing model (CAPM). The CAPM can be stated as follows

$$E(R_i) - R_f = \frac{\text{cov}(R_M, R_i)}{\text{var}(R_M)} [E(R_M) - R_f] = \beta_i [E(R_M) - R_f] \tag{11}$$

where R_M denotes the market portfolio. In the market portfolio all assets in the economy are weighted according to their relative total values. The CAPM claims that all expected asset returns are determined by two factors, the expected risk premium of the market, $(E(R_M) - R_f)/\text{var}(R_M)$, and the covariance of the returns with the market return. In a representative investor framework the CAPM can also be derived as a special case of the fundamental valuation equation if the representative investor has quadratic utility or all returns are multivariate normally distributed.

What does this line of reasoning imply for the winner-loser effect? The remarkable finding of the winner-loser effect is that loser firms perform better than winner firms during the test period. In a framework of rational asset pricing these differences in returns during the test period must be expected. Differences in expected returns are due to differences in the exposure with respect to systematic risk. Hence, for the test period the exposure of the loser portfolio to systematic risk must be larger than the exposure of the winner portfolio. In the general framework the exposure is measured by $\text{cov}(\phi, R_i)$. To implement this framework empirically, it is necessary to use observable variables rather than ϕ which cannot be observed directly. In the CAPM the exposure with respect to systematic risk is measured by β. If the winner-loser effect occurs within a CAPM framework it must hold that $\beta_L > \beta_M > \beta_W$. This hypothesis is pursued in the fourth chapter.

3.2
Unexpected Changes in Fundamentals and Unexpected Returns

The alternative hypothesis is that the winner-loser effect does not occur within a framework of rational asset pricing but is due to a surprise effect. Investors do not expect the loser firms to perform better than the winner firms during the test period. If this difference in the performance is not expected the question arises why it still occurs. One possibility is that the difference is due to unexpected changes in the fundamental performance of the winner and the loser firms.

The underperformance of the winner portfolio might be due to an unexpected poor performance in terms of fundamentals during the test period. Investors might be surprised by a deterioration of profits during the test period. As they have to adjust their expectations accordingly, this implies a subsequent underperformance of the winner portfolio. For the loser portfolio the reverse might be true. If profits improve unexpectedly this leads to a subsequent overperformance of the loser portfolio. If the fundamental performance of the companies shows the hypothesized pattern, to some extent the valuation is still consistent with rational asset pricing. Stock returns are in line with movements in fundamentals. Nevertheless, some systematic misconception remains as movements in fundamentals are not expected.

The hypothesis of a difference in the fundamental performance of the winner and the loser portfolio is pursued in the fifth chapter. A first interpretation of the relationship between stock returns and fundamentals is that unexpected movements in fundamentals for the winner and the loser portfolio are related to unexpected differences in returns. A framework for the analysis of the way in which fundamental variables such as dividends and profits are related to returns is provided in the accounting literature.

Starting with the seminal study of Ball and Brown (1968) returns have been related to changes in earnings and dividends. The intuition for this relationship is as follows. If stock prices are the sum of future dividends which are discounted appropriately then unexpected changes in dividends should lead to unexpected returns. Also my first approach in the fifth chapter is to relate returns to changes in earnings and dividends. However, in the accounting literature doubts have been raised whether changes in fundamentals are sufficient to capture the relevant information in stock returns. Alternatively, it has been claimed that also levels have explanatory power (Easton and Harris (1991)). To answer the question whether levels or changes in earnings are more important for the explanation of stock returns, Ohlson (1992) and Ohlson and Shroff (1992) have provided the following theoretical framework.

Starting point for their analysis is the random walk assumption for the process of earnings

$$x_{t+1} = Rx_t - (R-1)d_t + u_{t+1} \qquad (12)$$

x denote earnings, d dividends, and R is the cost of capital, which is equal to the expected gross return on the market value of capital, u is an error term. Contrary to the cross section of expected returns where the determination of the discount factor is crucial, in the accounting literature no special attention is paid to this question. Under the assumption that stock prices equal the present value of expected dividends, stock prices can be determined from equation (12) as

$$P_t = \psi x_t - d_t$$

where $\psi = R/R-1$ (Ohlson (1992), p. 6). Returns are calculated as $R_{t+1} = (P_{t+1} + d_{t+1})/P_t$. This implies

$$R_{t+1} = \psi \frac{x_{t+1}}{P_t} \qquad (13)$$

$$R_{t+1} = 1 + \psi \frac{\Delta x_{t+1}}{P_t} + \frac{d_t}{P_t} \qquad (14)$$

where Δx_{t+1} denotes the change in earnings $x_{t+1} - x_t$ (Ohlson and Shroff (1992), p. 214). From these two equations it can be observed that both earnings levels and changes in earnings can be used to explain returns. The explanatory power of both variables should be almost the same.

To be able to distinguish between the explanatory power of earnings levels and changes in earnings one has to deviate from the strict assumption of a random walk in earnings. This can be done by introducing an additional error term which follows an AR(1) process (Ohlson and Shroff (1992), p. 215)

$$x_{t+1} = Rx_t - (R-1)d_t + v_t + u_{1,t+1}$$
$$v_{t+1} = \gamma v_t + u_{2,t+1}$$

γ is assumed to be $0 \leq \gamma \leq 1$. The error terms $u_{1,t+1}$ and $u_{2,t+1}$ have zero mean and are unpredictable. To see how γ influences the relationship between earnings and returns I restrict my attention to the case that

$$\text{cov}\left(u_{1,t+1}, u_{2,t+1}\right) = 0$$

From these assumptions one can derive the value of an asset as

$$P_t = \psi x_t - d_t + \beta v_t \tag{15}$$

where $\beta = \psi / (R - \gamma)$ (Ohlson and Shroff (1992), p. 216). For the return the following result is obtained

$$R_{t+1} = R + \psi \frac{u_{1,t+1}}{P_t} + \beta \frac{u_{2,t+1}}{P_t} \tag{16}$$

For the analysis of the relationship between earnings and returns this equation has the following implications. The $u_{2,t+1}$ variable is a pure noise variable and independent of actual and past earnings. To be able to interpret the $u_{1,t+1}$ variable one can substitute the above equations (15) and (16) and obtains

$$\frac{u_{1,t+1}}{P_t} = \frac{x_{t+1} - \gamma x_t}{P_t} + \frac{\gamma}{\psi_t} \frac{d_t}{P} - \beta^{-1}$$

Under reasonable assumptions (Ohlson and Shroff (1992), p. 217) the second and third term on the right-hand side can be neglected. If earnings follow a pure random walk, then all past information should be reflected in current prices and hence $\gamma = 0$. In this case the earnings level variable is the variable which shows the closest correlation with returns. In the opposite case, if $\gamma = 1$, the earnings change variable is the variable which shows the closest correlation with returns. In all other cases of lower positive correlation a mixture between the earnings levels and changes in earnings variables will deliver the best regression results.

This analysis shows that depending on the process for earnings both earnings and changes in earnings have explanatory power for returns. For my analysis this has the following implications. In a first step I apply the intuitive approach which has also been the starting point in the accounting literature. In the fifth chapter I relate stock returns to movements in fundamentals. I turn to the more general approach as I compare the explanatory power of the CAPM β and fundamentals. In the regression analysis of chapter 6 I include both changes and levels in fundamentals as explanatory variables.

3.3
Fundamentals and Rational Asset Pricing

For my empirical investigation the theoretical discussion so far has the following implications: Within a framework of rational asset pricing the return on a winner-loser strategy must be due to a difference in the exposure with respect to systematic risk. This exposure is measured by the covariance between returns and the pricing kernel. To implement this approach empirically, stock returns are related to aggregate pricing variables. In the CAPM the exposure with respect to systematic risk is measured by β. To the extent that differences in β can explain differences in returns, the winner-loser effect can be explained within the CAPM as a special case of a framework of rational asset pricing.

The alternative approach is to relate stock returns to movements in fundamentals. The overperformance of the loser portfolio during the test period might be due to unexpected improvements of profits, the underperformance of the winner portfolio due to an unexpected deterioration of profits. The interpretation which I have proposed in the last subsection is as follows: If such a pattern can be observed, the winner-loser effect reflects unexpected movements in fundamentals. As these movements could have been expected, the winner-loser effect is not in line with rational asset pricing.

Relating stock returns to the CAPM β on the one hand side and to fundamentals on the other hand, the analysis so far implies a strict dichotomy. If the CAPM β can explain the winner-loser effect this implies that the winner-loser effect occurs within a framework of rational asset pricing. If fundamentals explain the winner-loser effect it is due to a surprise effect.

In this last part of my analysis I show that this dichotomy is artificial. I show that an alternative interpretation is available for the relationship between stock returns and fundamentals. Changes in fundamentals might proxy for changes in the exposure with respect to systematic risk.

The modelling approach which is pursued in this chapter is related to two strands of the literature: single-asset models and multi-asset models. Most models which relate asset returns to cash flows are stated for single-asset economies (e.g., Franke (1984), Stapleton and Subrahmanyam (1990)). The winner-loser effect however is an observation for the cross section of stock returns which has to be modelled in a multi-asset economy. An earlier example of this second approach is Lucas (1978). For modelling aggregate cash flows and the pricing process I refer to results from the single-asset literature. In particular, I rely on a result derived by Stapleton and Subrahmanyam (1990) for the pricing process: In a representative investor economy with constant relative risk aversion where aggregate cash flows follow a geometric random walk the pricing kernel is not autocorrelated. With respect to modelling multi-asset economies the approach pursued in this chapter is related to the asset pricing framework which has been provided by Stapleton and

Subrahmanyam (1978). But whereas their multi-period CAPM relies on constant absolute risk aversion my model relies on constant relative risk aversion.

After a preliminary remark I analyze the methodological setting of my empirical investigation and present my modelling framework. Then I investigate co-movement in expected excess returns and expected cash flows during the test period. Fourth, I discuss under which conditions we obtain comovement between realized returns and realized cash flows during the formation period. Finally, I turn to the question of intertemporal dependence. A final remark relates the analysis to the rational asset pricing framework which I have provided at the beginning of this chapter.

3.3.1
Preliminary Remark

The theoretical relationship between stock returns and fundamentals is far from direct. In a one period framework this can be shown as follows. Assume that the value of a company is paid back as cash at the end of the period. Let X^i denote this final cash flow of the company i, X^M is the market cash flow. Assume that the whole economy is financed by equity. R^i is the return on the company i, R^M the return on the market portfolio. ϕ is the pricing kernel.

The winner-loser hypothesis compares returns of the winner and loser portfolios with the return on a reference portfolio. To investigate these excess returns it is necessary to define a reference portfolio.[21] In the following I will refer to the market portfolio as the reference portfolio as this will facilitate the analysis considerably. This procedure does not exactly mirror my empirical analysis. In my empirical analysis I take the middle portfolio as the reference portfolio. However, other investigations have taken index portfolios as reference portfolios (most notably DeBondt and Thaler (1985) and Meyer (1994)). On a qualitative level the results of these investigations have been similar to my results. From an empirical point of view therefore this change in the reference portfolio should not harm the analysis.

To obtain a positive expected excess return the following equivalent conditions must hold:

---

[21] Note that these excess returns are different from the usual definition of an excess return as for example applied in the CAPM where we refer to $R^i - R_f$ as excess return.

$$E(R^i) - E(R^M) = \frac{E(X^i)}{E[\phi X^i]} - \frac{E(X^M)}{E[\phi X^M]} > 0 \Leftrightarrow$$

$$
\begin{aligned}
&E(X^i)\left[\operatorname{cov}(\phi, X^M) + E(\phi)E(X^M)\right] \\
&-E(X^M)\left[\operatorname{cov}(\phi, X^i) + E(\phi)E(X^i)\right] > 0 \Leftrightarrow
\end{aligned}
\tag{17}
$$

$$-\operatorname{cov}\left(\phi, \frac{X^i}{E(X^i)}\right) + \operatorname{cov}\left(\phi, \frac{X^M}{E(X^M)}\right) > 0$$

where $E(X^i), E(X^M), E(\phi X^i), E(\phi X^M)$ are all greater than 0.

$-\operatorname{cov}\left(\phi, X_i E(X_i)^{-1}\right)$ measures the exposure of the cash flows to systematic risk. An asset for which $\operatorname{cov}\left(\phi, X_i E(X_i)^{-1}\right)$ takes large negative values pays high cash flows in states where state contingent claims are cheap. The last inequality states the necessary condition to obtain an expected return which is larger than the market return. The exposure of the cash flows of company i must be larger than the exposure of the market cash flow.

In the following I turn to a more complete analysis of the relationship between stock returns and fundamentals in a two period setting.

3.3.2
A Two-Period Framework

Before I turn to the derivation of the asset pricing model I have a closer look at the setting of my empirical investigation. This research design conditions on the performance of stocks during a formation period and investigates whether stocks outperform or underperform the market portfolio during the subsequent test period. Although at first sight it seems to be the same whether we look at the formation period or the test period it is not quite: We condition on realized returns during the formation period whereas it is expected returns which we are interested in during the test period. Every realized return can be decomposed into an expected part and a residual, $R_{t+1}^i = E_t\left(R_{t+1}^i\right) + \varepsilon_{t+1}^i$. If expectations are unbiased the expectation of the residual must be equal to zero. This has different consequences for the formation and for the test period. In constructing the winner and the loser portfolio we condition on realized returns during the formation period. Hence, a stock might be in the winner portfolio because it has a high expected return or because it has a high residual. Conditional on these realized returns we observe returns during the test period. During the test period the expectation of the residual must be equal to zero if the market is efficient and market participants have rational expectations. Hence, realized returns must be equal to expected returns on average. We look for the following combination of realized and expected returns during the formation and during the test period:

portfolio	formation period	test period
winner	$R_1^i - R_1^M > 0$	$E_1(R_2^i) - E_1(R_2^M) < 0$
loser	$R_1^i - R_1^M < 0$	$E_1(R_2^i) - E_1(R_2^M) > 0$

where R_t^i denotes the return on a stock i in period t and R_t^M denotes the return on the market portfolio in period t. To get a valid model for the observed intertemporal structure of returns we are interested in realized returns in period 1 and expected returns in period 2. The return during the first period can be written as

$$
\begin{aligned}
R_1 &= \frac{X_1 + P_1}{P_0} \\
&= \frac{X_1 + E_1\left(\phi_1^2 X_2\right)}{E_0\left(\phi_0^1 X_1\right) + E_0\left(\phi_0^2 X_2\right)}
\end{aligned}
\tag{18}
$$

where ϕ_t^s denotes the pricing kernel for cash flows in period s valued in period t, R_1 is the return in period 1, and X_t is the cash flow in period t. The expected return during the second period can be written as

$$
E_1(R_2) = \frac{E_1(X_2)}{E_1\left(\phi_1^2 X_2\right)}.
$$

Since we are concerned with excess returns over the market return, $R_t^i - R_t^M$, we first discuss the properties of the market return. I use the market return as a benchmark and therefore I am not interested in the properties of the market return *per se*. To model it in a particularly simple way I apply a model where the market return in period t is independent of the market return in period $t+1$.[22] In the following I discuss a setting in which we obtain myopia for the market return. As can be seen from equation (18) the properties of the market return derive from the interplay between cash flows and the pricing kernel. In a representative investor economy the pricing kernel ϕ_t^s is equal to $U'(X_s)/E_t(U'(X_s))$. Stapleton and Subrahmanyam (1990) have shown that myopia applies in a representative investor framework under two conditions: (1) Either the cash flow follows an arithmetic random walk and the representative investor shows constant absolute risk aversion, or (2) the cash flow follows a geometric random walk and the investor shows constant relative risk aversion. In the following we rely on this second setting.[23] For the market cash flow the process is assumed to be as follows

---

[22] If this property holds for all stocks in an economy it implies myopia: In a multi-period framework it is sufficient to optimize one's portfolio period by period without taking into account future developments.

[23] In a framework which is solely based on the condition of no-arbitrage this second set of assumptions can be substituted by the assumption of constant elasticity of the pricing kernel (cf. Franke, Stapleton, and Subrahmanyam (1999)).

$$X_{t+1}^M = \eta_{t+1} X_t^M$$

where η_{t+1} is stochastic and intertemporally independent. For our model we do not need any further assumptions about the distribution of η_{t+1}. If η_{t+1} is normally distributed this is a geometric random walk. If we assume limited liability, then $\eta_{t+1} > 0$. A representative agent is assumed to exist and to exhibit constant relative risk aversion, $U = \sum_{t=1}^{2} \rho^t \frac{X_t^{1-\gamma}}{1-\gamma}$. Under these conditions equation (18) simplifies to[24]

$$R_1^M = \frac{X_1^M \left(1 + \dfrac{E_1\left(\phi_1^2 X_2^M\right)}{X_1^M}\right)}{E_0\left(\phi_0^1 X_1^M\right)\left(1 + \dfrac{E_0\left(\phi_0^2 X_2^M\right)}{E_0\left(\phi_0^1 X_1^M\right)}\right)}$$

$$= \frac{X_1^M}{E_0\left(\phi_0^1 X_1^M\right)} = \frac{\eta_1}{E_0\left(\phi_0^1 \eta_1\right)} \frac{X_0^M}{X_0^M} = \frac{\eta_1}{E_0\left(\phi_0^1 \eta_1\right)}.$$

The realized return on the market depends only on the market cash flow X_1^M and the pricing kernel ϕ_0^1 for the next period. This particularly simple myopic form of the market return is due to the combination of the power utility function and the specific stochastic process. More general utility functions like extended power utility functions and more complex stochastic processes lead to intertemporal dependence which hinders the above decomposition. The expected return on the market in period 2 is

$$E_1\left(R_2^M\right) = \frac{E_1\left(X_2^M\right)}{E_1\left(\phi_1^2 X_2^M\right)} = \frac{E_1\left(\eta_2\right)}{E_1\left(\phi_1^2 \eta_2\right)}.$$

For the cash flows of the portfolios I use a similar framework as for the market cash flow. In my model specification the stochastic increment for the portfolio is a function of the stochastic increment of the market cash flow, $X_{t+1}^i = f\left(\eta_{t+1}\right) X_t^i$. I restrict my attention to linear specifications of the function $f\left(\eta_{t+1}\right)$. To be able to

---

[24] This can be shown as follows. Under the above assumptions the pricing kernel can be determined as

$$\phi_t^s = \frac{U'\left(X_s^M\right)}{U'\left(X_t^M\right)} = \frac{\rho^s \left(X_s^M\right)^{-\gamma}}{\rho^t \left(X_t^M\right)^{-\gamma}} = \rho^{s-t} \prod_{k=t+1}^{s} \eta_k^{-\gamma}$$

and hence,

$$\frac{E_1\left(\phi_1^2 X_2^M\right)}{X_1^M} = \frac{E_1\left(\rho \eta_2^{-\gamma} X_1^M \eta_2\right)}{X_1^M} = E_1\left(\rho \eta_2^{1-\gamma}\right) = \frac{E_0\left(\rho \eta_1^{1-\gamma}\right) E_0\left(\rho \eta_2^{1-\gamma}\right)}{E_0\left(\rho \eta_1^{1-\gamma}\right)}$$

$$= \frac{E_0\left(\rho^2 \eta_1^{-\gamma} \eta_2^{-\gamma} X_0^M \eta_1 \eta_2\right)}{E_0\left(\rho \eta_1^{-\gamma} X_0^M \eta_1\right)} = \frac{E_0\left(\phi_0^2 X_2^M\right)}{E_0\left(\phi_0^1 X_1^M\right)}$$

interpret the cash flow structure, I relate these linear specifications to managerial effort as an additional explanatory variable. In addition to the stochastic market increments, η_{t+1}, contributions of the management determine the results. Additional managerial effort should lead to larger cash flows which in turn should increase the return. I investigate under which conditions this intuition works.

3.3.3
Expected Express Returns during the Test Period

The main aim of my analysis is to obtain reversals in stock returns which are driven by movements in cash flows. In this section my aim is defined more narrowly: I investigate expected excess returns during the test period.

The first specification of the portfolio cash flow which I analyze is $X_{t+1}^i = (a + b\eta_{t+1})X_t^i$. In this specification the growth rate of the cash flow consists of two components, an idiosyncratic component a and a component $b\eta_{t+1}$ which is proportional to the stochastic increment of the market cash flow. In this specification we assume b to be fixed. The extra effort of the management is captured by the a component. a is assumed to be stochastic and uncorrelated with the market cash flow and the pricing function. The extra effort of the management enters as a multiplicative component, the cash flow of the previous period is multiplied by a to get the new cash flow. The intuition is that the management contribution has a higher impact in larger companies which show already a large cash flow in period t. The condition for an expected excess return is as follows:

$$E_1\left(R_2^i\right) - E_1\left(R_2^M\right) = \frac{E_1(a) + E_1(b\eta_2)}{E_1\left[\phi_1^2(a+b\eta_2)\right]} - \frac{E_1(\eta_2)}{E_1(\phi_1^2\eta_2)} \quad > 0 \quad \Leftrightarrow$$

$$\left(E_1(a) + E_1(b\eta_2)\right)E_1\left[\phi_1^2\eta_2\right] - E_1(\eta_2)E_1\left[\phi_1^2(a+b\eta_2)\right] \quad > 0 \quad \Leftrightarrow$$

$$E_1(a)E_1\left[\phi_1^2\eta_2\right] + E_1(b\eta_2)E_1\left[\phi_1^2\eta_2\right] \quad\quad\quad\quad (19)$$

$$-E_1(a)E_1(\eta_2)E_1\left[\phi_1^2\right] - E_1(b\eta_2)E_1\left[\phi_1^2\eta_2\right] \quad > 0 \quad \Leftrightarrow$$

$$E_1(a)\,\mathrm{cov}\left(\phi_1^2, \eta_2\right) \quad > 0$$

As $\mathrm{cov}(\phi_1^2, \eta_2)$ is negative[25], $E_1(a)$ has to be negative. Or, if we reverse this statement, a positive contribution of the management decreases the expected return of the stock.

At first sight this result is surprising. Instead of increasing expected returns an additional cash flow which is due to managerial effort decreases the expected return below the market rate of return. Investigating the two cash flow components a and $b\eta_2$ more closely reveals the following. In terms of expected returns we

---

[25] $\mathrm{cov}(\phi_1^2, \eta_2)X_1^M = \mathrm{cov}(\phi_1^2, X_2^M) = \mathrm{cov}\left(\dfrac{U'(X_2^M)}{E(U'(X_2^M))}, X_2^M\right) < 0 \text{ for } U''(X_2^M) > 0.$

can distinguish two extreme cases. One where the component a is expected to be equal to zero and one where the component b is equal to zero. In the first case the expected return $E_1(R_2)$ can be determined as

$$E_1\left(R_2^i\right) = \frac{E_1\left(b\eta_2\right)}{E_1\left(\phi_1^2\left(b\eta_2\right)\right)} = \frac{E_1\left(\eta_2\right)}{E_1\left(\phi_1^2\eta_2\right)} = E_1\left(R_2^M\right)$$

Hence, the $b\eta_2$ component earns the market rate of return due to perfect correlation between X_2^i and X_2^M. In the second case the expected return $E_1\left(R_2^i\right)$ can be determined as

$$E_1\left(R_2^i\right) = \frac{E_1\left(a\right)}{E_1\left(\phi_1^2\left(a\right)\right)} = \frac{1}{E_1\left(\phi_1^2\right)} = R_2^f,$$

R_2^f is the risk free rate of return in period 2. As the a component does not bear any systematic risk it earns the risk-free rate of return. Now it is possible to understand our findings from above. If a positive cash flow aX_t^i is anticipated, the expected return decreases. The reason for this effect is that this component earns the risk-free rate. As a is assumed to be uncorrelated with the market cash flow and hence the pricing function, it does not bear any systematic risk. Therefore, its expected return is the risk-free rate. The component b earns the market return. Hence, a stock for which a positive cash flow a is expected is a portfolio which earns a mixture of the market return on the b component and the risk-free rate on the a component. Expected excess returns are negative. For the expected excess return to be positive signs reverse: With $E_1(a) < 0$ a stock is leveraged by the negative a component, and hence is expected to earn more than the market. This model specification implies that larger growth rates in cash flows, as long as they are driven by a positive a component, lead to a decrease in expected returns.

I therefore turn to a second model specification in which the additional managerial effort, which in this case is denoted by ε, is multiplied by the stochastic market component. In this second specification the cash flow in period $t+1$ is determined by $X_{t+1}^i = (b+\varepsilon)\eta_{t+1}X_t^i$. Here the effectiveness of the contributions of the management depends on the situation of the economy as a whole. For this specification of the cash flow we obtain the following equivalent condition for positive expected excess returns

$$E_1\left(R_2^i\right) - E_1\left(R_2^M\right) = \frac{E_1\left(\left(b+\varepsilon\right)\eta_2\right)}{E_1\left(\phi_1^2\left(b+\varepsilon\right)\eta_2\right)} - \frac{E_1\left(\eta_2\right)}{E_1\left[\phi_1^2\eta_2\right]} > 0 \iff$$

$$E_1\left(\left(b+\varepsilon\right)\eta_2\right)E_1\left(\phi_1^2\eta_2\right) - E_1\left(\phi_1^2\left(b+\varepsilon\right)\eta_2\right)E_1\left(\eta_2\right) > 0 \iff \qquad (20)$$

$$\operatorname{cov}\left(\varepsilon,\eta_2\right)E_1\left(\phi_1^2\eta_2\right) - \operatorname{cov}\left(\varepsilon,\phi_1^2\eta_2\right)E_1\left(\eta_2\right) \qquad > 0$$

Decisive for the valuation are covariances: A positive covariance between managerial effort, ε, and the macroeconomic activity, η_2, increases the expected return. The other component is the covariance between ε and $\phi_1^2\eta_2$. From a theoretical point of view it would be desirable to obtain a relationship where a positive covariance $\mathrm{cov}(\varepsilon,\eta_2)$ implies a negative covariance $\mathrm{cov}(\varepsilon,\phi_1^2\eta_2)$. However, in general no simple functional relationship between the two covariances exist.

$\phi_1^2 X_2^M = \phi_1^2 \eta_2 X_1^M$ is the price of future wealth. In a representative investor economy the correlation of ε with future aggregate economic activity and the correlation with the price of wealth are closely related. A simple analytical relationship between $\mathrm{cov}(\varepsilon,\eta_2)$ and $\mathrm{cov}(\varepsilon,\phi_1^2\eta_2)$ is only available if ε and η_2 are jointly normal. Then Stein's lemma can be applied. Under this condition it can be shown that if the representative agent shows relative risk aversion larger than 1, then $\mathrm{cov}(\varepsilon,\eta_2)$ and $\mathrm{cov}(\varepsilon,\phi_1^2\eta_2)$ show opposite signs.[26] With respect to the expected excess return a positive effect of $\mathrm{cov}(\varepsilon,\eta)$ is reinforced by the other covariance under this condition (cf. equation (20)).

In a third step I turn to a model which combines the two elements which I have described so far. Here the condition for a positive excess return is simply a combination of the two results which we have derived above:[27]

$$E[a]\mathrm{cov}(\phi_1^2,\eta_2) + \mathrm{cov}(\varepsilon,\eta_2)E[\phi_1^2\eta_2] - \mathrm{cov}(\varepsilon,\phi_1^2\eta_2)E[\eta_2] > 0 \qquad (21)$$

We can interpret this condition in the following way: Assume that the manager has a limited budget of extra activity which he can spread between a and ε. If he wants to maximize expected returns he has to focus his attention on activities

---

[26] If both ε and $X_2^M = \eta_2 X_1^M$ are jointly normally distributed, then Stein's lemma applies: $\mathrm{cov}(\varepsilon,f(X^M)) = E(f'(X^M))\mathrm{cov}(\varepsilon,X^M)$. This relationship can be applied to investigate the relationship between $\mathrm{cov}(\varepsilon,X_2^M)$ and $\mathrm{cov}(\varepsilon,\phi_1^2 X_2^M)$. If Stein's lemma can be applied then $\mathrm{cov}(\varepsilon,\phi_1^2 X_2^M) = E(d\phi_1^2 X_2^M / dX_2^M)\mathrm{cov}(\varepsilon,X_2^M)$. In a representative agent economy $\phi_1^2 = u'(X_2^M)/E_1(u'(X_2^M))$ and hence $\phi_1^2 X^M = u'(X^M)X^M / E(u'(X^M))$

$$\frac{d\phi_1^2 X_2^M}{dX_2^M} = \left(u''(X^M)X^M + u'(X^M)\right)\frac{1}{E(u'(X^M))}$$

$$= \left[\frac{u''(X^M)X^M}{u'(X^M)} + 1\right]\frac{u'(X^M)}{E(u'(X^M))}$$

$d\phi_1^2 X_2^M / dX_2^M$ is negative in the case of relative risk aversion larger than 1, a result which is favoured by empirical investigations of relative risk aversion. In this case a positive covariance between ε and X_2^M implies a negative covariance $\mathrm{cov}(\varepsilon,\phi_1^2 X_2^M)$ which reinforces the effect.

[27]

$$E[R^i] - E[R^M] = \frac{E(a) + E[(b+\varepsilon)\eta]}{E[\phi_1^2 a] + E[\phi_1^2(b+\varepsilon)\eta]} - \frac{E(\eta)}{E[\phi_1^2\eta]} > 0 \Leftrightarrow$$

$$E[a]E[\phi_1^2\eta] + E[(b+\varepsilon)\eta]E[\phi_1^2\eta] - E[\phi_1^2(a)]E(\eta) - E[(b+\varepsilon)\eta]E(\eta) > 0 \Leftrightarrow$$

$$E[a]\mathrm{cov}(\phi_1^2,\eta) + E(\varepsilon\eta)E[\phi_1^2\eta] - E(\varepsilon)E(\eta)E[\phi_1^2\eta] - E(\eta)\mathrm{cov}(\varepsilon,\phi_1^2\eta) > 0 \Leftrightarrow$$

$$E[a]\mathrm{cov}(\phi_1^2,\eta) + \mathrm{cov}(\varepsilon,\eta)E[\phi_1^2\eta] - \mathrm{cov}(\varepsilon,\phi_1^2\eta)E[\eta] > 0$$

which are positively correlated with the market. The management should concentrate on activities which are correlated with its core activities (i.e. increase $\mathrm{cov}(\varepsilon,\eta)$) and stop outside activities which are uncorrelated with its main business (i.e. a). The best is if it were able to go short in the a component which would increase the leverage of its actions.

If we assume condition (21) to hold the question arises whether this implies a comovement between excess returns and changes in fundamentals. For the market cash flow the expected growth rate is $E(\eta)$, for the stocks $E(a+(b+\varepsilon)\eta)$. We assume that the management can only influence ε and a. $E(\varepsilon)$ and $E(a)$ both might be positive. If we set b equal to one on average, the decisive condition to obtain a growth in cash flows for single stocks which is larger than for the market is

$$E(a+(1+\varepsilon)\eta)>E(\eta)\Leftrightarrow$$
$$E(a)+E(\eta)+\mathrm{cov}(\varepsilon,\eta)+E(\varepsilon)E(\eta)>E(\eta)\Leftrightarrow \qquad (22)$$
$$E(a)+\mathrm{cov}(\varepsilon,\eta)+E(\varepsilon)E(\eta)>0$$

Inequality (21) states the condition for a positive excess return. Inequality (22) states the condition for an excess growth rate in cash flows. If we compare the two conditions we obtain good news and bad news at the same time. For the a component our reasoning from above applies. A positive idiosyncratic contribution increases the cash flow, but as it earns the risk-free rate of return it decreases the expected return. Therefore, the ε component is not able to foster comovement of stock returns and cash flows. For the a component the result is more favourable. A positive covariance $\mathrm{cov}(\varepsilon,\eta)$ increases the expected return (cf. inequality (21)). At the same time it favours the inequality (22) to hold. This is the good news. The bad news is that neither condition implies the other. Neither do excess cash flows imply excess returns nor vice versa. Nevertheless, both observations help to explain each other.

3.3.4
Excess Returns during the Formation Period

I now turn to the formation period. Here the question arises under which conditions we obtain comovement between realized returns and realized changes in cash flows. For the test period we had to relate expected cash flows to expected returns. For the formation period we relate realized cash flows to realized returns. The analysis of realized returns turns out to be quite complicated, as I will demonstrate below. Nevertheless, it is quite likely that we obtain comovement between stock returns and fundamentals. This is due to the fact that any deviation of realized cash flows from expected cash flows has an immediate effect on realized returns which shows into the same direction. We can split the realized value of any variable into its expected part and a residual. Therefore, for the formation period

$$R_t = \frac{P_t + X_t}{P_{t-1}}$$

$$E(R_t) + \varepsilon_t^R = \frac{E(P_t + X_t) + \varepsilon_t^{PX}}{P_{t-1}}$$

whereas for the test period

$$E(R_{t+1}) = \frac{E(P_{t+1} + X_{t+1})}{P_t}$$

where P_t denotes the stock price in period t. In terms of expectations the same line of reasoning applies for both equations. As we investigate realized returns during the formation period, two residuals enter the equation: ε_t^{PX} on the right hand side which captures unexpected cash flows and unexpected changes in stock prices, ε_t^R on the left hand side which captures unexpected returns. Whereas the relationship between expected cash flows and expected returns turned out to be quite complicated, the relationship between the residual cash flows and the residual returns is likely to be closer. *Ceteris paribus,* an unexpected positive cash flow leads to an increase in realized returns. An unexpected negative cash flow leads to a decrease in realized returns. Hence, ε_t^X and ε_t^R are likely to show the same sign which reinforces comovement between realized returns and realized changes in cash flows.

One can try to decompose realized returns in a similar way as expected returns. Unfortunately, the analysis of realized returns delivers very inconvenient expressions which are difficult to handle. In my simplified framework I can show that the realized return is determined by three components and their interaction: the realized cash flow relative to its expectation, the change of expectation of cash flows in period 2 from period 0 to period 1 and finally a covariance term. I present a derivation of this decomposition below. The decisive question for the explanation of the winner-loser effect is the question how realized returns in the formation period are related to expected returns during the test period. I turn to this question in the next subsection.

Realized returns: A decomposition
If we analyze realized returns in greater detail even for our simple specification of the cash flow process the expression for the realized return during the formation period becomes quite complicated. We again assume for the cash flow process of the single stock: $X_{t+1}^i = \left(a_{t+1} + (b + \varepsilon_{t+1})\eta_{t+1}\right)X_t^i$ (In this two-period framework we have to introduce time indices for the management contribution.) To simplify the notation we denote $b + \varepsilon_{t+1}$ by c_{t+1}. Then the realized return becomes

$$R_1 = \frac{X_1 + E_1\left(\phi_1^2 X_2\right)}{E_0\left(\phi_0^1 X_1\right) + E_0\left(\phi_0^2 X_2\right)} =$$

$$\frac{\left(a_1 + c_1\eta_1\right)\left(1 + E_1\left(\phi_1^2\left(a_2 + c_2\eta_2\right)\right)\right)}{E_0\left(\phi_0^1\left(a_1 + c_1\eta_1\right)\right)\left(1 + E_0\left(\phi_1^2\left(a_2 + c_2\eta_2\right)\right)\right) + \text{cov}_0\left(\phi_0^1\left(a_1 + c_1\eta_1\right), \phi_1^2\left(a_2 + c_2\eta_2\right)\right)}.$$

The realized return has various interacting components which make it difficult to derive further implications in general. Instead we give some intuition for the components of this expression. We ask which factors drive large positive returns.

A first component of the realized excess return in period 1 is

$$\frac{\left(a_1 + c_1\eta_1\right)}{E_0\left(\phi_0^1\left(a_1 + c_1\eta_1\right)\right)}.$$

This fraction is similar to the expected return for the second period (cf. equation (19)) which we have analyzed above. The important difference is that realized cash flows enter the formula instead of expected cash flows. The numerator can be split into an expected part and a residual: $a_1 + c_1\eta_1 = E_0\left(a_1\right) + \varepsilon_1^a + E_0\left(c_1\eta_1\right) + \varepsilon_1^{cn}$, where ε_1^a denotes the residual of a_1, ε_1^{cn} denotes the residual of the product $c_1\eta_1$. For the expected part of the equation we obtain the same results as in the one-period framework. An increase in the expectation of the a component, $E_0\left(a_1\right)$, reduces the expected return and hence also the realized return on a stock. This is due to the effect that the expected return on the a_1 component is the risk-free rate of return. For an increase in the residual ε_1^a this is different. An increase in the residual ε_1^a increases the realized return as well as the realized cash flow. For the remaining parts of the fraction the effect is unambiguous. $E_0\left(c_1\eta_1\right)$ increases both returns and cash flows. The same holds for ε_1^{cn}.

The second component is

$$\frac{1 + E_1\left(\phi_1^2\left(a_2 + c_2\eta_2\right)\right)}{1 + E_0\left(\phi_1^2\left(a_2 + c_2\eta_2\right)\right)}.$$

This is the change in expectations due to information occurring in time 1. $\phi_1^2\left(a_2 + c_2\eta_2\right)X_1^i$ is the time 1 value of cash flows in period 2. If this value increases due to a change in expectations, this is already reflected in the realized return during the formation period.

The third component is $\text{cov}_0\left(\phi_0^1\left(a_1 + c_1\eta_1\right), \phi_1^2\left(a_2 + c_2\eta_2\right)\right)$. This is the covariance between the values of the cash flows in period 1 and in period 2. Remember $E_0\left[\phi_0^1\left(a_1 + c_1\eta_1\right)X_0^i\right]$ is the period 0 value of the cash flow in period 1 and $E_1\left[\phi_1^2\left(a_2 + c_2\eta_2\right)X_1^i\right]$ is the time 1 value of the cash flow in period 2. A positive covariance increases the price of an asset and decreases the realized return. This covariance is due to the geometric framework which we have chosen.

3.3.5
Intertemporal Dependence

The main aim of this chapter is to explain long-term reversals in the cross section of stock returns. So far we have restricted our attention to the analysis of co-movement between stock returns and fundamentals in a period by period approach. Realized returns have been related to realized cash flows during the formation period and expected returns have been related to expected cash flows during the test period. I now turn to an intertemporal analysis. In the empirical analysis we condition on realized returns during the formation period. Realized returns can be split into expected returns and the residual. Both parts, the expected return and the residual, might drive intertemporal dependence. Three types of models can be proposed: one where expected returns drive the results, a second one where residuals are the driving force and a third one where both components are decisive for the observed pattern of intertemporal dependence. For return reversals in winner portfolios we can summarize these models as follows

model	formation period	test period
type I	$E_0\left(R_1^i\right) - E_0\left(R_1^M\right) < 0$	$E_1\left(R_2^i\right) - E_1\left(R_2^M\right) < 0$
type II	$\varepsilon_1^i - \varepsilon_1^M > 0$	$E_1\left(R_2^i\right) - E_1\left(R_2^M\right) < 0$
type III	$R_1^i - R_1^M > 0$	$E_1\left(R_2^i\right) - E_1\left(R_2^M\right) < 0$

I discuss these three types of models in turn. All three types of models can be related to the pattern of management contributions. However, it is important to keep in mind the findings of the previous two sections: The decisive question for expected returns is whether management activity is correlated with macroeconomic activity. Large positive correlation implies expected excess returns. Large negative correlation or management activity which is uncorrelated with the market, i.e. a positive expected a component, imply an expected underperformance. In the following management performance is measured by its correlation with macroeconomic activity.[28]

---

[28] Instead of relating our theoretical reasoning to management contributions we could also relate it to the rise and decline of monopolistic structures. However, we have to be careful: As in the case of management performance the decisive question is how the rise and decline of monopolistic structures is correlated with macroeconomic activity. For a company to show cycles in returns it is neither necessary nor sufficient to observe extra profits which rise and decline over time. Decisive is that their exposure to systematic risk varies systematically over time.

The *type I* model proposes that the observed pattern in stock returns is due to the pattern of expected returns. Short-term persistence in excess returns is due to short-term persistence in expected returns. Long-term reversals in excess returns are due to long-term reversals in expected returns. For management performance this would imply that in the short run the management performance shows persistence whereas in the long run it shows reversals. From a theoretical point of view the question arises whether it is possible to formulate a process in expected returns which has the proposed properties. From a conceptual point of view such a process seems to be conceivable. For the sake of simplicity assume the following pattern of expected returns $+ + + - - - + + +$ etc where '+' denotes a period of expected returns above and '$-$' denotes a period of expected returns below the market return. Persistence can be observed from period 1 to period 2, as well as from period 2 to period 3. A reversal is observed from period 3 to period 4. Hence, the pattern which emerges is $(+, +); (+, +); (+, -); (-, -)$ etc. On average we observe persistence. This is different if we take a two period perspective. In our empirical investigation we look at overlapping samples. For this pattern the use of an overlapping sample delivers the following results if we look at time horizons of two periods $(2+, 0); (2+, 2-), (0, 2-); (2-, 0); (2-, 2+) \ldots$ This implies a reversal on average. Short-term persistence and long-term reversals in terms of management contributions then imply the following. Already in this simple deterministic scheme short-term persistence and long-term reversals can occur at the same time. Therefore, there is no theoretical obstacle to this pattern in expected returns.

In terms of management contributions we can interpret this finding as follows: Persistence in management performance in the short run implies that over a short-term horizon incentives for the management work in the same direction. A suitable incentive system induces the management to improve the performance of a company. The management fails to improve the company results if the incentive system is unsatisfactory. This is different in the long run, the incentives which are provided for the management are expected to reverse. A good management becomes tired. Shareholders do not succeed to motivate the management over longer time horizons. On the other hand poor performance of the management becomes punished in the long run. After an (expected) poor performance management performance is expected to improve: Either better incentive schemes are provided or a new management is employed. In a framework of rational asset pricing this pattern has to coincide with cycles in the exposure to systematic risk. High expected management performance has to be correlated with a high exposure to systematic risk, low expected management performance with a low exposure.

In the *type II* model the residual during the formation period drives the result. A large short-term residual implies that the expected return for the next short-term period increases. A large long-term residual implies that the expected return for the next long-term period decreases. This implies that investors infer from this period's returns something about future returns. In the short run residual returns are used to update expectations by a positive feedback rule. If in this period the return is larger than expected then the expected return for the next period increases. In the long run a negative feed-back rule is used to update expectations. In terms of management contributions this implies the following. If the management performs better than expected for a short horizon investors update their prior conception of the management quality. On the other hand, after a long period of overperformance investors assume that the management is exhausted and expects the management to underperform the market subsequently. Again, in a framework of rational asset pricing the expected management performance during the test period has to be correlated with the exposure to systematic risk. Management underperformance has to coincide with low exposure to systematic risk.

In the *type III* model the observed pattern of intertemporal dependence is due to a combination of the two mechanisms. For example short-term persistence could be driven by the short-term residual whereas long-term reversals could be driven by reversals in long-term expectations.

All three types of models provide possible theoretical explanations of the winner-loser effect in a framework of rational asset pricing. Whether one of these models can explain the winner-loser effect is an empirical question. Although I do not test for these three types of models directly, I use them as a conceptual framework of my empirical analysis in chapter 5. The process of expectation building is investigated in the second part of chapter 4 within a CAPM framework. There I investigate for the CAPM whether expected returns or the unexpected residual during the formation period determine the pattern of expected returns during the test period.

3.3.6
Final Remark and Summary

In this subsection I have developed an alternative interpretation of the relationship between stock returns and movements in fundamentals. Fundamentals might proxy for the exposure to systematic risk. I have derived the results in this section within a framework of rational asset pricing. Hence, they are just a special case of the framework which I have derived in the first part of this chapter.

Empirically, the question arises whether fundamentals can better approximate for the exposure to systematic risk than the CAPM β. If the assumptions of the CAPM hold, this cannot be the case. Fundamentals then only proxy for the CAPM β. The CAPM β will always deliver a better explanation in terms of expected returns than fundamentals. However, if the assumptions of the CAPM do not hold then fundamentals might deliver a better explanation of stock returns than the CAPM. Fundamentals might then approximate the exposure to systematic risk better than the CAPM β.

In a stylized setting this subsection has shown how expected changes in fundamentals may explain the winner-loser effect. Market cash flows are modelled as a geometric random walk. The growth rate of the cash flows of individual stocks depends upon the growth rate of the market cash flow in a linear way. I distinguish between an idiosyncratic component and a component which is correlated with the market cash flow. I relate this decomposition to the way in which the management contributes to the performance of a company. The setting of the winner-loser effect can be split into two parts: a conditioning formation period during which we observe realized returns and a subsequent test period during which we explore expected returns. First, we investigate comovement during the test period. To obtain a positive expected excess return, management activity has to be positively correlated with market growth rates. Expected excess growth in cash flows is implied by a high expected value for the product of the management contribution and the market growth rate. Although these conditions do not imply each other they reinforce each other. For comovement during the formation period the same line of reasoning applies. In addition deviations of realized cash flows from expected cash flows induce similar deviations of realized returns from expected returns. To obtain the winner-loser effect in a two period setting expected returns during the test period have to be correlated with the expected return or the residual during the formation period. In the first case the correlation between the management contribution and the market cash flow must change over time. In the second case unexpected management contributions during the formation period imply a correlation between management contributions and the market cash flow during the test period which has the opposite sign. Positive [negative] unexpected management contributions during the formation period lead to a negative [positive] correlation during the test period.

If the winner-loser effect is explained by movements in fundamentals, this does not necessarily imply that it is due to a surprise effect. Fundamentals might proxy for the exposure with respect to systematic risk. Then the winner-loser effect occurs within a framework of rational asset pricing.

3.4
Summary

Starting point for my theoretical analysis is the question whether it is possible to explain the winner-loser effect within the framework of rational asset pricing. If the winner-loser effect occurs within this framework, it must be due to differences in the exposure with respect to systematic risk. The excess return of the loser portfolio as compared to the winner portfolio must be due to a larger exposure with respect to systematic risk. The standard way how to explore this question is to relate stock returns to aggregate pricing variables. A special case is the CAPM where stock returns are related to the market return.

An alternative explanation of the winner-loser effect is that it is due to a surprise effect. Investors are surprised by the performance of stocks during the test period. This surprise may be driven by news in fundamentals. Unexpected improvements in dividends and profits for the loser firms lead to an overperformance of the loser firms in terms of returns. An unexpected deterioration for the winner firms leads to an underperformance of the winner firms. This alternative explanation relates stock returns to the performance in terms of fundamentals. Unexpected changes in fundamentals are related to unexpected returns.

In a last step I have returned to the framework of rational asset pricing. I have investigated the relationship between stock returns and changes in fundamentals within this framework. Expected returns are related to expected changes in fundamentals. It has been shown that fundamentals might proxy for the exposure to systematic risk. Even if the winner-loser effect is explained by movements in fundamentals, this does not necessarily imply that it is due to a surprise effect. The winner-loser effect might still occur within a framework of rational asset pricing.

In the subsequent chapters I apply this theoretical framework. First, I investigate whether the winner-loser effect can be explained by the CAPM. Stock returns are related to the market rate of return (chapter 4). Then I turn to fundamentals as explanatory variables (chapter 5). Finally, I compare the explanatory power of the CAPM and of fundamentals.

4 The CAPM and the Winner-Loser Effect

Long-term reversals in stock returns can have two implications. Most of the literature has attributed them to an inefficiency of the stock market which is caused by irrational behaviour of market participants. This chapter follows a different line of reasoning. In a rational asset pricing model excess returns should be due to an additional exposure to systematic risk. If after high [low] realized returns low [high] returns are expected, then long-term reversals are in line with capital market theory. To investigate this question it is necessary to measure the exposure to systematic risk. In this chapter I investigate to which extent the CAPM as the simplest asset pricing model can explain the observed excess returns.

Starting point is the observation of long-term reversals in the cross section of German stock returns. For a time horizon of 60 months we have found an excess return of 3.27% p.a. for a contrarian strategy. As this is the largest annual excess return which we could find, I take the period length of 60 months as a reference point. Table 14 presents differences in annualized returns for a contrarian strategy year by year.[29] In addition results are presented for the pooled sample.[30] Significant excess returns of the winner portfolio as compared to the loser portfolio are obtained for 6 out of 10 years. This difference is mainly driven by the difference in the performance between the middle and the winner portfolio. We obtain excess returns for all 10 periods, 7 of which are significant. For the difference between the loser and the middle portfolio the evidence is much weaker. Only in 7 cases we obtain excess returns, four of which are significant. For the pooled sample we find an overperformance of the loser portfolio as compared to the winner portfolio of 3.27%.

In this section I investigate the winner-loser effect within a CAPM framework. I investigate two questions. The first question is to which extent the CAPM is able to explain the winner-loser effect. The second question concerns the way in which expectations are built.

For the first step I take the theoretical reasoning from the first part of the previous section as a starting point. In a framework of rational asset pricing expected

---

[29] This table is derived from the findings in table 9 from the first chapter. Instead of presenting total returns over 60 months it presents differences in annualized returns. The reported levels of significance are based on t-statistics and are in general a bit more supportive than the Wilcoxon rank sum statistics which we have reported previously.

[30] For our investigation the results for the pooled sample is not just the average over the years as the number of stocks available increases over time and hence, the results of the single years have to be weighted to obtain the results for the pooled sample.

excess returns must be due to an additional exposure with respect to systematic risk. In the CAPM this exposure with respect to systematic risk is measured by the covariance of returns R_i with the return on the market portfolio R_M.

The second question concerns the process of expectation building. In a framework of rational asset pricing the difference in returns between the winner and the loser portfolio during the test period is expected. The observed reversals in stock returns can then be due to two factors. Either the winner-loser effect is due to reversals in expected returns. For the loser portfolio low expected returns are followed by large expected returns, for the winner portfolio large expected returns are followed by low expected returns. Alternatively, new information during the formation period is used to update expectations.

Table 14. Differences in returns on the winner, the middle, and the loser portfolio during a 60 months test period, yearly evidence, annualized returns. Portfolios are formed conditional on the performance during the previous 60 months

Year	Middle/Winner		Loser/Middle		Loser/Winner	
	ΔR_t	Sign.	ΔR_t	Sign.	ΔR_t	Sign.[a]
1968	1.5288%	**	3.1314%	*	4.6603%	***
1969	2.8430%	**	3.2459%	**	6.0890%	***
1970	2.2338%	*	0.7409%		2.9747%	**
1971	2.7929%	**	1.1443%		3.9372%	**
1972	3.2182%	*	−2.9438%		0.2744%	
1973	2.6117%		−3.3469%	†††	−0.7352%	
1974	−0.3479%		−4.3382%	††	−4.6861%	
1975	0.6075%		0.4636%		1.0711%	
1976	2.4625%	**	0.9766%	*	3.4391%	***
1977	2.5591%	*	3.0556%	**	5.5147%	***
pooled	2.1999%	***	1.0748%	*	3.2747%	***

[a] Significance of the t-statistic for a test of the difference in portfolio returns $(H_0 : \Delta R_t = 0)$; the level of significance is shown by the following symbols, *** (**, *): H_0 can be rejected against $H_1 : \Delta R_t > 0$ at a 1% (5%, 10%) significance level; ††† (††, †): H_0 can be rejected against $H_1 : \Delta R_t < 0$ at a 1% (5%, 10%) significance level

4.1
Explaining the Winner-Loser Effect

First, I investigate to which extent the CAPM is able to explain the winner-loser effect. This question has a cross sectional as well as a time series dimension. In the cross section large returns should be due to large exposures with respect to systematic risk. Intertemporally, reversals should be due to changes in this exposure. The main findings of this chapter add to the evidence that the CAPM can only explain a small fraction of expected stock returns. I find evidence for differences in the exposure with respect to systematic risk. However, they are too small to explain the cross section of stock returns. A reason for this finding might be that the CAPM is only partially able to capture the exposure with respect to systematic risk. This section follows a standard research design: First, we derive our hypotheses. Second, we present the results of our empirical investigation which are then discussed. A summary concludes.

4.1.1
Hypotheses

I derive two sets of hypotheses. The first set of hypotheses concerns the question to which extent we can explain the cross section of excess returns within the CAPM. The second set of hypotheses relates to the intertemporal pattern of returns. If a strategy earns an excess return in a framework of rational asset pricing, the strategy has to have an exposure to systematic risk which justifies the observed excess return.

From the condition of no-arbitrage we obtain (cf. equation (7))

$$E(R_i) - R_f = \left[E(R_M) - R_f\right] \frac{\text{cov}(\phi, R_i)}{\text{cov}(\phi, R_M)} \tag{23}$$

where R_i denotes the random return on an individual stock, R_M the random return on the market portfolio, R_f the risk-free rate of return and ϕ denotes the pricing kernel. From an empirical point of view it is difficult to determine the covariance between returns and the pricing kernel directly. Therefore, we resort to an equilibrium framework where a representative investor exists. Under the restrictive assumptions of the capital asset pricing model[31] the no-arbitrage condition implies

$$E(R_i) - R_f = \left[E(R_M) - R_f\right] \frac{\text{cov}(R_i, R_M)}{\text{var}(R_M)} = \left[E(R_M) - R_f\right] \beta_i$$

The first two hypotheses are concerned with the cross section of stock returns during the test period. As the exposure with respect to systematic risk is measured by $\beta_i = \text{cov}(R_i, R_M)/\text{var}(R_M)$, I investigate whether I can observe significant differences in β between the winner, loser, and middle portfolios which are in line with the observed excess returns.

Hypothesis I: *The portfolios have different exposure to systematic risk. As the loser portfolio shows the best performance during the test period, it has the highest exposure. Hence, $\beta_L > \beta_M > \beta_W$ where $\beta_L(\beta_M, \beta_W)$ denote the β of the loser (the middle, the winner) portfolio during the test period.*

---

[31] Returns have to be jointly normal or the representative investor has to have quadratic utility.

Hypothesis I does not ensure that the CAPM can explain the observed behaviour of stock returns. In addition, the size of the difference in β is important: the difference in β has to be multiplied by the risk premium of the market portfolio to find out whether it is large enough to explain the observed excess returns.

Hypothesis II: *The difference in exposure to systematic risk multiplied by the average risk premium explains the observed differences in return.*

The second set of hypotheses is concerned with the intertemporal dimension: Reversals in stock returns imply a cyclical behaviour of stock returns where high returns follow low returns and vice versa. In a rational asset pricing framework this implies that the exposure to systematic risk should change systematically over time.

Hypothesis III: *For the winner portfolio from the formation to the test period the exposure to systematic risk declines. For the loser portfolio it increases.*

4.1.2
Estimation Results

In this section I investigate my hypotheses for long-term reversals with a time horizon of 60 months. At the heart of the analysis is the estimation of a CAPM regression

$$R_{jt} - R_{ft} = \alpha_j + \beta_j \left(R_{Mt} - R_{ft} \right) + \varepsilon_{jt} \tag{24}$$

where R_{jt} denotes the return on the stock j. R_{Mt} is the market rate of return and R_{ft} is the risk-free rate of return. As market index I use the DAFOX, for the risk-free rate I use the monthly money market rate.

To test for the hypothesis I estimate equation (24) for all stocks during the test period by an OLS regression. The estimation is based on the 60 monthly returns during the test period. I compare the average β coefficient for the portfolios j and k by a t-test

$$t = \frac{\bar{\beta}_j - \bar{\beta}_k}{\sqrt{\dfrac{\sigma_j^2}{n_j} + \dfrac{\sigma_k^2}{n_k}}}$$

where $\bar{\beta}_j$ is the average value for β for portfolio j, σ_j is the standard deviation of β within the portfolio and n_j the number of observations.

The results for the first hypothesis are presented in table 15. The table shows the differences in β and the level of significance for a t-test. $\Delta\beta$ is the difference in portfolio β and ΔR_t is the difference in yearly returns during the test period. For the pooled sample the β of the loser portfolio exceeds the β of the winner portfolio by a highly significant 0.2045. Also the differences between the winner and the middle portfolio as well as the differences between the middle and the loser portfolio are highly significant. Similar to the differences in returns the larger part of this difference (about 75%) is due to the difference between the winner and the middle portfolio.

On a yearly basis the evidence is weaker but still supportive. For the years 1968-1970 and 1975-1977 the β of the loser portfolio is larger than the β of the winner portfolio. For the years 1973 and 1974 signs reverse. Both the β and the return on the winner portfolio are larger than for the loser portfolio. Also the annual evidence for the difference between the middle and the winner portfolio β is consistent with our first hypothesis. The evidence for the difference between the loser and the middle portfolio β is considerably weaker. In three out of ten cases the difference is close to 0. Still, in eight cases the sign of the difference in β is in line with the sign of the difference in returns.

Table 15. Differences in β between portfolios during the test period for a time horizon of 60 months

Year	Middle/Winner			Loser/Middle			Loser/Winner		
	$\Delta\beta^a$	Sign.[b]	ΔR_t^c	$\Delta\beta^a$	Sign.[b]	ΔR_t^c	$\Delta\beta^a$	Sign.[b]	ΔR_t^c
1968	0.2306	***	1.53%	0.1213		3.13%	0.3520	***	4.66%
1969	0.2260	***	2.84%	0.2792	***	3.25%	0.5051	***	6.09%
1970	0.1911	**	2.23%	0.4045	***	0.74%	0.5956	***	2.97%
1971	0.0678		2.79%	-0.1280		1.14%	-0.0602		3.94%
1972	0.1321	*	3.22%	-0.0788		-2.94%	0.0533		0.27%
1973	0.0105		2.61%	-0.0729		-3.35%	-0.0624		-0.74%
1974	0.0511		-0.35%	-0.2377	†††	-4.34%	-0.1866	†	-4.69%
1975	0.2370	***	0.61%	-0.0124		0.46%	0.2247	**	1.07%
1976	0.2045	***	2.46%	0.1587	***	0.98%	0.3632	***	3.44%
1977	0.1596	**	2.46%	0.1008	**	3.06%	0.2604	***	5.51%
pooled	0.1510	***	2.20%	0.0535	***	1.07%	0.2045	***	3.27%

[a] average difference in the portfolio β during the test period
[b] Significance of the t-statistic for a test of the difference in β; $H_0 : \Delta\beta = 0$, the level of significance is shown by the following symbols, *** (**, *): H_0 can be rejected against $H_1 = \beta_W < \beta_M < \beta_L$ at a 1% (5%, 10%) significance level; ††† (††, †): H_0 can be rejected against $H_1 = \beta_W > \beta_M > \beta_L$ at a 1% (5%, 10%) significance level
[c] difference in yearly returns during the test period

By and large, I obtain supportive evidence for the first hypothesis, $\beta_L > \beta_M > \beta_W$. Differences in β can be observed for the pooled sample as well as on a yearly basis.

In the next step I investigate whether the difference in β is sufficient to explain the observed excess returns. I compare the distribution of realized excess returns, ΔR_t, with the distribution of estimated excess returns, $\Delta\hat{R}_t$. Excess returns are calculated as differences in portfolio means. The estimated excess returns are calculated as $\Delta\hat{R} = \Delta\bar{\beta}(R_M - R_f)$. $\Delta\bar{\beta}$ is the average difference in portfolio β which I multiply with the average risk premium $R_M - R_f$ during the 60 months of the investigation. To calculate the estimated excess return I do not include the intercept α as this intercept captures the part of the expected return which is not explained by the CAPM. According to the CAPM differences in expected returns are only due to differences in the exposure to market risk which is captured by β.

Table 16. Excess Returns: Explained and Unexplained

Portfolios	Mean[a]			Sum of Squares[b]		
	ΔR_t	$\Delta\hat{R}_t$	$\Delta\hat{R}_t / \Delta R_t$	$\Sigma(\Delta R - \Delta\bar{R})^2$	$\Sigma(\Delta\hat{R} - \Delta\bar{R})^2$	expl.
L/W[c]	3.27%	0.82%	25.07%	414.5%^{2}	120.3%^{2}	29.02%
M/W[c]	2.20%	0.48%	21.82%	160.2%^{2}	27.9%^{2}	17.42%
L/M[c]	1.07%	0.34%	31.77%	137.1%^{2}	27.5%^{2}	20.06%

[a] $\Delta R_t (\Delta\hat{R}_t)$ is the observed (estimated) difference in returns, $\Delta\hat{R}_t / \Delta R_t$ is the part of the excess return which is explained by the estimation. The third column presents the ratio between the estimated and the observed difference in returns
[b] Comparison between the observed sum of squares $\Sigma(\Delta R - \Delta\bar{R})^2$ and the estimated sum of squares $\Sigma(\Delta\hat{R} - \Delta\bar{R})^2$. $\Delta\bar{R}$ is the mean difference in returns, $\Delta\hat{R}$ is the estimated difference in returns. expl. (= explained) is the ratio between the estimated sum of squares and the observed sum of squares
[c] L/W (M/W, L/M) difference in returns between loser and winner portfolio (middle and winner portfolio, loser and middle portfolio)

I investigate the question to which extent the CAPM is able to explain the winner-loser effect in two ways. First, I compare the average realized excess return ΔR_t with the estimated excess return $\Delta\hat{R}_t$. Results for this calculation are presented on the left hand side of table 16. I compare again differences between the winner, the middle, and the loser portfolio. For a 60 months horizon I observe a difference in returns between the winner and the loser portfolio of 3.27%. 0.82% is the estimated value. Hence, only 25% oxcess return is explained by the CAPM. The explanatory power for the middle/winner and the loser/middle difference is similar.

The second way how to look at the explanatory power is to look at the sum of squares. On the right hand side of table 16 I present the total sum of squares $\Sigma(\Delta R - \Delta\bar{R})^2$, the explained sum of squares $\Sigma(\Delta\hat{R} - \Delta\bar{R})^2$, and R^2. $\Delta\bar{R}$ is the average difference in all periods. The last column expl. (=explained) is the ratio between the explained sum of squares and the observed sum of squares. It captures the explained part of the total variation in ΔR. For the difference between the winner and the loser portfolio 29% of the total variations in returns is captured by the CAPM. For the difference between the winner and the middle portfolio and between the loser and the middle portfolio the results are a bit worse.

Taken together, the evidence supports the second hypothesis only weakly. Both the major part of the observed excess return as well as the major part of its variation remain unexplained.

Table 17. Differences in β from the formation to the test period

Year	Loser Portfolio		Winner Portfolio	
	$\beta_{t+1} - \beta_t$	Sign.[a]	$\beta_{t+1} - \beta_t$	Sign.[a]
1968	0.165543	**	0.138382	
1969	0.189281	**	−0.045114	
1970	0.184114	*	−0.209626	**
1971	0.116473		−0.077039	
1972	0.053304		0.058554	
1973	0.074348		0.094163	
1974	0.053208		−0.153158	
1975	0.285845	**	−0.220991	**
1976	0.022623		−0.175394	**
1977	−0.103390		0.320658	***
pooled	0.099563	***	0.106112	***

[a] Significance of the t-statistic for a test of a change in β from the formation to the test period; $H_0 : \beta_{t+1} - \beta_t = 0$, the level of significance is shown by the following symbols, *** (**, *): For the loser portfolio (winner portfolio) H_0 can be rejected against $H_1 : \beta_{t+1} - \beta_t > 0$ $\left(H_1 : \beta_{t+1} - \beta_t < 0 \right)$ at a 1% (5%, 10%) significance level

Turning to the intertemporal development, table 17 investigates changes in β from the formation to the test period. For every stock I estimate the CAPM regression (24) by means of an OLS regression for the 60 monthly returns during the formation period, and for the 60 monthly returns during the test period separately. For the loser portfolio it is tested whether there is an increase in β, for the winner portfolio it is tested whether there is a decrease in β by means of a t-test. For the pooled sample I find significant changes: For the loser portfolio I find an increase in beta of 9.96 percentage points. For the winner portfolio I observe a decrease in beta of roughly the same size. However, as I investigate the results on a yearly base the evidence weakens considerably. For the loser portfolio all but one observation have the right sign, but only 4 out of 10 observations are significant. For the winner portfolio the evidence for an intertemporal change in returns is again significant in 4 out of 10 cases. However, more observations show the wrong sign. Taken together, I find supportive evidence for my third hypothesis. For the loser portfolio β increases from the formation to the test period. For the winner portfolio it decreases. Again the evidence for the pooled sample is considerably stronger than for the year by year observations.

4.1.3
Discussion

The findings of this section show that the CAPM can only explain part of the long-term reversals in stock returns. On a qualitative level the evidence for the first and the third hypothesis is supportive. For the pooled sample $\beta_L > \beta_M > \beta_W$ during the test period. From the formation to the test period β increases for the loser portfolio and decreases for the winner portfolio. On a yearly basis the evidence is weaker but still supportive. However, the differences in β are too small to explain the differences in returns. Both in terms of the mean as well as the variation in excess returns the CAPM can only explain less than 30% of the winner-loser effect.

These findings are in line with the findings for the American market. Chan (1988) and DeBondt and Thaler (1987) observed differences in portfolio β which were too small to explain the observed differences in returns. If the difference in returns is not explained by differences in the portfolio β, the question arises why this difference is not exploited by means of an arbitrage strategy. One possibility is that institutional rigidities prevent this. The second possibility is that the CAPM does not capture the differences in the exposure to systematic risk.

Institutional rigidities could be one reason. To exploit the difference between the return on the winner and the loser portfolio it is necessary to buy the loser portfolio and to sell the winner portfolio. A possible obstacle could have been short-selling restrictions. For a 5 year horizon buying the loser portfolio delivers only an excess return of 1.07% as compared to an investment into the middle portfolio. Short selling of the winner portfolio adds a return of 2.20% to the return of the strategy. About 75% of the success of a winner-loser strategy can be attributed to the short selling of the winner portfolio. Short selling restrictions existed in the German stock market at the time which is investigated. Therefore, this part of the excess return has not been available to most investors. Still, it would have been a rational strategy for the investors who held the winner portfolio to have sold it. These investors might have had other reasons not to sell their stocks. For institutional investors who have kept their stocks at purchase prices on their balance sheets selling would have implied large profit realizations and as a consequence large tax payments which they may have tried to avoid. In addition the selling of large stakes would have led to large price movements which might have made this strategy unprofitable. Another reason not to sell could have been strategic ownership of companies in the same industry. It is an interesting question to which extent the winner stocks have been held by institutional investors or by companies which are in the same industry.

An alternative explanation is that the CAPM does not capture differences in the exposure to systematic risk. In this case the question arises whether it is possible to develop better asset pricing models than the CAPM. The empirical flaws of the

CAPM are well-known.[32] From a theoretical point of view the CAPM only holds under very restrictive assumptions. A representative investor has to make his decisions according to a quadratic utility function or stock returns have to be jointly normally distributed. Neither of these assumptions is very attractive. The assumption of joint normality of stock returns does not hold empirically: the distribution is leptokurtic. Quadratic utility of the representative investor implies increasing absolute risk aversion. Rich investors would have to invest a lower absolute amount of money into a risky asset than a poor investor, a property which does not hold in reality.[33]

To derive alternative asset pricing models, we can go back to the no-arbitrage condition for asset returns (equation (23)). From there we can derive the more general insight that the expected return of an asset depends on the exposure of this asset to a systematic risk factor. This exposure is measured by the covariance of the return of the asset with this factor. In the most general case this systematic risk factor is the pricing kernel, ϕ. Unfortunately, we cannot observe ϕ directly. To test for equation (23) one has to relate ϕ to observable variables. Under the restrictive assumptions of the CAPM ϕ is related to the return on the market portfolio, R_M. Under alternative assumptions ϕ has been related to other variables. Breeden (1979) derives a consumption CAPM where ϕ is related to growth rates in macroeconomic consumption. From a theoretical point of view the consumption CAPM is attractive because it includes macroeconomic variables and hence offers a more complete view of the economy. However, its empirical performance is quite weak. If we look at the time series behaviour of consumption and stock returns it is not difficult to see why this is the case. Consumption is much more smoothed than stock returns. But as in this model the covariance between stock returns and growth rates in macroeconomic consumption is the measure of risk exposure, it is not likely to capture much of the total variation in returns. Therefore, empirically one is likely to obtain better results if one sticks with a partial equilibrium approach. An extension along these lines is the arbitrage pricing theory (APT) due to Ross (1976). In the APT the pricing kernel is related to a multifactor explanation. Empirically, different risk factors have been proposed. A three factor model which has become quite popular has been proposed by Fama and French (1996). They explain the cross section of stock returns by the return on the market portfolio, size and the book to market ratio. The return on the market portfolio can be interpreted as a systematic risk factor in the same way as in the CAPM. With respect to size Fama and French find that small stocks earn a risk premium. This can be interpreted as a liquidity premium for thin trading as there is usually less liquidity in small stocks. Unfortunately, we lack such a plausible

---

[32] For a recent overview see Elton and Gruber (1995), chapter 15.

[33] Moreover, the assumption of a representative investor makes it impossible to explain the variety of derivative financial instruments which we observe in the real world. E.g., Franke, Stapleton, and Subrahmanyam (1998) explain the existence of options by investors which face different amounts of background risk. In such an economy a representative investor does not exist.

interpretation of the book to market ratio. This nourishes the suspicion of data mining. A complementary approach is pursued in the next chapter. I relate the observed pattern in stock returns to movements in fundamentals.

4.2
Expectation Building

In this section I investigate the process of expectation building. Within a framework of rational asset pricing the winner-loser effect is characterized by a sequence of realized and expected returns. For the winner portfolio large realized returns are followed by low expected returns, $R_{i,1} > R_{M,1}$ and $E(R_{i,2}) < E(R_{M,2})$. The reverse pattern obtains for the loser portfolio. In the following I decompose the realized return during the formation period into two components, the expected return and a residual, $R_{i,1} = E(R_{i,1}) + \varepsilon_{i,1}$. I investigate whether the expected return or the residual drive the observed reversals. This question has already been raised in the discussion on intertemporal dependence in the last part of chapter 3.

In the first case the winner-loser effect is due to reversals in expected returns. For the winner portfolio large expected returns are followed by low expected returns. The opposite pattern obtains for the loser portfolio. Alternatively new information during the formation period is used to update expectations. Large residuals are followed by low expected returns for the winner portfolio. Low residuals are followed by large expected returns for the loser portfolio.

This section is structured as follows. In the first theoretical part I show that the proposed decomposition can be applied more generally to any form of negative autocorrelation. In the second part I present my hypothesis and the results.

4.2.1
Theory

The winner-loser effect is a special finding of negative autocorrelation in stock returns. In this section I show that the proposed decomposition of the realized stock returns into an expected part and a residual can be applied to any form of autocovariance. My investigation whether the winner-loser effect is driven by expected returns or the residual is a special application of this decomposition.

Before I derive my hypothesis I show that any autocovariance can be decomposed into a covariance of the expected values and a covariance of the expected value in period 1 with the residual in period 2.

$$\mathrm{cov}\left(R_{t+1}, R_t \,|\, I_{t-1}\right) = \mathrm{cov}\left(x_t, x_{t-1} \,|\, I_{t-1}\right) + \mathrm{cov}\left(x_t, \varepsilon_t \,|\, I_{t-1}\right)$$

This can be seen as follows. For the realized return we can write

$$R_t = E\left(R_t \,|\, I_{t-1}\right) + \varepsilon_t = x_{t-1} + \varepsilon_t \qquad (25)$$

where x_{t-1} is the expected part and ε_t is the unexpected part of the return. Now we determine the covariance between R_{t+1} and R_t at time $t-1$.

$$\operatorname{cov}\left(R_{t+1}, R_t \middle| I_{t-1}\right) = \operatorname{cov}\left(x_t + \varepsilon_{t+1}, x_{t-1} + \varepsilon_t \middle| I_{t-1}\right)$$
$$= \operatorname{cov}\left(x_t, x_{t-1} \middle| I_{t-1}\right) + \operatorname{cov}\left(x_t, \varepsilon_t \middle| I_{t-1}\right) + \qquad (26)$$
$$\operatorname{cov}\left(\varepsilon_{t+1}, x_{t-1} \middle| I_{t-1}\right) + \operatorname{cov}\left(\varepsilon_{t+1}, \varepsilon_t \middle| I_{t-1}\right)$$

By definition,

$$\operatorname{cov}(x, y) = E(xy) - E(x)E(y) = E_y\left[yE_x\left(x \middle| y\right)\right] - E(x)E(y)$$

If we decompose the last two covariances of (26) we obtain

$$\operatorname{cov}\left(x_{t-1}, \varepsilon_{t+1} \middle| I_{t-1}\right) = E\left[x_{t-1}E\left(\varepsilon_{t+1} \middle| x_{t-1}, I_{t-1}\right) \middle| I_{t-1}\right] - E\left(\varepsilon_{t+1} \middle| I_{t-1}\right)E\left(x_{t-1} \middle| I_{t-1}\right) \quad (27)$$
$$\operatorname{cov}\left(\varepsilon_t, \varepsilon_{t+1} \middle| I_{t-1}\right) = E\left[\varepsilon_t E\left(\varepsilon_{t+1} \middle| \varepsilon_t, I_{t-1}\right) \middle| I_{t-1}\right] - E\left(\varepsilon_{t+1} \middle| I_{t-1}\right)E\left(\varepsilon_t \middle| I_{t-1}\right) \quad (28)$$

From the law of iterated expectations we know (cf. Dothan (1990), p. 81)

Axiom 1 (Law of iterated expectations) *If a partition* **f** *is coarser than a partition* **g** *then for any random variable* x

$$E\left[E\left(x \middle| \mathbf{g}\right) \middle| \mathbf{f}\right] = E\left(x \middle| \mathbf{f}\right)$$

Applying the law of iterated expectations to R_{t+1} we obtain $E\left(\varepsilon_{t+1} \middle| I_t\right) = 0$. For information sets **f** which are coarser than I_t we obtain

$$E\left[E\left(\varepsilon_{t+1} \middle| I_t\right) \middle| \mathbf{f}\right] = E\left(\varepsilon_{t+1} \middle| \mathbf{f}\right) = 0$$

Turning to the information sets $I_{t-1}, \left(x_{t-1}, I_{t-1}\right)$, and $\left(\varepsilon_t, I_{t-1}\right)$, all these information sets provide partitions which are coarser than I_t and can be denoted by **f**. The expectation of ε_{t+1} under these information sets is equal to 0.

Therefore, both covariances in equations (27) and (28) are equal to 0 and the covariance between R_{t+1} and R_t reduces to

$$\operatorname{cov}\left(R_{t+1}, R_t \middle| I_{t-1}\right) = \operatorname{cov}\left(x_t, x_{t-1} \middle| I_{t-1}\right) + \operatorname{cov}\left(x_t, \varepsilon_t \middle| I_{t-1}\right) \qquad (29)$$

We have two possible sources of negative autocovariance in asset returns: either autocovariances between the expected return in period t and the expected return in period $t+1$ or the autocovariance between the unpredicted part of the return in period t, ε_t, and the expected return in period $t+1$.

4.2.2
Hypothesis and Empirical Results

In this section I apply the proposed decomposition to the winner-loser effect. The winner-loser effect is a special finding of negative autocorrelation in stock returns.

For the winner [loser] portfolio low [high] returns are expected during the test period. The expected return during the test period has to be correlated with the realized return during the formation period. As the realized return during the formation period can be split up into an expected part and a residual, $R_t = E(R_t) + \varepsilon_t$, the expected return during the test period can be correlated with either part. To explore which part of the realized return is the decisive part which drives the results during the test period, we condition on the expected part $E(R_t)$ and the residual ε_t separately.

The difference in expected returns during the test period is either due to the pattern of expected returns during the formation period or the pattern of residuals. The hypothesis which I pursue in this section is that the winner-loser effect is due to the residual during the formation period. This implies that investors update their expectations. The expected return during the formation period is unlikely to be decisive. If expected returns were driving the results this would imply a pattern where large expected returns are followed by low expected returns and vice versa. It is more likely that investors use new information from the formation period to update their expectations. Therefore, I can state my hypothesis as follows.

Hypothesis IV: *The winner-loser effect is due to new information which arises during the formation period. The residual during the formation period is decisive to obtain a return reversal during the test period.*

To test for this hypothesis I change the design of my research strategy. In the standard design of the winner-loser effect returns during the test period were observed conditional on past returns. Realized returns can be split into an expected part and a residual, $R_t = E(R_t) + \varepsilon_t$. Instead of conditioning on realized returns during the formation period I condition on the expected return and the unexplained residual separately. Both values, the expected return and the residual, are obtained from a CAPM regression for the formation period. The CAPM regression

$$R_{jt} - R_{ft} = \alpha_j + \beta_j \left(R_{Mt} - R_{ft} \right) + \varepsilon_{jt}$$

is run asset by asset on monthly data from the 60 months of the formation period. Within the CAPM, α_j should be equal to zero. Hence, α_j captures the excess return over R_f which is not explained by the CAPM. It is also known as *Jensen's* α. I first condition on α_j: stocks are sorted into quintiles according to α_j. This time the winner portfolio is the portfolio of stocks with the largest values for α_j. I test for differences in the performance of these portfolios during the test period. In a second step I condition on the expected return. Within the CAPM the expected return on any stock is $\beta_j \left[E(R_M) - R_f \right]$. As $E(R_M) - R_f$ is the same for all stocks I sort stocks according to β_j into quintiles. Again, I test for differences in the performance across portfolios during the test period.

Table 18 presents the results for conditioning on the residual. A picture emerges which is very similar to the traditional winner-loser effect. In fact the average success of the contrarian strategy is even larger than before. If we look at the pooled result we obtain an excess return of 5.49% (as compared to 3.27% which we obtained previously). Again the major part of this difference can be attributed to the difference between the middle and the winner portfolio (3.81%). If we take a closer look at the evidence on the yearly base the results are again fairly supportive in a similar way as our previous findings. The difference between the winner and the loser portfolio is significant for most of the years. In fact the evidence is slightly more supportive than before. For the difference between the loser and the middle portfolio the evidence is again very weak.

Table 18. Differences in returns on the winner, the middle, and the loser portfolio during a 60 months test period, yearly evidence, annualized data. In comparison to table 14 portfolios are built conditional on Jensen's α during the formation period

Year	Middle/Winner		Loser/Middle		Loser/Winner	
	Diff.	Sign.	Diff.	Sign.	Diff.	Sign.[a]
1968	5.8695%	***	1.2282%		7.0977%	***
1969	4.4114%	**	6.5307%	***	10.9421%	***
1970	5.6049%	***	1.3115%		6.9164%	**
1971	3.1959%	*	2.2851%		5.4810%	*
1972	3.0419%		1.7686%		4.8105%	*
1973	3.1025%		2.6578%		5.7603%	**
1974	2.6932%		−2.7539%	†	−0.0607%	
1975	2.7964%	*	−2.1834%		0.6130%	
1976	0.9126%		3.3386%		4.2512%	
1977	7.0981%	***	3.4499%		10.5480%	***
pooled	3.8055%	***	1.6851%	**	5.4906%	***

[a] cf. Table 19

Table 19 presents the results for conditioning on the expected return. A very different picture emerges. The sign for the difference in portfolio returns reverses: Conditional on expected returns the newly defined loser portfolio underperforms the newly defined winner portfolio by a significant 3.32%. The driving force of this result is that the newly defined loser portfolio underperforms the middle portfolio by a highly significant 3.42%. The difference between the winner and the middle portfolio is insignificant. On a yearly base we find that the difference between the loser and the middle portfolio is significant in most of the years whereas the evidence is weaker for the difference between the winner and the loser portfolio.

The results are in line with my hypothesis. The decisive factor for the excess return during the test period is the residual during the formation period. To exploit the difference in returns between the winner and the loser portfolio one can buy the loser portfolio and sell the winner portfolio short. The standard winner-loser strategy is to condition on total realized returns. One can increase the return of this strategy if one conditions on the residual of a CAPM regression instead.

Table 19. Differences in returns on the winner, the middle, and the loser portfolio during a 60 months test period, yearly evidence, annualized data. In comparison to table 14 portfolios are built conditional on the CAPM β during the formation period

Year	Middle/Winner ΔR_t	Sign.	Loser/Middle ΔR_t	Sign.	Loser/Winner ΔR_t	Sign.[a]
1968	−1.2424%		−3.5792%	††	−4.8216%	††
1969	1.4632%		−5.0778%	††	−3.6146%	
1970	2.5882%		−4.7657%	†	−2.1775%	
1971	0.1339%		−0.3185%		−0.1846%	
1972	1.8115%		−1.7598%		0.0517%	
1973	3.8798%	*	−1.4548%		2.4250%	
1974	2.4378%		−1.4605%		0.9773%	
1975	−2.3416%		−3.1917%	††	−5.5333%	††
1976	−3.7434%	†	−6.8786%	†††	−10.6220%	†††
1977	−1.5983%		−4.6473%	††	−6.2456%	†
pooled	0.0971%		−3.4212%	†††	−3.3241%	†††

[a] Significance of the t-statistic for a test of the difference in portfolio returns; the level of significance is shown by the following symbols, *** (**, *): $H_0 : \Delta\beta = 0$, the level of significance is shown by the following symbols, *** (**, *): H_0 can be rejected against $H_1 = \beta_W < \beta_M < \beta_L$ at a 1% (5%, 10%) significance level; ††† (††, †): H_0 can be rejected against $H_1 = \beta_W > \beta_M > \beta_L$ at a 1% (5%, 10%) significance level

4.2.3
Discussion

This finding contributes to our understanding of the process of expectation building. In the literature the process of expectation building is often formulated exogenously.

E.g., following Campbell (1991) Campbell, Lo, and MacKinlay (1997) (p. 265 f.) formulate the expected return process as

$$E_t\left(R_{t+1}\right) = R + x_t$$
$$x_{t+1} = \gamma x_t + \xi_{t+1}, \qquad -1 < \gamma < 1$$

where R_{t+1} is the stock return of period $t+1$, R is a constant return and ξ_t a zero mean variable. x_t follows a first-order autoregressive (AR(1)) process. If γ is close to one the process is highly persistent: Shocks ξ_t from past periods determine future expectations for a long time. In this model the random increment ξ_{t+1} drives the process of expected returns. It is determined exogenously and cannot be observed directly.

In this model the expected return of the previous period is

$$E_{t-1}(R_t) = R + x_{t-1}.$$

This implies for the expected return process

$$E_t(R_{t+1}) = R + \gamma x_{t-1} + \xi_t$$
$$= E_{t-1}(R_t) + (\gamma - 1)x_{t-1} + \xi_t. \tag{30}$$

One can substitute for x_{t-1} further backwards; $x_{t-1} = \gamma x_{t-2} + \xi_{t-1}$.

My findings suggest an alternative way how to model the process of expected returns. My findings suggest that expected returns are a function of past realized returns. This suggests a process of adaptive expectation building. New information during the formation period should be used to update expectations. Expected returns are a function of realized returns during the last period, $E_t(R_{t+1}) = f(R_t) = f(E_{t-1}(R_t) + \varepsilon_t)$ where $\varepsilon_t = E_{t-1}(R_t)$. Assume a linear functional form

$$E_t(R_{t+1}) = a_1 E_{t-1}(R_t) + a_2 \varepsilon_t. \tag{31}$$

ε_t is the residual return during the formation period. My findings have the following implications for the coefficients a_1 and a_2. High expected returns during the formation period imply high expected returns during the test period (cf. table 19). Hence, a_1 is positive. A high residual during the formation period leads to a small expected return during the test period (cf. table 18). Hence, a_2 is negative.

Equation (31) is similar to equation (30). The main difference is that ξ_t is a variable which is specified exogenously and cannot be observed, whereas $\varepsilon_t = R_t - E_{t-1}(R_t)$ is the residual return during the formation period which can be observed. In addition the model of Campbell et al. includes an additional lagged variable, $(\gamma - 1)x_{t-1}$. However equation (31) can also be extended to include further lagged variables.

My findings suggest a process of adaptive expectation building. Whether adaptive expectation building or the process suggested by Campbell et al. are better able to explain the pattern in expected returns is an empirical question. It should be explored further.

4.3
Summary

Starting point of this chapter has been the observation of long-term reversals in the cross section of German stock returns. For a return period of 60 months we have found an excess return of 3.27% p.a. for a contrarian strategy. We investigate to which extent the CAPM explains this pattern. We find significantly different exposures with respect to market risk between the winner and the loser portfolio. The β of the loser portfolio exceeds the β of the winner portfolio by 0.2045. However, this difference is not sufficient to explain the observed difference in excess returns. The estimated excess return is only 0.82% p.a. Intertemporally we observe a change in β from the formation to the test period. The success of a contrarian strategy can be enhanced if we condition on the residual of a CAPM regression instead of the realized return during the formation period. The process of expected returns appears to be driven by exogenous shocks to realized returns during the formation period.

As the CAPM can only explain a small part of the observed excess return, we have to look for alternative model specifications which might perform better empirically. In the next chapter I relate the observed pattern in stock returns to movements in fundamentals.

Appendix: Methodology
This chapter has applied a fairly simple methodology to test for the CAPM. From the point of view of econometric methodology three concerns can be raised.[34] First, to estimate the β coefficients it has been proposed to estimate a system of regressions simultaneously (Greene (1997), pp. 648 ff. and Campbell, Lo, and MacKinlay (1997), pp. 189 ff.). This has the advantage that the covariances between the errors can be used to obtain more precise estimates. However, the estimated coefficients from an OLS regression on an asset by asset level lead to the same estimators (Campbell, Lo, and MacKinlay (1997), p. 190). Therefore, the differences in β are the same whether a system of regressions is estimated or OLS. A difference between the two approaches only occurs for the inference for hypothesis I and hypothesis III. An estimation of a system of equations could lead to more precise estimates. An even more general approach which in addition could account for intertemporal dependence is the GMM approach which has been proposed by MacKinlay and Richardson (1991). This approach is beyond the scope of this analysis and deserves a mongraph on its own.

The second concern is to which extent the analysis suffers from an errors-in-variables problem. The β which enter the analysis of hypothesis II are the result of an estimation and not the true β. The estimated instead of the true β is multiplied by the risk premium. Therefore, this analysis might suffer from an errors-in-variables problem. In the literature this problem has been addressed in two

---

[34] I am grateful to Prof. Winfried Pohlmeier for his comments on these questions.

ways. Fama and MacBeth (1973) use portfolios instead of individual stocks in order to obtain more precise estimates. An alternative method is to correct for the errors-in-variables explicitly by adjusting the standard errors (Litzenberger and Ramaswamy (1979) and Shanken (1992)).

The third concern is whether the design of the analysis biases the results. β is estimated conditional on the returns during the formation period. For the winner portfolio, the distribution of the estimator $\hat{\beta}$ is $F\left(\hat{\beta}(R_{it}) \mid R_{iF} > R_{MF}\right)$ where R_{MF} is the market return during the formation period, R_{iF} is the return of a winner stock i during the formation period. In general, this distribution will be different from the unconditional distribution of $\hat{\beta}$ on which the tests of this chapter rely.[35]

---

[35] For an in depth treatment of these "data snooping" problems see Lo and MacKinlay (1999), chapter 8.

5 Fundamentals and the Winner-Loser Effect

The main finding of the previous chapter has been that the CAPM is insufficient to explain the winner-loser effect. As the CAPM β can only explain a small part of the observed excess return, the question arises how we have to interpret this finding. Two interpretations can be offered.

First, this finding can be interpreted as an indicator that it is not possible to explain the winner-loser effect within a framework of rational asset pricing. Then the winner-loser effect is due to irrational behaviour of market participants. This line of reasoning has already been introduced by DeBondt and Thaler (1985). They claimed that the winner-loser effect is due to an overreaction to company news. According to their interpretation investors become too optimistic in the case of current positive news. They become too pessimistic in the case of current negative news.

One way to investigate this claim is to relate stock returns to movements in fundamentals. Investors might overinterpret changes in fundamentals during the formation period. If they observe improvements in fundamentals for the winner portfolio, investors might interpret these improvements to be permanent although they are only temporary. As this becomes clear during the test period investors adjust their expectations accordingly. As a consequence high returns during the formation period are followed by low returns during the test period. For the loser portfolio declines in fundamentals are taken to be permanent although they are only temporary. As fundamentals improve again during the test period investors adjust their expectations: low returns during the formation period are followed by high returns during the test period.

However, a second interpretation is also possible. Although the CAPM fails to explain major parts of the winner-loser effect it might still be possible that the winner-loser occurs within a framework of rational asset pricing. If this is the case the relationship between stock returns and fundamentals has to be interpreted in a different way. If fundamentals help to explain the cross section of expected returns within a framework of rational asset pricing, they must capture part of the exposure with respect to systematic risk.

Investigating the relationship between stock returns and fundamentals cannot answer the question which of these two interpretations is appropriate. Either the winner-loser effect is due to irrational behaviour of market participants. Then the pattern of fundamentals may help to explain how the irrational behaviour arises. Alternatively, the winner-loser effect occurs within a framework of rational asset pricing. Then the pattern in fundamentals must capture the exposure with respect to systematic risk. To answer this question, more research is needed to which extent aggregate pricing variables are able to capture the observed pattern in stock returns. This analysis is pursued in chapter 6.

This section is organized as follows. First, I relate the observed pattern in stock returns to movements in fundamentals. I discuss whether it is possible to find a pattern in fundamentals which is related to the observed overperformance and subsequent underperformance of winner stocks and the reverse behaviour of loser stocks. Starting point for my analysis is the hypothesis that the winner-loser effect cannot be explained within a framework of rational asset pricing and is due to an overreaction to news in fundamentals. Second, I reverse this question and ask whether one can use fundamental variables to distinguish between well performing and poorly performing stocks. In the third section I investigate whether fundamentals capture changes in the exposure to systematic risk. A summary concludes.

5.1
Movements in Fundamentals

This section relates the winner-loser effect to movements in cash flows. Proxies for a company's cash flows include dividends, a company's reported profits and profit components. I use the portfolio approach from the second chapter: stocks are sorted into five portfolios according to their performance in terms of stock returns during a formation period. I investigate the behaviour of dividends and profits for these portfolios. In a rational asset pricing model stock prices are the sum of future cash flows discounted at an appropriate rate. If we investigate the process for cash flows as the driving force of excess returns there are two possible sources for an excess return.[36] Either the realized cash flow is larger than the

---

[36] This can be seen as follows. To obtain an excess return the question is under which conditions we obtain a return R' which is larger than $E(R_M)$, the expected rate of return on the market portfolio. Assume the discount rate, R, to be equal to the expected market rate of return, $E(R_M)$. The price of a stock is determined by

$$P(t) = \sum_{\tau=t+1}^{\infty} \frac{E_t[X(\tau)]}{(1+R)^{\tau-t}}$$

where $P(t)$ is the price of an asset at time t, $X(\tau)$ is the dividend in period τ and R denotes the appropriate risk-adjusted discount factor which is assumed to be constant. The return on this stock is determined by expected cash flow, or the expectations concerning future cash flows have changed.

Starting point for my analysis is the hypothesis of DeBondt and Thaler that the winner-loser effect is due to an overreaction to current news. Investors mistake transitory movements in fundamentals to be permanent. For the winner portfolio they observe an increase in fundamentals. Although investors believe this increase to be permanent, it turns out to be transitory. Investors are surprised by a deterioration during the test period. Stock prices are adjusted accordingly which results in an underperformance in terms of returns relative to the market. The reverse pattern obtains for the loser portfolio. Investors take a deterioration of fundamentals during the formation period to be permanent, although it is only transitory. The unexpected improvements lead to a subsequent overperformance of the loser portfolio. From this reasoning I can state the following hypothesis.

Fundamental Hypothesis
For the winner-loser effect excess returns are parallelled by changes in fundamentals. For the winner portfolio the excess return during the formation period is parallelled by an increase in dividends and profits. The subsequent underperformance during the test period is parallelled by a decrease in fundamentals. For the loser portfolio the reverse pattern obtains.

In the framework of DeBondt and Thaler the Fundamental Hypothesis is due to irrational behaviour of market participants. Nevertheless, it is also possible to interpret this hypothesis within a framework of rational asset pricing. Then changes in fundamentals should proxy for changes in the exposure with respect to

$$1 + R'(t+1) = \frac{X(t+1) + P(t+1)}{P(t)}$$

$$= \frac{X(t+1) + \sum_{\tau=t+2}^{\infty} \frac{E_{t+1}[X(\tau)]}{(1+R)^{\tau-(t+1)}}}{\sum_{\tau=t+1}^{\infty} \frac{E_t[X(\tau)]}{(1+R)^{\tau-t}}}$$

$$= \frac{X(t+1) + \sum_{\tau=t+2}^{\infty} \frac{E_{t+1}[X(\tau)]}{(1+R)^{\tau-(t+1)}}}{\left(E_t[X(t+1)] + \sum_{\tau=t+2}^{\infty} \frac{E_t[X(\tau)]}{(1+R)^{\tau-(t+1)}} \right) \frac{1}{(1+R)}}$$

$$= \frac{X(t+1) + \sum_{\tau=t+2}^{\infty} \frac{E_{t+1}[X(\tau)]}{(1+R)^{\tau-(t+1)}}}{\left(E_t[X(t+1)] + \sum_{\tau=t+2}^{\infty} \frac{E_t[X(\tau)]}{(1+R)^{\tau-(t+1)}} \right)} (1+R)$$

To obtain a return R' which is larger than $R = E(R_M)$ the fraction on the right hand side has to be larger than 1. This can have two reasons: Either $X(t+1) > E_t(X(t+1))$, i.e. the realized cash flow is larger than the expected cash flow, or $\sum_{\tau=t+2}^{\infty} \frac{E_{t+1}[X(\tau)]}{(1+R)^{\tau-(t+1)}} > \sum_{\tau=t+2}^{\infty} \frac{E_t[X(\tau)]}{(1+R)^{\tau-(t+1)}}$, i.e the expectations concerning future cash flows have changed.

systematic risk. Decreases should proxy for decreases in this exposure. As long as no final answer can be given whether the winner-loser effect occurs within a framework of rational asset pricing it remains an open question which of the two interpretations applies.

The analysis proceeds as follows. First evidence is presented for the development of dividends per nominal equity and payout ratios, i.e. dividends as part of the profit of a company. Second, evidence is presented for profits per nominal equity. In addition, profit is split into three components: ordinary income, financial income, and extraordinary income.

5.1.1
Dividends

Stock prices in an efficient capital market are the sum of all future cash flows discounted at an appropriate rate. The most straightforward way how to investigate the cash flows of a company is to explore the behaviour of dividends. I take this as a starting point for my investigation. The main focus of my analysis however will be on profits. Profits as a measure of fundamental performance have the advantage that they abstract from the decision of the firm whether to pay dividends or whether to retain profits. As I pursue an in depth analysis of the behaviour of corporate profits in a second step, I restrict my analysis of dividends to a graphical presentation.

I discuss the case of a 60 months period; in the second chapter the largest excess return has been reported for this period length. The analysis is pursued for dividends per nominal equity. Dividends per nominal equity is calculated as the total amount of dividends over the book value of equity. The concept of this ratio is similar to dividends per share. However, dividends per nominal equity is a more precise measure for payments on the available equity. First, the capital subscribed per share can differ; this is not captured if we calculate dividends per share. Second, dividends per nominal equity do also account for capital surplus and earned surplus which is also equity available to the company. Another alternative measure would have been the dividend price ratio. Here it can be argued that nominal equity is likely to be a better measure of the available equity than stock prices. Stock prices are a market based measure of the available equity. As they reflect future earnings prospects they fluctuate according to changes in expectations. As I investigate the process of cash flows one main question is whether this process is expected. Therefore, I do not want expectations of cash flows to enter the analysis in this second indirect way. For the purpose of my analysis nominal equity is a more suitable measure of the available equity.

Figure 3 presents on its left-hand side evidence for dividends paid per nominal equity for a period length of 60 months. As the change in dividends is supposed to proxy for the change in expectations, dividends are reported starting in year 0 which is one year before the start of the formation period. Reported are the medians of the assets in the five portfolios which are obtained by sorting assets according to their returns as presented in the second chapter. Again an overlapping sample is used. Results are centered around the mean for each year which is set equal to 0. The beginning of the test period after year 5 is indicated by a dashed vertical line.

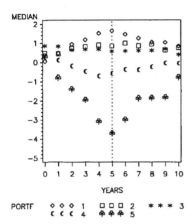
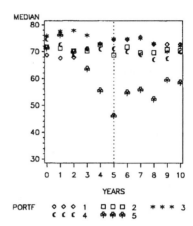

Figure 3. Changes in dividends per nominal equity (left graph) and levels of dividends per profit (in %) (right graph), medians for a period length of 60 months. The left graph shows the median dividend per equity adjusted for the market mean in %. The right graph shows the median of the dividend paid as a percentage of total profits. Portfolios are built according to the performance of assets during the test period and enumerated 1 (winner) to 5 (loser). The dotted line marks the end of the formation period and the beginning of the test period

For the graphical analysis a characteristic pattern emerges for the extreme portfolios.

For the winner portfolio I observe a slight increase in dividends per nominal equity of 1.8 percentage points during the formation period. During the test period the level of dividends decreases again to almost the level of the sample mean. A more dramatic development can be observed for the loser portfolio. During the formation period dividends per nominal equity decrease by four percentage points relative to the mean. During the test period they increase again up to almost the level of the sample mean. The increase does not occur steadily over time but occurs during the first, the second, and the fifth year. For the less extreme portfolios the evidence is weaker. For the fourth portfolio a decrease of half a percentage point is followed by an increase of the same size during the test period. For the second and the third portfolio no characteristic pattern can be observed. By and large, for the winner and the loser portfolio the evidence supports my hypothesis of a parallel movement of stock returns and changes in fundamentals.

There is a long controversy in financial economics whether the payout decision of a company is informative (see Miller (1986) for an overview). Dividends are generally supposed to be used as a signal to indicate future profitability. Evidence for the payout ratio of my sample is presented on the right-hand side of figure 3.[37] Except for the loser portfolio we cannot observe any particular pattern in the payout ratio. The average payout ratio is at a level of around 70%. For the loser portfolio we find a down-turn in the payout ratio during the formation period to a level of below 50% and a subsequent up-turn to a level of around 60%. This implies that the development in dividends exacerbates the development in corporate earnings. Dividends are used as a signalling device: As the management foresees a further deterioration in the business environment of a company it might reduce its dividend payments even more dramatically than to just reduce it in proportion to the deterioration of the reported earnings.

5.1.2
Profits

The preliminary evidence on dividends suggested that movements in fundamentals show into the same direction as excess returns. I now extend my analysis to movements in corporate earnings. First, I present again graphical evidence for a period of 60 months. Then I turn to a more complete picture of the development of profits over different period lengths.

Figure 4 presents evidence for the development of profits per nominal equity for a period length of 60 months. Profits per equity are reported starting in period 0 which is one period before the start of the formation period. The left-hand graph presents means, the right-hand graph medians for the portfolios. After year 5 the test period starts which is indicated by a dashed vertical line.

Both figures show evidence which is largely in line with the hypothesis. During the formation period changes in profits move in parallel with stock returns. The winner portfolio (# 1) outperforms the other portfolios in terms of profits over the entire period. At the end of the formation period the difference between the sample mean and the mean of the winner portfolio is about 9 percentage points. For the median the evidence is a bit weaker. The reverse picture emerges for the loser portfolio. The loser portfolio (# 5) underperforms the other portfolios in terms of profits over the entire period. The difference between the sample mean and the mean of the loser portfolio is also about 9 percentage points. Again for the medians the evidence is a bit weaker.

---

[37] If profits are zero or negative the question arises how to define the payout ratio. In the graphical analysis I have neglected all observations which show negative profits. This results in a high payout ratio. In chapter 7 of this monograph I provide an additional analysis of the payout ratio which uses a different convention. There I define the payout ratio to be 100% if dividends are paid although profits are zero or negative, if no dividends are paid the payout ratio is defined to be 0%. Despite this different definition the pattern which emerges is similar (cf. Table 40).

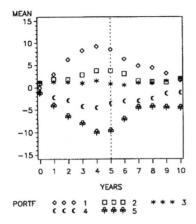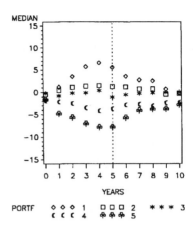

Figure 4. Changes in profits per nominal equity (in %) - means and medians for a period length of 60 months. The left graph shows the mean profit per nominal equity adjusted for the market mean, the right graph shows the median profit per equity adjusted for the market mean. In both cases portfolios are built according to the performance in terms of stock returns during the test period and enumerated 1 (winner) to 5 (loser). The dotted line marks the end of the formation period

If we look at the intertemporal evidence we find that the spread between the performance of the portfolios in terms of fundamentals widens almost during the entire formation period. It has its peak one period before the end of the formation period. During the test period the pattern reverses. The maximum spread between profits occurs already in period 4, i.e. one period before the end of the formation period. This may be due to the lag in the publication of accounting data. Accounting results are published and hence become public knowledge only after the reporting period. Therefore, looking at the flow of information one can argue that the change in reported income from period t to period $t + 1$ should be the driving factor for asset returns in period $t + 2$ which is the period in which results are reported. After period 4 the performance in terms of fundamentals becomes again closer. The difference diminishes most dramatically from period 5 to period 7. In addition, one can observe that there is a larger spread between the means than between the medians whereas the pattern is the same in both cases. This indicates that the distribution is skewed to the left. Extreme observations exacerbate the development of the means as compared to the medians.

In table 20 I investigate whether the observed pattern in profits is significant. For the reference period of 60 months earnings per nominal equity increase from 17.09% to 23.45% during the formation period for the winner portfolio. During the test period earnings per nominal equity decrease from 23.45% to 16.51%. Both developments are highly significant. For the loser portfolio we observe opposite developments. The earnings per nominal equity decrease from 17.19% to 9.71% and increase afterwards again to a level of 13.91%. For 60 months changes in fundamentals and excess returns show into the same direction. If we turn to other period lengths the following picture emerges. In the first chapter we have reported reversals in returns for period lengths from 36 to 84 months. In the case of 24 months we have found reversals in returns which were not significant. For almost all of these period lengths we find highly significant reversals in fundamentals. (Only for the loser portfolio in the case of 84 months I find no evidence for a reversal.) We can interpret this as supportive evidence for our claim that stock returns are driven by movements in fundamentals. The evidence is different in the case of 12 months. For 12 months we have reported persistence in stock returns. For fundamentals we obtain slight evidence for a reversal for the winner portfolio. This implies that other forces than movements in fundamentals are likely to drive short-term persistence.

Taken together, long-term reversals are parallelled by movements in fundamentals. This is different for short-term persistence for which no equivalent movement in fundamentals can be found.

Table 20. Comparison of profits per nominal equity for both the winner and the loser portfolio. For the winner portfolio it is tested whether there is an increase in profits per equity during the formation period (Diff 01), and whether there is a decrease in profits per equity during the test period (Diff 12). For the loser portfolio signs are reversed

Months[a]		Median 0[b]	Median 1	Median 2	Diff. 01[c]	Diff. 12
12	Winner	18.519201	20.122582	18.972006	***	†
	Loser	13.367782	11.309053	11.294813	***	
24	Winner	18.956 305	22.274058	19.210361	***	***
	Loser	13.780458	10.138748	12.639700	***	***
36	Winner	19.285331	22.815780	17.849518	***	***
	Loser	15.116683	8.729665	12.443798	***	***
48	Winner	18.757261	22.571603	17.606517	***	***
	Loser	15.371968	9.068226	12.991873	***	***
60	Winner	17.088534	23.451051	16.505258	***	***
	Loser	17.191224	9.712143	13.913457	***	***
72	Winner	17.217695	23.968369	16.886795	***	***
	Loser	18.987706	11.436529	13.891054	***	**
84	Winner	18.309177	21.931708	15.982386	**	***
	Loser	21.412881	12.190914	12.910992	***	

[a] Respective length of the test and the formation period. The test is done for all periods where a winner-loser effect has been observed

[b] Median 0: median of the distribution at the beginning of the formation period; Median 1: median of the distribution at the end of the formation period; Median 2: median of the distribution at the end of the test period

[c] Test for a shift in the distribution during the formation period (H_0: no shift in the distribution); level of significance *** (**, *): H_0 can be rejected at a 1% (5%, 10%) significance level against H_1: a shift which is parallel to the development in returns. †: H_0 can be rejected at a 10% significance level against H_1: a shift into the opposite direction of the development in returns. Tests are based on the Wilcoxon rank sum statistic

5.1.3
Profit Components

This section analyzes which factors are the driving forces behind profits by look-ing at their components: *ordinary income* is income generated by activities of the company's core business, *financial income* is income generated from financial assets held by the company as well as from its borrowings and lendings, and *ex-traordinary income* are the remaining parts of total profits which are obtained aperiodically or as profits gained from re-evaluation of assets. The positions of the income statement which are subsumed under the heading of extraordinary income are those supposed to leave most space for managerial discretion. The tables pre-sent the definition of the variables which I use.

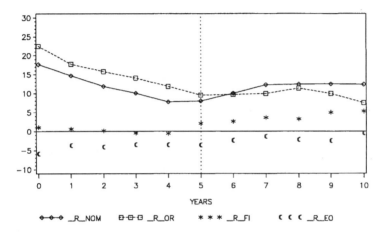

Figure 5. Components of profit per equity (in %) - means for the 60 months loser portfolio. The graph shows the components of profits per nominal equity _r_nom: its components are deno-ted by _r_or for ordinary income per equity, _r_fi for financial income per equity, _r_eo for extraor-dinary income per equity. The graph differs from figure 4 as there is no adjustment for the mar-ket mean. The dotted line marks the end of the formation period

First, I present graphical evidence for the winner and the loser portfolio. The evi-dence presented in figure 5 shows the components of profits for the loser portfolio for a period length of 60 periods where the evidence is particularly clear-cut.[38] Total and ordinary income move mainly in parallel indicating that ordinary in-come is indeed the driving force behind total profits. Financial income moves mainly in the same direction but with a smaller amplitude. Financial income in-cludes payments from short-term investments in the capital market and payments on bank loans. It also includes payments from subsidiaries and other affiliated

---

[38] In the graphical evidence we use means whereas in the tables we report medians. This causes slight differences in the figures presented. However, the qualitative results remain the same.

companies. If subsidiaries and affiliated companies operate in the same or related industries as the company itself, profits and hence payments from these companies should show a similar pattern as the ordinary income of the company itself. The remaining idiosyncratic components dilute a closer relationship with total profits. The extraordinary component does not show a particular pattern.

operating income	
= Rohertrag	*gross proceeds*
− Löhne and Gehälter	*wages and salaries*
− soziale Abgaben	*social contributions*
− Aufwendungen für Altersversorgung und Unterstützung	*pensions and assistance*
− Abschreibungen auf Sachanlagen und immaterielle Werte	*depreciation on tangible assets*
− sonstige Aufwendungen	*other expenses*
+ sonstige Enträge (ohne ausserordentliche Erträge)	*other income (less extraordinary expenses)*
financial income	
= Erträge aus Gewinnabführungsverträgen	*income from profit-transfer agreements*
+ E. aus Beteiligungen	*inc. from affiliated companies*
+ E. aus anderen Finanzanlagen	*inc. from other investments*
+ sonstige Zinsen und ähnliche Erträge	*inc. from interest*
+ E. aus Abgängen u. Zuschreibungen zum Anlagevermögen	*gains from sale of plant property valuation adjustment of plant property and investment*
− Abschreibungen auf Finanzanlagen	*writedowns of investments*
− Zinsen and ähnliche Aufwendungen	*interest expenses*
− Aufwendungen aus Verlustübernahme	*transfer of losses from affiliates*
extraordinary income	
= Erträge aus der Auflösung von Rückstellungen	*transfers from the reduction of prior provisions*
+ E. aus der Auflösung von Sonderposten mit Rücklageanteil	*transfers from special reserves*
+ Erträge aus Herabsetzung der Pauschalwertberichtigung	*transfers from the reduction of the global value adjustment*
+ ausserordentliche Erträge	*extraordinary income*
+ sonstige andere Erträge	*other income*
− Verluste aus dem Abgang von Anlagevermögen	*losses on retirements of fixed assets*
− Einstellungen in den Sonderposten mit Rücklageanteil	*transfer to special reserves*
− Abschreibungen auf Konsolidierungsausgleichsposten	*depreciation of excees arising in consolidation (good will)*
− Abschr. auf Forderungen	*depreciation on accounts receivable*
− sonstige andere Aufwendungen	*other expenses*
− eigene Gewinnabführungen	*profit transfers*
− Sonstige Steuern	*other taxes*

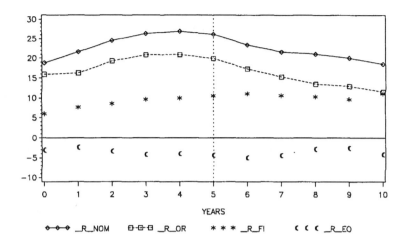

Figure 6. Components of profit per equity (in %) - means for the 60 months winner portfolio. The graph shows the components of profits per nominal equity _r_nom: its components are denoted by _r_or for ordinary income per equity, _r_fi for financial income per equity, _r_eo for extraordinary income per equity. The graph differs from figure 4 as there is no adjustment for the market mean. The dotted line marks the end of the formation period

The reverse pattern of an upswing during the formation and a downswing during the test period is obtained for the winner portfolio (figure 6). Again the driving force behind profits per nominal equity appears to be the ordinary income. Profits and ordinary income move in parallel both during the formation period and during the test period. Ordinary income accounts for approximately three quarters of profits. For the two other profit components no particular pattern can be observed. For the entire time horizon I obtain large positive values for financial income and small negative values for extraordinary income.

To gain insight whether these observed movements are significant for the whole range of winner and loser portfolios for different period lengths, the statistical results are presented in tables 21 to 23. It is tested whether components of profits show into the same direction as the winner-loser effect. I restrict my attention to the periods of 36 to 84 months for which I have obtained significant results for the winner-loser hypothesis. Median 0 is the median at the beginning of the formation period, median 1 is the median for the last period of the formation period and median 2 is the median for the last period of the test period. The signs in the table relate to Wilcoxon rank sum statistics which test for a shift in the distribution.

Table 21. Comparison of ordinary income per equity in the winner and the loser portfolio. For the winner portfolio it is tested whether there is an increase in ordinary income per equity during the formation period (Diff 01), and whether there is a decrease in ordinary per equity during the test period (Diff 12). For the loser portfolio signs are reversed [Legend cf. table 23]

Months[a]		Median 0[b]	Median 1	Median 2	Diff. 01[c]	Diff. 12
36	Winner	17.340107	17.799408	12.190948		***
	Loser	17.793454	10.434634	11.154543	***	
48	Winner	14.931042	17.535992	10.405748	*	***
	Loser	19.878422	12.103770	11.020308	***	
60	Winner	12.574685	15.613656	8.215639	*	***
	Loser	22.531904	13.328041	12.333540	***	
72	Winner	12.888029	19.278288	9.739323		***
	Loser	24.598339	12.505230	12.430171	***	
84	Winner	12.734226	18.526871	6.150616		***
	Loser	25.164046	11.653258	11.905733	***	

Table 22. Comparison of financial income per equity in the winner and the loser portfolio [Legend cf. table 23]

Months[a]		Median 0[b]	Median 1	Median 2	Diff. 01[c]	Diff. 12
36	Winner	2.525759	5.281051	5.876993	***	
	Loser	0.078236	−0.737188	1.958435		***
48	Winner	3.069113	6.506074	7.243495	***	
	Loser	−0.107795	−0.971278	2.825393		***
60	Winner	2.949549	7.328136	8.278270	***	
	Loser	−0.956129	0.520874	2.180942		***
72	Winner	2.663451	7.328136	8.088793	***	
	Loser	0.284075	0.379598	3.293125		***
84	Winner	2.382626	7.285952	9.709642	***	
	Loser	0.933825	0.592866	3.293199		***

For ordinary income I obtain the following results (table 21). First I have a look at our reference period of 60 months. For the winner portfolio ordinary income moves from 12.6% to 15.6% during the formation period and diminishes to a level of 8.2% during the test period. Both movements are significant. The movement during the test period is highly significant. For the loser portfolio a highly significant movement can only be observed for the formation period. Ordinary income decreases from 22.5% to 13.3%. For the test period no significant movement can be found. Interestingly, for all other period lengths we obtain the same pattern of significant results: I obtain a significant decrease both for the loser portfolio during the formation period and for the winner portfolio during the test period. Sometimes I obtain slightly significant increases for the winner portfolio during the formation period. Movements in ordinary income seem to drive the results in the case of downturns in the economic performance.

A different picture emerges in the case of financial income (table 22). For our reference period of 60 months financial income per nominal equity increases for the winner portfolio during the formation period from 2.9% to 7.3%. It increases further to a level of 8.3% during the test period. However, this change is no longer significant. The opposite picture emerges in the case of the loser portfolio. During the formation period the level stays roughly constant at ± 0, and increases afterwards to a level of 2.2%. This increase is highly significant. Other period lengths deliver again the same results: I obtain highly significant increases both for the winner portfolio during the formation period and for the loser portfolio during the test period. These findings have the interesting implication that upswings and downswings in the fundamental performance are driven by different profit components. Whereas downswings are driven by ordinary income, upswings are driven by movements in financial income.

Table 23. Comparison of extraordinary income per equity in the winner and the loser portfolio

Months[a]		Median 0[b]	Median 1	Median 2	Diff. 01[c]	Diff. 12
36	Winner	−0.072444	0.004696	0.029450		
	Loser	−0.218910	0.363842	0.109649	†††	
48	Winner	0.081270	−0.167416	0.161483	†	††
	Loser	−0.422394	0.070259	0.019917	††	
60	Winner	−0.141726	−0.262044	0.135278		††
	Loser	−0.364665	0.004055	0.043785	††	
72	Winner	−0.296445	−0.212068	−0.086615		
	Loser	−0.718088	−0.015116	−0.561672	††	
84	Winner	−0.296445	−1.075193	−0.014498		††
	Loser	−0.827383	0.122805	−0.012240	†††	

[a] Respective length of the test and the formation period. The tests are done for all periods where a winner-loser effect has been observed

[b] Median 0: median of the distribution before the formation period; Median 1: median of the distribution at the end of the formation period; Median 2: median of the distribution at the end of the test period

[c] Test for a difference in the central moments of the distributions at the point of time 0 and 1; level of significance: *** (**, *): The hypothesis of no shift in the distribution can be rejected at a 1% (5%, 10%) significance level on the basis of the Wilcoxon rank sum statistic. H_1: a shift which is parallel to the development in returns; ††† (††, †): The hypothesis of no shift in the distribution can be rejected at a 1% (5%, 10%) significance level. H_1: a shift into the opposite direction of the development in returns

As we turn to extraordinary income a completely different picture emerges (table 23). For the reference period of 60 months for the winner portfolio we observe a small decrease during the formation period and a small but significant movement from -0.26% to 0.13% during the test period. The reverse picture emerges for the loser portfolio. A small but significant increase from -0.36% to 0.0% can be observed during the formation period. A further increase during the test period is insignificant. This implies that most of the time extraordinary income moves into the opposite direction as compared to total income. Again a similar picture emerges across the different period lengths. The increase in extraordinary profit is significant both for the loser portfolio during the formation period and for the winner portfolio during the test period. Although the absolute size of the movements in extraordinary income is small, the observed pattern is strikingly different from the pattern in total profits: In most cases movements in extraordinary income reverse movements in total profits. With respect to extraordinary income management has the most space for discretion. It may use this space in order to smooth total profits.

Taken together, a similar pattern emerges across the different period lengths. The driving components of total profits are ordinary and financial income. Downswings in the total performance are driven by movements in ordinary income, upswings are driven by movements in financial income. The extraordinary income is used to smooth total profits.

5.1.4
Summary

Long-term reversals in the cross section of stock returns are parallelled by movements in fundamentals. We have investigated whether it is possible to observe changes in cash flows which show into the same direction as excess returns: By and large, the reported evidence is supportive. For long-term reversals we have found small but consistent movements in dividends. For the winner portfolio, an increase during the formation period is followed by a decrease during the test period. The reverse pattern can be observed for the loser portfolio. The same pattern on a larger scale can be observed for movements in total profits. For an investment horizon of 5 years we obtain the following results. Profits per nominal equity increase from 17.09% to 23.45% during the formation period. Afterwards they decrease again to a level of 16.51%. The reverse pattern can be observed for the loser portfolio: After an initial level of 17.19% profits per nominal equity decrease to a level of 9.71%. Afterwards they increase again to a level of 13.91%. Similar findings are obtained for other time horizons. No comovement is obtained for short-term persistence in stock returns. In a second step we have investigated the importance of different profit components. The driving factors for movements in total profits are ordinary income and financial income. Ordinary income plays the important role in the case of downswings in the performance and financial income plays the important role in the case of upswings. Extraordinary income is used to smooth total profits.

5.2
Differences between the Winner and the Loser Portfolio -
A Binary Choice Approach

Stock returns have been the starting point of our investigation so far. We have sorted stocks into portfolios according to their performance during the formation period. Reversals in the portfolio performance are parallelled by movements in fundamentals. In this section I reverse the direction of the investigation. I explore whether it is possible to use movements in fundamentals to distinguish between winner and loser firms. I estimate a logit model which sorts stocks into the winner and the loser portfolio according to their performance in terms of fundamentals. In the previous section I have investigated the behaviour of different fundamental variables (dividends, profits, and profit components) in a variable by variable approach. In this section I apply a multivariate approach. I determine the probability that given a set of fundamental variables an observation belongs to the winner or to the loser portfolio. I explore this question by means of a binary choice model, a method which is presented in greater detail below. The analysis is pursued separately for the formation and for the test period. For the formation period increases in dividends or profits should make it more likely that a stock belongs to the winner portfolio. For the test period the opposite result holds.

The main hypothesis of this section is that it is possible to distinguish between the winner and the loser portfolio by means of fundamentals. From our previous findings it appears that stock returns during the formation as well as during the test period were driven by changes in fundamentals.

Hypothesis I: *Winner and loser firms in both the formation and the test period can be identified by changes in profit components.*

To investigate this hypothesis we first restrict our attention to a scarcely specified model which only includes changes in profit components as explanatory variables *(model I)*. In order to obtain a more complete view of the factors which determine stock returns I include two other sets of explanatory variables. First, I include the volatilities of the profit components. A larger volatility could mean that there is a larger idiosyncratic risk which might be difficult to hedge. If investors want to be compensated for bearing this risk this should increase the return. Second, I include characteristics of the balance sheets of the winner and the loser firms. One reason for this is to control for leverage. An increase in leverage should induce an increase in the expected return. Another reason is that we want to investigate whether there are other factors which determine stock returns. The second more complete model includes these variables and the changes in profit components *(model II)*. Applying this model we investigate the following hypothesis.

Hypothesis II: *The predictive power of a model to identify winner and loser firms through movements in profit components can be enhanced by including additional fundamental variables.*

The analysis proceeds as follows. First, we explain the binary choice model. Second, we turn to our empirical findings and their discussion. A summary concludes this section.

5.2.1
Econometric Methodology

In a model of binary choice the observations are attributed to two classes of observations.[39] It is investigated to which extent a set of explanatory variables is able to attribute observations to the correct classes. In a second step the estimated model can be used to make predictions to which class a new observation belongs. The estimated function has the form

$$\pi(y \text{ belongs to class } 1) = F(\beta'x)$$

π is the probability that an observation y belongs to class 1, x is the vector of explanatory variables and β the vector of parameters which has to be estimated. I estimate the probability that an observation belongs to the winner portfolio. For this estimation I only include stocks which belong either to the winner or the loser portfolio. Therefore it must hold that $\pi(y = winner) = 1 - \pi(y = loser)$.

Different functions F are discussed in the literature. The most common are the probit and the logit function. For my investigation the logit function turns out to fit my set of data best.

$$\pi(y = winner) = \frac{e^{\beta'x}}{1+e^{\beta'x}} = \Lambda(\beta'x)$$

The joint probability function is estimated using a maximum likelihood estimation. The likelihood function can be written as

$$L = \prod_{i=1}^{n}\left[F(\beta'x)\right]^{y_i}\left[1-F(\beta'x)\right]^{1-y_i}$$

$$\ln L = \sum_{i=1}^{n}\left[y_i \ln F(\beta'x_i)+(1-y_i)\ln(1-F(\beta'x_i))\right]$$

For a general function F the first order conditions for this model turn out to be nonlinear. Then a solution can only be obtained by numerical iteration. In the special case of the logit function the optimality conditions are linear. The optimality conditions are (Greene (1997) p. 883)

---

[39] For a comprehensive overview of the binary choice model cf. Greene (1997), pp. 873-896, on which I rely in my presentation.

$$\frac{\partial \ln L}{\partial \beta} = \sum_{i=1}^{n} (y_i - \Lambda_i) x_i = 0$$

Λ_i is the value of the logistic function for x_i. These optimality conditions are estimated using a maximum likelihood estimation.

For the interpretation of a binary choice model a special feature must not be neglected. Unlike in the case of the ordinary regression we cannot interpret the parameter estimates as marginal effects. The expected value conditional on the vector x is

$$E(y|x) = 0[1 - F(\beta'x)] + 1F(\beta'x)$$
$$E(y|x) = F(\beta'x)$$

For the marginal effect we obtain

$$\frac{\partial E(y|x)}{\partial x} = \frac{dF(\beta'x)}{d(\beta'x)} \beta = f(\beta'x)\beta$$

For the logistic function (cf. Greene (1987, p. 876))

$$\frac{\partial E(y|x)}{\partial x} = \Lambda(\beta'x)[1 - \Lambda(\beta'x)]\beta$$

Hence the marginal effect of a change in x does not only depend on β, but also on x.

5.2.2
Estimation Results

In this section I estimate the logistic regression equation

$$\pi(y = winner) = \frac{e^{\beta'x}}{1 + e^{\beta'x}} = \Lambda(\beta'x) \tag{32}$$

for different sets of explanatory variables x.

The empirical evidence is presented in two steps. First, I present classification results and evidence on the goodness of fit. Second, I present the estimation results. I investigate the question whether it is possible to distinguish between the winner and the loser portfolio for the winner and the loser portfolio separately. Afterwards I present evidence for the goodness of fit. The investigation is pursued for an investment horizon of 60 months for both the formation and the test period.

Formation Period

For the formation period I investigate the logistic regression equation (32) for two sets of explanatory variables x. The first set of explanatory variables does only include changes in ordinary income, changes in financial income, and changes in extraordinary income. Two further sets of variables are included in the second broader set of explanatory variables. First, I include the variations of the profit components as explanatory variables. Second, I also include changes in other variables. On the asset side of the balance sheet I include changes in fixed assets and in financial assets. On the liabilities side I use changes in the following equity components: capital stock, earned surplus *(Rücklagen),* and other equity components, as well as changes in reserves and accrued liabilities. Starting from this specification the variance of financial income, changes in fixed assets, and changes in financial assets were excluded from the final specification which fitted the data best and provided the best attribution of stocks to the winner and the loser portfolio. The final specification can be obtained from table 25.

First, I present evidence for the simple and the extended specification in terms of classification tables. Classification tables show to which extent we can discriminate between the winner and the loser portfolio using fundamental characteristics of these stocks. Probabilities are estimated that stocks belong to the winner or the loser portfolio. If the estimated probability to belong to the winner portfolio is above 50% the stock is attributed to the winner portfolio. The classification table shows the evidence in terms of matching frequencies. The elements on the main diagonal show the number of correct matches. Winner firms are correctly sorted into the winner portfolio, loser firms are correctly sorted into the loser portfolio. The failures to match are reported in the off diagonal.

Table 24. Classifications - Formation Period

| | model I[a] | | model II[b] | |
	winner	loser	winner	loser
winner	184 66.43%	93	212 79.40%	55
loser	67	210 75.81%	52	204 79.69%
match	71.12%		79.54%	

[a] explanatory variables: changes in profit components
[b] explanatory variables: changes and variation in profit components, change in equity and assets components (cf. table 25)

In the empirical investigation we restrict our attention to the case of 60 months, the period lengths for which we have found the largest excess return for a contrarian strategy. Table 24 presents results for the formation period. On the left hand side we present evidence for a scarce specification of our model which only includes changes in profit components as explanatory variables. The benchmark of a random match is 50%. For model I we obtain a match of 71.12%. Hence, roughly 20% of the stocks are sorted into the right portfolios in addition to the 50% which are already matched by random. In addition we observe that the matching results are better for the loser portfolio (75.81%) than for the winner portfolio (66.43%).

We can improve the classification results if we turn to the second model specification. Results are presented on the right hand side of the table. Here we obtain a classification result which attributes 79.54% of the observations correctly. In this case the classification for the winner and the loser portfolio is equally successful. In summary, we find supportive evidence for both of our hypotheses: For the formation period changes in profits are informative to evaluate the performance of stocks and we can improve the explanatory power of our analysis if we include more variables than just changes in profits.

Table 25 presents the estimation results for the second specification. The table presents estimators and standard deviations for the three groups of explanatory variables: changes in profit components, the variation in profit components, and changes in other balance sheet variables.

Table 25. Estimation Results - Logistic Regression for the Formation Period

Variables[a]	Formation Period	
	coeff.	std.
intercept	−0.8495	0.1786
Changes in Profit Components		
Δ ord.inc.	16.5248	2.2788
Δ fin. inc.	15.4685	2.5494
Δ extraord.inc.	14.5768	2.8886
Variation in Profit Components		
σ^2 ord. inc.	−7.0157	2.0582
σ^2 extraord. inc.	11.4382	2.7352
Changes in Other Balance Sheet Variables		
Equity		
- capital stock	2.7866	0.7702
- earned surplus	1.57889	0.4543
- other equity components	−2.3665	0.9898
reserves and accrued liabilities	0.63403	0.2057

[a] Results of a logistic regression. Stocks are sorted into 5 portfolios according to their performance during a 60 months formation period. The analysis is restricted to the top quintile (the "winner portfolio") and the bottom quintile (the "loser portfolio"). The probability of a stock to belong to the winner portfolio is regressed on the set of explanatory variables in the first column

The coefficients which we obtain are in line with our previous findings.[40] We find large positive coefficients for the formation period and large negative coefficients for the test period. We estimate a coefficient for changes in ordinary income of 16.52, a coefficient for changes in financial income of 15.46 and a coefficient for changes in extraordinary income of 14.57. For changes in ordinary and financial income this is the result which we have expected from our previous analysis. The contrarian movement of the extraordinary income which we have observed on a single variable level does not reappear on a multivariate level. Instead we observe the same sign for all profit components. In addition to changes in profit components we find a significant influence of the volatility of the profit components during the formation period. A high volatility of the ordinary income decreases the probability that a stock belongs to the winner portfolio. A high volatility of the extraordinary income increases this probability. These findings might indicate that investors appreciate characteristics of the business policy which are reflected in these volatilities. If investors interpret the ordinary income as indicator of future business conditions they might appreciate if firms show less uncertainty with respect to these conditions. With respect to the volatility of the extraordinary profit investors might appreciate a business policy which uses the available space for discretionary actions to diminish and enhance the extraordinary income from time to time. The increased return might also reflect a preference for transparency which is reflected in higher volatility of the extraordinary profit. During the test period the volatility of the profit components has no additional explanatory power.

For two of the three equity components I obtain positive coefficients. Increases in capital stock and in earned surplus render it more likely that a firm belongs to the winner portfolio. This can be interpreted as follows. Winner firms are more likely to enhance their equity during the formation period both by issuing new stocks and by retained earnings. In addition a positive coefficient is also obtained for reserves and accrued earnings. Firms in the winner portfolio are also more likely to increase their reserves during the formation period.

Test Period
I repeat the analysis for the test period. I estimate again the logistic regression function (32) for two sets of explanatory variables. The first set of explanatory variables are again changes in profit components. But whereas in the previous investigation I used changes in profits during the formation period, in this section I use changes in profits during the test period. For the second specification I start again with the same three sets of variables as in the previous section, this time variables are taken from the test period. The specification for the test period which delivers the best classification results includes the following variables: changes in all three profit components, changes in capital stock, earned surplus, and other equity components. The variations in profit components during the test period

---

[40] As we have already mentioned above the coefficients have to be interpreted with care. Unlike in a standard regression they do not represent the marginal effects. We therefore restrict our attention to the sign and neglect the absolute size of the coefficients.

were excluded from the final specification as they did not improve the classification results. The exact specification can be observed from table 27.

The classification results for the test period are presented in table 26. Based on changes in profit components alone, a matching of 54.35% is obtained which is hardly more than the 50% which is obtained from random matching. Interestingly, the result for the winner firms is substantially better (62.82%) as compared to the loser portfolio (45.82%). We can improve the classification results up to a matching frequency of 63.15% if we include other variables. Although not to the same extent as before the matching frequency for the winner portfolio is still slightly better (66.16% as compared to 60.08%). In contrast to our findings for the formation period this could imply that a more pronounced development in fundamentals can be observed for the winner portfolio. In summary, for the test period we find only weak evidence for changes in profits alone to be informative. However, we find substantial discriminatory power for a broader set of accounting variables and hence supportive evidence for the second hypothesis.

Table 26. Classification Results – Test Period

	model I[a]		model II[b]	
	winner	loser	winner	loser
winner	174 62.82%	103	174 66.16%	89
loser	149	126 45.82%	103	155 60.08%
match	54.35%		63.15%	

[a] explanatory variables: changes in profit components
[b] explanatory variables: changes and variation in profit components, change in equity and assets components (cf. table 27)

The classification results for the test period have turned out to be considerably weaker than the results for the test period. This difference does not come as a surprise if we think of the research design of the winner-loser effect. During the formation period stocks are sorted according to their realized returns. This implies that we can increase the explanatory power of the probit analysis up to a level of 100% if we use returns instead of changes in fundamentals. We can think of changes in fundamentals to proxy for this development in returns. For the test period such a benchmark is not available. If we use the returns during the test period to differentiate between winner and loser portfolios, we obtain a matching rate of 57.07%. Therefore, it is not surprising if the explanatory power for fundamentals is of about the same size.

Table 27 presents the estimation results for the second specification. In the same way as table 25, it presents estimators and standard deviations for the set of explanatory variables which were included in the final regression. For changes in all three profit components I obtain negative coefficients. Decreases in all three profit components make it more likely that the stock belongs to the winner portfolio during the test period. At least for the ordinary and financial income this is in line with the pattern which we have observed in the previous section. The winner firms showed a poorer performance in terms of fundamentals during the test period.

Table 27. Estimation Results - Logistic Regression for the Test Period

Variables[a]	Test Period	
	coeff.	std.
intercept	−0.1301	0.1081
Changes in Profit Components		
Δ ord.inc.	−3.4513	1.315
Δ fin. inc.	−4.172	1.486
Δ extraord.inc.	−3.4125	1.542
Changes in Other Balance Sheet Variables		
Equity		
- capital stock	−1.164	0.565
- earned surplus	−0.4932	0.1821
- other equity components	2.0455	0.6055
fixed assets	1.5283	0.3457
financial assets	−0.3018	0.1133

[a] Results of a logistic regression. Stocks are sorted into 5 portfolios according to their performance during a 60 months formation period. The analysis is restricted to the top quintile (the "winner portfolio") and the bottom quintile (the "loser portfolio"). The probability of a stock to belong to the winner portfolio is regressed on the set of explanatory variables in the first column

For other balance sheet variables I obtain the following results. For capital stock and earned surplus I obtain a negative coefficient. As compared to loser firms winner firms are less likely to increase their equity by issuing new capital or retaining of earnings. For the asset side of the balance sheet the evidence is inconclusive. For fixed assets I obtain a positive coefficient, for financial assets a negative coefficient.

Goodness of Fit
In addition to the estimation results I present evidence for the goodness of fit of the estimated models. The goodness of fit of our model is investigated using a test statistic due to Hosmer and Lemeshow (1989) which is related to the classification tables presented above. For the classification table the only relevant information is

whether the estimated winner probability is larger or below 50%. Hosmer and Lemeshow use the whole distribution of estimated probabilities to infer whether the model is correctly specified. For each observation I obtain an estimated probability $\hat{\pi}$. The observations are sorted according to the estimated probabilities and classified approximately into deciles. For every decile I compare the estimated frequency of winner stocks to the observed frequency of winner stocks. The estimated frequency is calculated as $n_j \bar{\pi}_j$, which is the number of observations in the decile n_j multiplied by the average estimated winner probability for this decile $\bar{\pi}_j$. The difference between the actual number of observations, o_j, and the estimated number of observations, $n_j \bar{\pi}_j$, is at the heart of the test statistic of Hosmer and Lemeshow (1989). They show that

$$\hat{C} = \sum_{j=1}^{10} \frac{\left(o_j - n_j \bar{\pi}_j\right)^2}{n_j \bar{\pi}_j \left(1 - \bar{\pi}_j\right)}$$

is χ^2 distributed with 8 degrees of freedom.

Table 28. Classification Results for the Model I for the Test Period

Deciles	winner firms		loser firms	
	# obs.	estimated	# obs.	estimated
1	16	18.21	39	36.79
2	24	24.76	31	30.24
3	28	26.51	27	28.49
4	24	28.09	32	27.91
5	32	28.81	24	27.19
6	30	29.44	26	26.56
7	29	29.97	27	26.03
8	32	30.02	23	24.98
9	32	31.22	24	24.78
10	30	29.96	22	22.04
Test Statistic $\hat{C}^a$	2.95		P-value	0.9375

a $\hat{C} = \sum_{j=1}^{10} \frac{\left(o_j - n_j \bar{\pi}_j\right)^2}{n_j \bar{\pi}_j \left(1 - \bar{\pi}_j\right)}$ is χ^2 distributed with 8 degrees of freedom. This implies a P-value of 0.9375. For a rejection of the model the probability of an error would be 93.75%

Table 28 shows results for the scarcely specified model I for the test period. On the left hand side I present the actual number of observations and the estimated number of observations for the winner portfolio. On the right hand side I present the actual number of observations and the estimated number of observations for the loser portfolio. We can observe that the actual numbers and the estimated numbers are quite close. I obtain a test statistic of 2.95. This implies a P-value of 93.75%. Hence, we cannot reject the H_0 that the model is correctly specified. For a rejection the probability of an error would be 93.75%. For the other model specifications the evidence is even more supportive. The P-values for the formation period are 98.39% for the first scarce model specification and 99.84% for the second model specification. For the test period I obtain a P-value of 98.85% for the second specification. Hence, there is no evidence that any of the models is misspecified.

5.2.3
Summary

This section has used fundamentals to distinguish between winner and loser firms. The analysis has been led by two hypotheses: The first hypothesis has been that it is possible to distinguish between winner and loser stocks according to changes in fundamentals alone. The second hypothesis has been that other variables have explanatory power as well. For the formation period we have found supportive evidence for both of these claims: 71.12% of the observations have been correctly classified using changes in profits alone. This result could be improved up to a level of 79.54% if other variables were included. The signs of the estimated probit regression were also supportive: Increases in profit components increased the probability that the asset belonged to the winner portfolio. For the test period the evidence has been considerably weaker: only 54.35% of the observations were correctly classified. Again this explanatory success could be increased considerably up to a level of 63.15% if other explanatory variables were included. The analysis of the estimated discrimination function has shown that also other factors help to discriminate between well and poorly performing stocks. Taken together, these findings imply that changes in the fundamental performance contain information which contributes significantly to the performance in the stock market. A good [poor] performance in terms of fundamentals implies a good [poor] performance in the stock market.

5.3
Movements in Fundamentals and Changes in the Exposure to Systematic Risk

The previous two sections have provided evidence for comovement between stock returns and changes in fundamentals. What does this comovement imply? At the heart of the theoretical discussion of the winner-loser effect is the question whether the observed reversals in stock returns occur in a framework of rational asset pricing. This question remains as I observe comovement of stock returns and fundamentals. Again two interpretations are available.

The most obvious interpretation is that return reversals and the observed comovement are due to a systematic misconception. Investors wrongly assume that earnings follow a random walk. They do not anticipate the observed reversals in cash flows. For the former winner firms the assumption of a random walk is over-optimistic. Investors are surprised by the subsequent decrease in cash flows and adjust their expectations accordingly. This induces low returns and an underperformance of the winner firms. For the loser firms the opposite holds. Investors are too pessimistic at the end of the formation period, and are surprised by the subsequent increases in cash flows. Again they adjust their expectations accordingly. This induces an overperformance of the loser firms relative to the market.

On the other hand there is also an alternative interpretation. In the theoretical part of this monograph I have developed a model of rational asset pricing in which I relate stock returns to changes in fundamentals. Within this framework it is possible to obtain reversals in excess returns which are due to a change in the exposure with respect to systematic risk. However, although stock returns are related to changes in cash flows, it is not changes in cash flows *per se* which are important for excess returns. The driving force for excess returns is the covariance of cash flows with the pricing kernel. A necessary condition for the winner-loser effect to occur in a framework of rational asset pricing is that the observed changes in cash flows also imply a change in the exposure with respect to systematic risk. A positive excess return should be due to a high exposure; a negative excess return should be due to low exposure.

5.3.1
Hypothesis

In this section I investigate this question by means of a regression analysis. The hypothesis which I pursue is as follows.

Hypothesis
Changes in cash flows indicate changes in the exposure with respect to systematic risk. For the winner portfolio the exposure with respect to systematic risk increases during the formation period, for the loser portfolio this exposure decreases.

The idea of the subsequent analysis is to relate changes in cash flows to the pricing kernel, ϕ. As I cannot run a regression on the pricing kernel directly I relate changes in cash flow variables to common pricing factors by the following regression equation,

$$\Delta X = \alpha + \Delta\beta\phi' \tag{33}$$

where ΔX are changes in cash flows and ϕ' is a common pricing factor which proxies for the pricing kernel ϕ. $\Delta\beta$ denotes the regression coefficient which is supposed to proxy for changes in the exposure with respect to systematic risk. From the regression equation a change in this exposure induces a change in cash flows of ΔX. Alternatively, a change in cash flows of ΔX can be taken as an indicator for the change in the exposure with respect to systematic risk of $\Delta\beta\phi'$.

For the winner portfolio the exposure with respect to systematic risk should decrease during the formation period. For the loser portfolio this exposure should increase. For the middle portfolio I do not expect any change in the exposure. I test for the following hypotheses: As the portfolios should show different developments in the exposure with respect to systematic risk I test for these differences by a pairwise comparison of the estimated $\Delta\beta$. For long-term reversals I test three hypotheses: whether the $\Delta\beta_W$ of the winner portfolio is smaller than the $\Delta\beta_M$ of the middle portfolio, whether the $\Delta\beta_M$ of the middle portfolio is smaller than the $\Delta\beta_L$ of the loser portfolio, and finally whether the $\Delta\beta_W$ of the winner portfolio is smaller than the $\Delta\beta_L$ of the loser portfolio. For investment horizons which are equal or larger than 36 months I investigate the hypothesis of long-term reversals. For investment horizons of 12 months and 24 months, I investigate the opposite hypothesis of short-term persistence.

For the formation of portfolios I rely again on the setting from the previous sections: according to their performance during a formation period stocks are sorted into 5 portfolios of equal size. The best performing stocks are in the winner portfolio, the worst performing stocks are in the loser portfolio. The three middle portfolios are summarized into one portfolio.

I investigate my hypothesis within the framework of the CAPM. I relate changes in cash flows to the market return

$$\Delta X = \alpha + \Delta\beta R_M \qquad (34)$$

Unfortunately, this limits the potential explanatory power of my analysis to the explanatory power of the CAPM. However, I do not have any better way available to approximate the pricing kernel ϕ.

I investigate two specifications of the regression model (34). As cash flow variables ΔX I use both dividends as well as earnings per nominal equity. As market risk factor ϕ' I use the return on the DAFOX, a value weighted market index which I have already used in the previous chapter. Results are presented in tables 29 and 30.

5.3.2
Results

Table 29 presents the results for the profits regression in which changes in profits per nominal equity are related to the market index,

$$\Delta\Pi = \alpha + \Delta\beta R_M.$$

$\Delta\Pi$ are changes in earnings during the formation period and R_M is the market return. The results are presented according to the period length which is investigated. On the left hand side I present the estimates of the $\Delta\beta$ coefficients for the different portfolios, on the right hand side I present the results for the comparison of the $\Delta\beta$ coefficients. WM is a comparison of the $\Delta\beta$ coefficients for the winner and the middle portfolio, ML for the middle and the loser portfolio, and WL for the difference between the winner and the loser portfolio. This analysis is pursued by means of a dummy regression. The numbers on the right hand side are the levels of significance. For a period of 60 months the difference between the winner and the middle portfolio is significant at a level of 8.33 %.

Table 29. Changes in Profits as Proxies for Changes in β

M.	Parameter Estimates			Level of significance[a]		
	$\Delta\beta_W[^b]$	$\Delta\beta_M[^b]$	$\Delta\beta_L[^b]$	$WM[^c]$	$ML[^c]$	$WL[^c]$
12	0.0970	0.0063	−0.0219	0.0037	0.2044	0.0022
24	0.0667	0.0068	0.0072	0.9894	0.4830	0.9687
36	0.0278	0.0021	0.0647	0.8494	0.0056	0.1122
48	−0.0076	−0.0078	0.0612	0.5035	0.0031	0.0136
60	−0.0426	−0.0054	0.0371	0.0833	0.0550	0.0077
72	−0.0365	−0.0057	0.0190	0.1248	0.1786	0.0457
84	−0.0201	−0.0216	0.0139	0.5226	0.0929	0.1497

[a] For the time horizons of 12 months, I test for persistence $\beta_W > \beta_M > \beta_L$, for longer time horizons for reversals $\beta_W < \beta_M < \beta_L$

[b] Estimators from the regression $\Delta X = \alpha + \Delta\beta R_M$, ΔX are changes in profits during the formation period, R_M is the return on the market portfolio (DAFOX) during the formation period. The regression is run for the winner, middle and loser portfolios separately. $\Delta\beta_W (\Delta\beta_M, \Delta\beta_L)$ is the estimated coefficient for the winner (middle, loser) portfolio

[c] $WM(ML, WL)$: Comparison of $\Delta\beta_W$ and $\Delta\beta_M$ ($\Delta\beta_M$ and $\Delta\beta_L, \Delta\beta_W$ and $\Delta\beta_L$)

The $\Delta\beta$ values which I obtain for my reference period of 60 months are $\Delta\beta_W = -0.0426$, $\Delta\beta_M = -0.0054$, and $\Delta\beta_L = -0.0371$. This is in line with my hypothesis: For the winner portfolio I obtain a reduction in the exposure with respect to market risk, for the middle portfolio the exposure stays roughly the same, and for the loser portfolio the exposure increases. From the right hand side of the table we can see that all these developments are significant: The difference between the winner and the middle portfolio is significant at a level of 8.33%, between the middle and the loser portfolio at a level of 5.50%. The most significant difference is between the winner and the loser portfolio with a level of significance below 1%. This supports my hypothesis that changes in fundamentals also imply a difference in the exposure with respect to systematic risk.

For other period lengths the evidence is somewhat weaker, albeit in many cases it is significant and shows into the right direction. For the shorter period of 12 months I obtain persistence in $\Delta\beta$. For this investment horizon the winner portfolio shows an increase in the exposure with respect to systematic risk of 0.097 and the loser portfolio shows a decrease of −0.0219. The difference between the winner and the middle portfolio as well as the difference between the winner and the loser portfolio is highly significant. For the period length of 24 months I find the same pattern of a significant increase of $\Delta\beta$ for the winner portfolio as compared to the middle portfolio as well as compared to the loser portfolio. However, the implications of these findings are different. For 12 months, they imply a change in the exposure which is in line with the observed excess return. For 24 months, there is no corresponding excess return.

For longer periods we can observe reversals. For 36 and 48 months, I obtain significant differences between the middle and the loser portfolio. The full pattern of the hypothesis, $\Delta\beta_W < \Delta\beta_M < \Delta\beta_L$, can be observed for the period lengths of 60 and 72 months, although this pattern is fully significant only for the reference period of 6 months. For a period of 8 months it is no longer the full pattern of the hypothesis which can be observed: there is almost no difference between the performance of the winner and the middle portfolio. The only difference which is weakly significant is the difference between the middle and the loser portfolio.

By and large, the picture which emerges is in line with my hypothesis. The $\Delta\beta$ coefficients have the same sign as the excess returns. For long horizons I observe an increase in systematic risk for the loser portfolio and a decrease for the winner portfolio. The reverse movement can be observed for short-term horizons. Therefore, it can be argued that changes in earnings can be taken as proxies for changes in the exposure with respect to systematic risk.

Table 30 presents the equivalent analysis for dividends. The regression equation relates changes in dividends ΔD to the market return,

$$\Delta D = \alpha + \Delta\beta R_M.$$

The table is organized in the same way as the previous table: It presents the values of the estimated $\Delta\beta$ coefficients and the level of significance for a pairwise comparison of the estimated $\Delta\beta$.

By and large, a similar picture emerges as I use changes in dividends instead of changes in earnings. For a period of 12 months, I find similar results for earnings as for dividends. The $\Delta\beta$ coefficients are 0.0236 for the winner portfolio, 0.0057 for the middle portfolio, and -0.0169 for the loser portfolio. Although these coefficients are smaller than the coefficients which I have obtained in the case of changes in earnings the differences between all coefficients are significant. Interestingly, the same pattern emerges for a 24 months period, again $\Delta\beta_W > \Delta\beta_M > \Delta\beta_L$. Again, for 24 months there is no pattern in returns which corresponds to this pattern in $\Delta\beta$.

Partial evidence for reversals in the $\Delta\beta$ coefficient is obtained for periods of 48 and 60 months. In both cases $\Delta\beta_W$ is significantly smaller than $\Delta\beta_W$. For 60 months also the difference between $\Delta\beta_W$ and $\Delta\beta_L$ is highly significant. The full pattern of the reversal hypothesis, $\Delta\beta_W < \Delta\beta_M < \Delta\beta_L$, can be observed for a period of 72 months, where all differences in $\Delta\beta$ are significant, and somewhat weaker for 84 months where the difference between $\Delta\beta_M$ and $\Delta\beta_L$ is not significant.

Table 30. Changes in Dividends as Proxies for Changes in β

M.	Parameter Estimates			Level of significance[a]		
	$\Delta\beta_W[b]$	$\Delta\beta_M[b]$	$\Delta\beta_L[b]$	$WM[c]$	$ML[c]$	$WL[c]$
12	0.0236	0.0057	-0.0169	0.0034	0.0003	0.0000
24	0.0169	0.0046	0.0102	0.9959	0.9989	0.9999
36	0.0053	0.0002	0.0015	0.8783	0.3842	0.7629
48	-0.0063	-0.0021	0.0002	0.0226	0.6740	0.1017
60	-0.0147	-0.0019	0.0019	0.0000	0.4982	0.0006
72	-0.0117	-0.0006	0.0067	0.0047	0.0436	0.0002
84	-0.0098	-0.0020	0.0015	0.0450	0.4585	0.0706

[a] For the time horizons of 12 months, I test for persistence $\beta_W > \beta_M > \beta_L$, for longer time horizons for reversals $\beta_W < \beta_M < \beta_L$

[b] Estimators from the regression $\Delta X = \alpha + \Delta\beta R_M$, ΔX are changes in profits during the formation period, R_M is the return on the market portfolio (DAFOX) during the formation period. The regression is run for the winner, middle and loser portfolios separately. $\Delta\beta_W (\Delta\beta_M, \Delta\beta_L)$ is the estimated coefficient for the winner (middle, loser) portfolio

[c] $WM(ML, WL)$: Comparison of $\Delta\beta_W$ and $\Delta\beta_M$ ($\Delta\beta_M$ and $\Delta\beta_L$, $\Delta\beta_W$ and $\Delta\beta_L$)

By and large, the evidence is again supportive for my hypothesis. Similar to a change in earnings an increase in dividends can be taken as a proxy for a change in the exposure to systematic risk into the same direction.

5.3.3
Discussion

What are the implications of these findings? In the theoretical part of this monograph I have shown that comovement between return reversals and changes in fundamentals might imply that the winner loser effect occurs within a framework of rational asset pricing. Within this framework it is not changes in cash flows which are important *per se* but how changes in cash flows are related to changes in the exposure with respect to systematic risk. This section has provided evidence that both changes in dividends as well as changes in earnings are related to changes in the exposure with respect to systematic risk.

These findings support the point of view that the winner-loser effect occurs within a framework of rational asset pricing. However, the results have to be interpreted with care for three reasons. The first reason is that the investigation has only been pursued on a qualitative level. I find evidence for a change in the exposure to systematic risk, but do not analyze the size of this change. One decisive question is whether the size of this change is sufficient to explain the differences in excess returns.

The second limitation of my empirical analysis is that it sticks to the CAPM framework. I approximate the exposure of changes in cash flows to systematic risk by the exposure to the market return. In the fourth chapter of this monograph the CAPM has turned out to have only limited explanatory power. Therefore, a more general analysis has to investigate whether there are better ways how to approximate the exposure to the pricing kernel. In other asset pricing models, as e.g. the APT, this exposure is measured by other common pricing factors as interest rates, GDP growth, or exchange rates.

The third limitation is due to an even more fundamental problem. It concerns the potential explanatory power of fundamentals in a framework of rational asset pricing. As we have seen in the theoretical part of this monograph the expected excess return is determined by

$$E(R_i) - R_f = \left(E(R_M) - R_f\right)\frac{\mathrm{cov}(R_i, \phi)}{\mathrm{cov}(R_M, \phi)}$$

The exposure with respect to systematic risk is measured by $\mathrm{cov}(R_i, \phi)$. As the pricing kernel cannot be observed directly this exposure has to be approximated by the covariance of the return, R_i, with a common pricing factor ϕ', $\mathrm{cov}(R_i, \phi')$. In the CAPM the only relevant pricing factor is the return on the market portfolio. Empirically returns are related to aggregate pricing variables by means of a regression.

The approach which has been pursued in this section is different. Instead of relating returns to a common pricing factor, I have related returns to idiosyncratic variables: i.e. changes in fundamentals such as dividends and profits. In a second step I have argued that these idiosyncratic variables can be thought to approximate for changes in the exposure with respect to systematic risk. This indirect approach uses changes in fundamentals as an intermediate variable. In the end stock returns should be determined by cash flows. Nevertheless, from an empirical point of view the question arises whether changes in fundamentals can provide additional explanatory power has compared to the direct approach. The crucial information for the explanation of excess returns is contained in the covariance, $\mathrm{cov}(R_i, \phi)$.

The analysis which I have pursued in this section has been to relate R_i to changes in fundamentals ΔX_i in a first step. In a second step ΔX_i is related to an aggregate pricing variable which is supposed to approximate the exposure with respect to systematic risk. This is an indirect way to approximate the exposure of the returns R_i to systematic risk. Decisive from a theoretical point of view is the question how to approximate the kernel ϕ by aggregate pricing variables. To explain the winner-loser effect in a framework of rational asset pricing it is necessary to relate stock returns to aggregate pricing variables.

This result has far reaching consequences. From the point of view of rational asset pricing the approach which is pursued in this chapter cannot lead to superior results as compared to standard asset pricing models which relate returns to aggregate pricing variables directly. If idiosyncratic variables contain additional information this can only be due to misspecification of the model or to irrational behaviour of market participants.

5.3.4
Summary

In this section I have investigated whether changes in cash flows approximate for changes in the exposure with respect to systematic risk. Both for earnings per nominal equity as well as dividends per nominal equity I have found supportive evidence for this claim. Changes in fundamentals correspond to short-term persistence and long-term reversals in the exposure with respect to systematic risk.

On a qualitative level these findings can be taken as evidence for the claim that changes in fundamentals proxy for changes in the exposure with respect to systematic risk. However this analysis suffers from a fundamental problem. In a framework of rational asset pricing excess returns are due to the exposure to systematic risk. The standard asset pricing approach is to test for this relationship directly. In my analysis I have related excess returns to movements in fundamentals which are then related to the market return as an aggregate pricing factor. Unfortunately, this second indirect approach can never deliver better results than to relate stock returns to aggregate pricing variables directly. To find out whether the winner-loser effect occurs within a framework of rational asset pricing, stock returns have to be related to aggregate pricing variables.

5.4
Summary

For the winner-loser effect stock returns are parallelled by movements in fundamentals. This is the main finding of this chapter. For the winner portfolio an increase in dividends and profits during the formation period is followed by a decrease. For the loser portfolio the reverse pattern obtains. A decrease in dividends and profits during the formation period is followed by an increase. In addition I have shown that movements in fundamentals can be used to distinguish between stocks in the winner and the loser portfolio.

The observed pattern in fundamentals can be interpreted in two ways. If movements in fundamentals are not anticipated then the winner-loser effect is due to a surprise effect. Alternatively changes in fundamentals might proxy for changes in the exposure with respect to systematic risk. Then the winner-loser effect occurs within a framework of rational asset pricing. I show that within the CAPM changes in fundamentals proxy for changes in the exposure in the portfolio β. Of course, this can only provide limited evidence for the claim that the winner-loser effect occurs within a framework of rational asset pricing. The CAPM can only explain a small part of the observed reversals in the cross-section of stock returns.

Although the observed pattern in fundamentals enhances our understanding of the winner-loser effect, it cannot answer the question whether the winner-loser effect occurs within a framework of rational asset pricing. To answer this question an investigation is needed which relates stock returns to the pricing kernel directly or uses other aggregate pricing variables than the market return to approximate the exposure with respect to systematic risk.

6 Fundamentals versus Beta - What Drives Stock Returns?

Ever since people have invested their money into stocks they have been interested in the forces which drive stock returns. First, an analysis of these forces helps the investor to understand why stock returns have developed in a certain way during the past. Second, it might help him to make better investment decisions during the future. The main question of this chapter is which are the variables which explain the cross section of stock returns. I relate the cross section of stock returns to two sets of explanatory variables, the CAPM β and size on the one hand and to fundamentals on the other hand. I have already used these variables to explain stock returns in previous chapters. Starting point there has been the observed time series pattern. The main part of the analysis has concentrated on the explanation of long-term reversals in the cross section of excess returns. The CAPM showed only limited explanatory power whereas the pattern in fundamental variables was in line with lie pattern of excess returns. This evidence suggests that fundamentals explain the cross section of stock returns better than the CAPM β. In this chapter, I test for differences in the explanatory power directly.

The investor can approach the problem to determine the forces which drive stock returns in two ways. First, he can predict stock returns in period $t+1$ using information up to time t. As this approach uses only information which occurs before this period I call this the *ex ante* approach. However, in an efficient stock market the decisive information for a change in stock prices from time t to time $t+1$ (and hence for returns) is most likely to occur during that period. In the second approach the investor explains stock returns in period $t+1$ using information up to period $t+1$. In this case he investigates returns after the contemporaneous information has become available and therefore I call this the *ex post* approach. Both the *ex ante* and the *ex post* approach provide interesting information but for different reasons. The main motivation for the ex ante approach is to find out whether it is possible to earn excess returns conditional on past information.[41] The ex ante approach does not use contemporaneous information which is most likely to determine stock returns. Therefore, we expect the explanatory power of an ex ante regression to be low. This is different for the ex post regression. An

---

[41] Predictable excess returns raise again the question of capital market efficiency. As we have seen in the first chapter predictability does not necessarily imply an inefficiency of the capital market. Alternatively, the explanatory variables might capture the exposure with respect to systematic risk.

improvement in business conditions during the return period should be revealed both in profits and returns. Although it is likely that we obtain more powerful results in the case of the ex post regression the question arises why an investor should be interested in this type of analysis. If past information is already reflected in current stock prices, the ex post analysis seems to be of merely historical interest. However, this is not completely true. An investigation of realized returns helps the investor to make projections in the following way: It helps him to evaluate consequences of an unexpected development of exogenous variables. E.g., assume that the announced profit of a company is smaller than expected. From his investigation of past returns the investor might have a more precise idea of the new equilibrium price than other market participants. Hence, even the ex post analysis is useful to make limited predictions. It helps to predict the impact of unexpected news.

In this chapter I investigate stock returns both from an ex ante and from an ex post perspective. The empirical investigation is split into two parts. In the first part I investigate which variables explain the cross section of stock returns best. This part of the analysis is a linear regression of 5 year returns and is based on data for individual stocks. The second part of the investigation is concerned with the model specification. I discuss the following three questions. First, I ask in which way the time horizon influences our regression results. I explore how the regression results change if we analyze returns for one, two or more years instead of 5 year returns. Second, I investigate in which way the results change if we base the analysis on portfolios instead of individual stocks. Third, I test whether the linear framework which we have applied so far is appropriate. In both parts I apply a standard research design which presents hypotheses, empirical results, and a discussion where appropriate. A summary concludes.

6.1
Fundamentals versus Beta: A Horse Race

In this section I investigate whether the CAPM β and size or whether fundamentals explain the cross section of stock returns better. The analysis is based on the data set which has already been used in the first section of this monograph. I use an overlapping sample of 5 year returns from the most liquid segment of the German stock market from 1968 to 1986.

6.1.1
Hypotheses

I explain stock returns using two sets of variables, fundamentals and variables derived from asset pricing theory. One central question is which of the two groups of variables is more important in explaining stock returns. This question has very different implications from an ex ante and from an ex post perspective. From an ex ante perspective asset pricing theory claims that all the relevant information is captured by the exposure to the nondiversifiable pricing factors. In the CAPM this is the covariance between asset returns and the market return. Of course, this does not mean that other factors might not be able to capture at least part of this exposure as well. Nevertheless, from an ex ante perspective we expect the explanatory power of the asset pricing variables to be at least as good as the explanatory power of the fundamental variables. The perspective is different if we investigate stock returns from an ex post perspective. Realized returns are the sum of the expected return and an unexpected residual. This residual is driven by information which arrives after the point of time when the expectation has been built. Most of the time this information will be company specific and hence will not be captured by the covariance of the return with the market portfolio. This is different for fundamental variables. Company specific information is likely to be revealed in the fundamental performance of a company.

Ex post regression
My main hypothesis concerns the relative importance of fundamentals and more traditional measures of exposure with respect to systematic risk, like the CAPM β and size[42]. From our reasoning above I can state my hypothesis for the ex post regression as follows.

Hypothesis I: *Fundamental variables are more important for the explanation of stock returns ex post than the CAPM β or size.*

The following hypotheses take a closer look at the way in which fundamentals explain stock returns. The most simple time series process which we can assume for fundamentals is a random walk. Then new information which occurs from time t to time $t+1$ is revealed in changes in fundamentals. Therefore, I expect changes in dividends or profits to be among the significant variables which explain stock returns.

Hypothesis II: *Changes in dividends and changes in profits are significant explanatory variables in explaining realized stock returns.*

In the fifth chapter of this monograph I have found a characteristic pattern of the underlying fundamental variables. The direction of changes in total profits seemed to be driven by ordinary and financial income whereas extraordinary profits were used to smooth the reported profits. There I could show that at least part of these movements were significant as I analyzed these movements variable by variable.

---

[42] Size has been found to contribute to the explanation of stock returns empirically (Banz (1981)). Small companies earn an excess return which cannot be explained by other variables. This excess return is supposed to capture a liquidity premium. Fama and French (1996) also include size as a significant explanatory factor in a three factor model. Therefore, I include size as an established explanatory factor together with the CAPM β.

Therefore, I can state two hypotheses with respect to the profit decomposition. The first hypothesis is that the profit decomposition is informative. The second hypothesis is that the pattern of the profit decomposition which I have found on a variable by variable basis also holds for a multivariate regression.

Hypothesis III: *A decomposition of profits into their components is informative. The fraction of the variation in returns which can be explained by the profit components is larger than the fraction which can be explained by profits alone.*

Hypothesis IV: *Changes in ordinary and financial profits are significant explanatory variables. Their regression coefficients are positive. The regression coefficient for changes in extraordinary income are negative.*

The most general regression which I run to explain the cross section of stock returns includes both contemporaneous as well as past variables. The hypotheses which I have stated so far concern contemporaneous variables. The only past variable for which I formulate a specific hypothesis are past returns. Starting point for my investigation in the first chapter has been the observation of long run reversals in excess returns. Former winner firms underperformed the market subsequently, former loser firms overperformed the market. Returns on winner and loser firms show negative autocorrelation. Even if returns on other firms do not show any autocorrelation this implies that it should be possible to observe negative autocorrelation for the entire cross section on average.

Hypothesis V: *For long run returns the autoregressive coefficient is negative.*

Ex ante regression
For the ex ante regression our main hypothesis reverses: Ex ante all relevant information should be captured by aggregate pricing variables. In a rational asset pricing model expected excess returns are driven by the covariance of the return with respect to systematic risk. Empirically, this covariance should be captured by the covariance of returns with aggregate pricing variables. In the CAPM the exposure with respect to systematic risk is captured by the CAPM β. As I have explained above I use size as an additional aggregate pricing variable. Of course, also fundamentals might capture part of this covariance. However, ex ante they should not explain stock returns better than the asset pricing variables.

Hypothesis I': *Variables from asset pricing models are at least as successful in explaining stock returns ex ante as fundamental variables.*

The previous hypotheses II - IV in the ex post regression are concerned with the explanatory power of the fundamental variables. There is no reason to assume that these hypotheses also hold for the ex ante regression. Nevertheless, I will take a closer look at the signs which I obtain for changes in different fundamental variables. With respect to past returns the same reasoning applies as for the ex post regression.

Hypothesis V': *For long run returns the autoregressive coefficient is negative.*

6.1.2
Estimation Results

At the center of my investigation is the question which set of variables can explain the cross section of stock returns best. The comparison of the explanatory power of different sets of variables is pursued in an economic setting which is known as the General to Specific or LSE methodology and which has been introduced by Hendry, Pagan, and Sargan (1984). According to this methodology one has to use the most general specification of a model available to avoid a misspecification of the model. This methodology is by now standard of the practice of econometric modelling. We discuss the regression results for the most general model specification available, first in the case of the ex post regression, then in the case of the ex ante regression. Afterwards I turn to my main hypotheses I and I' and compare the explanatory power of the two sets of variables.

Ex post regression
First, I present results for the ex post regression: Both contemporaneous and past variables are included into the analysis. I run the ex post regression in two specifications, the first includes profit components, the second includes profits as an aggregate. Starting point for the first specification is the following regression equation.

$$
\begin{aligned}
R_t = \alpha_0 &+ \beta_1 R_{t-1} + \beta_2 \left[\beta \left(R_{Mt} - R_{ft} \right) \right] + \beta_3 \text{size}_{t-1} \\
&+ \beta_4 \sum D_t + \beta_5 \Delta D_t + \beta_6 \sum D_{t-1} + \beta_7 \Delta D_{t-1} \\
&+ \beta_{8a} \sum \Pi(o)_t + \beta_{8b} \sum \Pi(f)_t + \beta_{8c} \sum \Pi(x)_t \\
&+ \beta_{9a} \Delta \Pi(o)_t + \beta_{9b} \Delta \Pi(f)_t + \beta_{9c} \Delta \Pi(x)_t \\
&+ \beta_{10a} \sum \Pi(o)_{t-1} + \beta_{10b} \sum \Pi(f)_{t-1} + \beta_{10c} \sum \Pi(x)_{t-1} \\
&+ \beta_{11a} \Delta \Pi(o)_{t-1} + \beta_{11b} \Delta \Pi(f)_{t-1} + \beta_{11c} \Delta \Pi(x)_{t-1}
\end{aligned}
\tag{35}
$$

where R_t are stock returns for a 5 year period and R_{-1} are returns for the previous 5 years. β is the β from a CAPM regression for the return period.[43] $R_{Mt} - R_{ft}$ is the risk premium for the 5 year return period, where R_{Mt} is the return

---

[43] As in previous sections the market index used for the CAPM regression is the DAFOX which has been provided by the *Karlsruhe Kapitalmarkt Datenbank*. The CAPM β is estimated by an OLS regression.

on the DAFOX and R_{ft} is the riskfree rate. As there has been substantial variation in the risk premium, $\beta(R_{Mt} - R_{ft})$ is likely to capture more of the return R_t than β alone. Size is the logarithm of the sum of total assets at the beginning of the formation period. The fundamental variables which are included in the analysis are dividends D as well as profit components. $\Pi(o)$ is ordinary income, $\Pi(f)$ financial income, and $\Pi(x)$ extraordinary income. Fundamental variables are always included in two forms, a cumulative one as well as a difference. Cumulative means that we accumulate the values of the relevant variable over a time period of 5 years, e.g., $\sum D_t = D_1 + D_2 + ... + D_5$. Difference means that we take the difference between the realization of the variable at the beginning and the end of the 5 year period, e.g., $\Delta D_t = D_5 - D_0$. In the ex post regression these variables are included both for the 5 years of the return period as well as for the previous 5 years.

Starting point for the second specification is the regression equation

$$R_t = \alpha_0 + \beta_1 R_{t-1} + \beta_2 \left[\beta(R_{Mt} - R_{ft})\right] + \beta_3 \text{size}$$
$$+ \beta_4 \sum D_t + \beta_5 \Delta D_t + \beta_6 \sum D_{t-1} + \beta_7 \Delta D_{t-1} \qquad (36)$$
$$+ \beta_8 \sum \Pi_t + \beta_9 \Delta \Pi_t + \beta_{10} \sum \Pi_{t-1} + \beta_{11} \Delta \Pi_{t-1}$$

where I use profits Π instead of profit components. Starting from equations (35) and (36) I have tested for the regression specifications which maximize the adjusted R^2.

For the specification which includes profit components results are presented on the left hand side of table 31, for the second specification which includes aggregate profits results are presented on the right hand side. For the variables which were excluded from the final specification the entries are left blank. Table 31 presents the regression coefficients in three blocks. The upper part of the table contains the intercept and the coefficients for the lagged return, $\beta(R_{Mt} - R_{ft})$ and size. The middle part contains contemporaneous fundamentals, the lower part lagged fundamentals. In the last rows the adjusted R^2 and the number of observations are presented.

From table 31 I observe an explanatory power for both specifications of roughly 32%. Hence, about one third of the total variation in stock returns can be explained ex post.

Concerning my hypotheses, I obtain the following three findings. The first finding refers to the first block of variables in the upper part of the table, the second and third findings concern the fundamental variables. In both specifications I find the following results for lagged returns, , β , and size I find the following results. In accordance with hypothesis V I obtain as a first main finding a negative coefficient for the regression on the lagged return which is highly significant. This implies that for long run returns the negative autocorrelation which we have found in a single variable context also holds in a multivariate regression. For $\beta(R_{Mt} - R_{ft})$ the coefficient is positive and highly significant. Size has a positive coefficient which is also significant. This is a surprising result as it contradicts previous findings from the literature (Banz (1981)).

Table 31. The ex post regression: 5 year returns are related to the entire set of explanatory variables both contemporaneous and from the previous 5 years. The table presents the specifications which maximize the adjusted R^2

Specification regressor	Specification I[a] coeff.	std.	sign.[c]	Specification II[b] coeff.	std.	sign.[c]
intercept	0.1604	0.1869		0.1073	0.1819	
return $[t-1]$[d]	-0.2600	0.0362	***	-0.2120	0.0383	***
$\beta(R_M - R_f)[t]$	1.4671	0.1237	***	1.4427	0.1230	***
size $[t-1]$	0.0319	0.0145	**	0.0476	0.0141	***
Fundamentals $[t]$[e]						
Dividends						
diff.[f]	6.5424	0.5888	***	5.8720	0.6164	***
Profits						
cum.[g]	n.a.	n.a.		0.9011	0.0700	***
Profit components ordinary profits						
cum.	0.4167	0.0380	***	n.a.	n.a.	
financial profits						
cum.	0.4974	0.0481	***	n.a.	n.a.	
extraordinary profits						
cum.	0.4175	0.0609	***	n.a.	n.a.	
Fundamentals $[t-1]$						
Dividends						
diff.	3.5947	0.5487	***	2.6178	0.6386	***
Profits						
cum.				-0.1965	0.0733	***
diff.				0.4704	0.2213	**
Profit components extraordinary profits						
cum.	0.1849	0.0471	***			
adj. R^2		32.17%			32.76%	
# of obs.		1300			1300	

[a] Specification I includes profit components. All parameters which are reported are included in the final specification of the model. Variables which are not relevant for the specification are marked by "n.a" (not applicable). For variables which are excluded from the regression the entries are left blank

[b] Specification II includes aggregate profits. The exact specification can be seen from the table

[c] level of significance for a t-test: *** (**, *) implies that the hypothesis of the regression coefficient to be equal to 0 can be rejected at a 1% (5%, 10%) significance level

[d] index $t-1$: variables from the previous 5 years, e.g. the returns for the 5 years prior to the test period

[e] index t: contemporaneous variables, e.g. cumulative profits from the 5 years of the test period

[f] diff. = difference: $D_5 - D_0$

[g] cum. = cumulative: $\sum_{t=1}^{5} D_t$

Turning to the central part of the analysis I can state the two findings with respect to fundamentals. According to hypothesis II we expect large and positive values for changes in dividends and profits. Indeed, I find differences in dividends to be large and to be highly significant for both specifications. Therefore, we cannot reject hypothesis II. The second major finding with respect to fundamentals concerns the explanatory power of the profit decomposition. It turns out that this decomposition is not informative. On the contrary, the adjusted R^2 decreases slightly if we include profit components due to the increased number of variables. Therefore, I can reject hypothesis III. Furthermore, if we turn to the regression on the profit components we have also to reject hypothesis IV, at least partially. Contrary to my hypothesis it is not differences in profit components which are included but cumulative profit components and we cannot detect any significantly different movement for the extraordinary profits.

I have stated my hypotheses with respect to differences in fundamentals rather than levels. However, I do not only obtain significant coefficients for differences in fundamentals, but also for levels. Both profits as well as profit components enter the regression equation as levels rather than as differences. From our discussion in chapter 3 this finding does not come as a surprise. The analysis of the relationship between unexpected returns and fundamentals in section 3.2 has shown that levels may have explanatory power as well. The alternative explanation within a framework of rational pricing relates levels in fundamentals to the exposure with respect to systematic risk. Firms which show high levels in fundamentals are perceived to bear more systematic risk. As this systematic component is captured only imperfectly by $\beta\left(R_{Mt} - R_{ft}\right)$, the systematic risk also shows up in the coefficients for the levels in fundamentals which turn out to be significant. In addition, I find that also some of the past fundamental variables are significant. This finding can be interpreted along the same lines.

Ex ante regression
In a second step I test for the ex ante regression. This regression is more restrictive than the ex post regression as contemporaneous variables are excluded. Starting point for the first specification is the regression equation

$$
\begin{aligned}
R_t = {}& \alpha_0 + \beta_1 R_{t-1} + \beta_2 \alpha + \beta_3 \beta + \beta_4 \text{size}_{t-1} \\
& + \beta_5 \sum D_{t-1} + \Delta\beta_6 \Delta D_{t-1} \\
& + \beta_{7a} \sum \Pi(o)_{t-1} + \beta_{7b} \sum \Pi(f)_{t-1} + \beta_{7c} \sum \Pi(x)_{t-1} \\
& + \beta_{8a} \Delta\Pi(o)_{t-1} + \beta_{8b} \Delta\Pi(f)_{t-1} + \beta_{8c} \Delta\Pi(x)_{t-1}
\end{aligned}
\tag{37}
$$

Contrary to equation (35) this regression does not contain any contemporaneous explanatory variables. It includes the lagged return, size, dividends and profits. In addition I use two variables from a CAPM regression, α and β. For the 5 years of monthly returns which precede the return period I run a CAPM regression $R_t - R_f = \alpha + \beta\left(R_M - R_f\right) + \varepsilon$ for every stock. As in previous sections, R_f is the monthly money market rate and R_M is the return on the DAFOX. According to the CAPM, β should capture the variation in expected returns. However, often α, which is also known as Jensen's α is found to be significant. Therefore, both α and β are included into the regression. Note that in the case of the ex ante regression it is β rather than $\beta\left(R_{M_{t-1}} - R_{f_{t-1}}\right)$ which is included. For the ex ante regression there is no reason to assume that $\beta\left(R_{M_{t-1}} - R_{f_{t-1}}\right)$ increases the explanatory power as compared to β. The second specification again includes profits instead of profit components.

Starting from equation (37) and its modification for the second specification I present again the specification which maximizes the adjusted R^2. Results for the ex ante regression are presented in table 32. The upper part of the table presents the results for the intercept α_0, the lagged return, Jensen's α, the CAPM β, and size. The lower part presents the results for fundamentals.

From table 32 I obtain an explanatory power for the ex ante regression which is considerably lower than for the ex post regression. Instead of 32% in the ex post regression, it is 7.96% in the first specification (including profit components) and 5.24% for the second specification (excluding profit components).

Concerning my hypotheses I obtain the following three findings. The first two findings refer to the first set of variables. The third finding refers to fundamentals. As in the previous regression the coefficient of the lagged return turns out to be significant and negative. This is in line with hypothesis V'. The property of negative long run autocorrelation in stock returns seems to be a phenomenon which is robust for different empirical specifications of the model. The second main finding for the forecasting analysis also belongs to the first set of variables: The predictive power of the variables derived from the CAPM is almost zero. For the first specification neither Jensen's α nor β turn out to be significant explanatory factors. For the second specification it is only β which turns out to be significant, but at a low level. Another finding from the first set of variables is that size has a positive coefficient which is highly significant. As in the ex post regression this finding is at odds with the literature (Banz (1981), Fama and French (1996)).

The third finding concerns the explanatory power of the fundamental variables. Contrary to my previous findings, for the forecasting regression I find that including the profit decomposition increases the explanatory power from 5.24% to almost 8%. In the ex post regression the profit decomposition did not add to the explanatory power. All relevant information was reflected in aggregate profits. For the ex ante regression the profit decomposition contains additional information. In an efficient capital market this implies that profit components deliver more accurate estimates of the exposure with respect to systematic risk than aggregate profits. Another interesting finding is that lagged cumulative dividends show negative signs in both specifications. This can be related to our findings from the fourth chapter. There an increase in fundamentals anticipated a drop in returns and vice versa. Although in my regressions this reversal does not show up in the differences of dividends we find a significant coefficient for the cumulated dividends. This could capture part of the observed reversal.

Table 32. The ex ante regression: 5 year returns are related to the entire set of explanatory variables from the previous 5 years. The table presents the specifications which maximize the adjusted R^2

Specification regressor	Specification I[a]			Specification II[b]		
	coeff.	std.	sign.[c]	coeff.	std.	sign.[c]
intercept	0.1978	0.2232		0.2356	0.2217	
return $[t-1]$	−0.3445	0.0567	***	−0.3249	0.0574	***
Jensen's α $[t-1]$	0.2200	4.7588		5.9467	4.7668	
β $[t-1]$	0.0415	0.0582		0.0988	0.0582	*
size $[t-1]$	0.0487	0.0168	***	0.0492	0.0167	***
Fundamentals $[t-1]$						
Dividends						
cum.[d]	−0.8375	0.1813	***	−0.3295	0.1368	**
diff.[e]	1.6418	0.6188	***	1.2933	0.6615	*
Profits						
cum.	n.a.	n.a.				
diff.	n.a.	n.a.		0.6337	0.2620	**
Profit components $[t-1]$						
ordinary profits						
cum.	0.1989	0.0571	**	n.a.	n.a.	
diff.	0.2564	0.1272	***	n.a.	n.a.	
financial profits						
cum.	0.4165	0.0730	***	n.a.	n.a.	
diff.				n.a.	n.a.	
extraordinary profits						
cum.	0.3093	0.0711	***	n.a.	n.a.	
diff.				n.a.	n.a.	
adj. R^2		7.96%			5.24%	
# of obs.		1300			1300	

[a] Specification I includes profit components. All parameters which are reported are included in the final specification of the model. Variables which are not relevant for the specification are marked by "n.a" (not applicable). For variables which are excluded from the regression the entries are left blank

[b] Specification II includes aggregate profits. The exact specification can be seen from the table

[c] level of significance for a t-test: *** (**, *) implies that the hypothesis of the regression coefficient to be equal to 0 can be rejected at a 1% (5%, 10%) significance level

[d] cum. = cumulative: $\sum_{t=1}^{5} D_t$

[e] diff. = difference: $D_5 - D_0$

Hypotheses I and I'

I now turn to the central question of this chapter: Which is the set of variables which can explain returns best, fundamentals or variables from asset pricing models? To answer this question we face the following methodological problem: In the regressions which we have presented above part of both sets of variables has turned out to be significant. Therefore, omitting these variables necessarily leads to the problem of misspecification. Unfortunately, it is not possible to solve this problem. I run regressions on the two sets of explanatory variables separately, first for the CAPM variables and size, second for fundamentals. The CAPM variable for the ex post regression is $\beta(R_M - R_f)[t]$, the CAPM variables for the ex ante regressions are Jensen's $\alpha[t-1]$ and $\beta[t-1]$. An additional variable which has shown considerable explanatory power in the previous regressions has been the lagged return. Therefore, I run these regressions in two forms. The first reduced form is

$$R_t = \alpha_0 + \beta'X_t \tag{38}$$

where X_t is the vector of the explanatory variables, either size and the CAPM variables or the fundamental variables which are included both as cumulative values and as differences. The second specification includes the lagged return:

$$R_t = \alpha_0 + \beta'X_t + \gamma R_{t-1} \tag{39}$$

Results are presented in table 33. The upper part of table 33 presents the results for the ex post regression. The lower part presents the results for the ex ante regression.

The top row shows the explanatory power for the ex post regression which maximizes the adjusted R^2 (cf. table 31). The rows below show the explanatory of the restricted regressions, first for $\beta(R_M - R_F)$ and size, second for fundamentals. The first column presents the adjusted R^2 for the regression (38). The second column presents the adjusted R^2 for the regression (39).

For hypothesis I, I find very supportive evidence for the *ex post* regression: whereas the variables from asset pricing explain 9.81% of the observed variation in stock returns, the fundamental variables explain 22.93%. Hence, two thirds of the 32.76% we can explain if we take all the information together is due to fundamentals, only one third can be attributed to $\beta(R_M - R_F)$ and size. I obtain a similar result if I include the lagged return in the regression: For both regressions the explanatory power increases slightly by 1.5 to 2 percentage points.

For the *ex ante* regression I have tested the reverse hypothesis: I expect asset pricing variables to show at least as much explanatory power as fundamentals. We have to reject this hypothesis. The explanatory power of each set of variables alone is small. Still, fundamentals with an adjusted R^2 of 3.10% have more predictive power than asset pricing variables with an adjusted R^2 of 1.64%. This difference in explanatory power increases as we include lagged returns into the regression equation. For fundamentals and lagged returns we obtain an adjusted R^2 of 7.50%. For β and size we obtain an explanatory power of 3.39%. Alternatively we can state our results as follows. Starting from a level of explanatory power of 7.96% for the complete regression we lose half of a percentage point if we exclude asset pricing variables whereas we lose 4.57 percentage points or more than half of the explanatory power if we exclude fundamental variables from the regression. Our findings support hypothesis I, but reject hypothesis I'.

Table 33. Explanatory power: Adjusted R^2 for different model specifications for 5 year returns

	ex post regression	
Reference case all variables	32.76%	
	$R_t = \alpha_0 + \beta'x\,[^a]$	$R_t = \alpha_0 + \beta'x + \gamma R_{t-1}\,[^b]$
size, CAPM: $\beta(R_M - R_f)[t]$	9.81%	11.72%
fundamentals	22.93%	25.21%
	ex ante regression	
Reference case all variables	7.96%	
	$R_t = \alpha_0 + \beta'x\,[^c]$	$R_t = \alpha_0 + \beta'x + \gamma R_{t-1}\,[^d]$
size, CAPM: α, β $[t-1]$	1.64%	3.39%
fundamentals	3.10%	7.50%

[a] Adjusted R^2 for the regression $R_t = \alpha_0 + \beta'x$ where x are either size and $\beta(R_M - R_f)$, or fundamentals

[b] Adjusted R^2 for the regression $R_t = \alpha_0 + \beta'x + \gamma R_{t-1}$ where x are either size and $\beta(R_M - R_f)$, or fundamentals. R_{t-1} is the lagged 5 year return

[c] Adjusted R^2 for the regression $R_t = \alpha_0 + \beta'x$ where x are either size, Jensen's α and β, or fundamentals

[d] Adjusted R^2 for the regression $R_t = \alpha_0 + \beta'x + \gamma R_{t-1}$ where x are either size, Jensen's α and β, or fundamentals. R_{t-1} is the lagged 5 year return

6.1.3
Summary

In this section, I investigate which variables explain the cross section of stock returns best. Fundamentals turn out to have more explanatory power than the CAPM β and size. I distinguish between two types of regressions. Most of the information which determines stock returns from time t to time $t+1$ is revealed during that period. Including this information leads to an adjusted R^2 of 32.76% [*ex post* regression], excluding this information to an adjusted R^2 of 7.96% [*ex ante* regression]. In the ex post regression fundamentals contribute two thirds of the explanation (adj. R^2: 22.93%) whereas the contribution of $\beta(R_M - R_F)$ and size is about one third (adj. R^2: 9.81%). Also, in the ex ante regression fundamentals contribute the major part of the explanation. Almost no explanatory power is lost if Jensen's α, β and size are omitted from the regression (adj. R^2 with β 7.96%, without β 7.50%). Substantial explanatory power is lost if fundamentals are excluded from the regression (adj. R^2 without fundamentals 3.39%). For both regression approaches we observe significant negative autocorrelation in returns. The interesting finding from the point of view of economic theory is the explanatory power of fundamentals for the ex ante regression.

If fundamentals add substantial explanatory power, the question arises what this implies from the point of view of economic theory. Two interpretations are available. Either fundamentals capture the exposure with respect to systematic risk. This is the case of rational asset pricing. On the other hand if fundamentals capture idiosyncratic components which are independent of systematic risk this implies that a framework of rational asset pricing is not sufficient to explain the cross section of stock returns.

6.2
Time Horizon and Portfolio Effects, Nonlinearities

In the previous section I have explored returns for an investment horizon of five years in a linear regression framework on a stock by stock basis. In this section I investigate in which way the time horizon, portfolio effects, and the linear specification of the model influence our results.

6.2.1
Hypotheses

Instead of investigating returns for an investment horizon of five years we investigate stock returns for shorter time horizons. Aggregating returns over time should eliminate transitory components. For the ex post regression the question arises whether transitory components in returns also appear as transitory components in fundamentals. As accounting figures are usually assumed to be smoothed, they are not likely to capture these transitory components. Therefore, the explanatory power of regressions over longer time horizons should increase.[44] For the ex ante regression the hypothesis depends on the question whether it is easier to forecast transitory or permanent components of stock returns. As the transitory component is likely to be more noisy and hence more difficult to forecast we maintain the hypothesis for the ex ante regression that the explanatory power increases for longer time horizons.

---

[44] This hypothesis is in line with previous findings in the literature. For longer time horizons Easton, Harris, and Ohlson (1992) have claimed that "accounting earnings can explain most of security returns". Similar results have been found for German data by Harris, Lang, and Möller (1994). In the accounting literature there is a long discussion about the relationship between stock returns and earnings. For time horizons of one year this relationship has been found to be weak (Lev (1980)). Various attempts have been made to increase the explanatory power of this relationship. Beaver, Lambert, and Morse (1980) group stocks into portfolios according to their performance. However, conditioning on information on the dependent variables causes problems from an econometric point of view. Attempts to increase the explanatory power by means of a respecification of the model have been made by Beaver, Lambert, and Ryan (1987) (reverse regression) and Beaver, McAnally, and Stinson (1997) (simultaneous equations). The most powerful way how to increase the explanatory power of short horizon regressions is to increase the time horizon (Easton, Harris, and Ohlson (1992)).

Hypothesis VI (Time Horizon Effects): *The explanatory power of both the ex post as well as the ex ante regression increases for longer time horizons.*

In the next step we aggregate stocks into portfolios instead of investigating them on a stock by stock basis. The variation in stock returns can be thought to be composed of a common and of an idiosyncratic component. If stocks are aggregated into portfolios, part of the idiosyncratic return component should be diversified. For a regression of portfolios the common component should be more important than for a regression on a stock by stock basis. For the regressions on a stock by stock basis the question arises whether the explanatory variables keep track of the idiosyncratic component. We have to distinguish between the ex post and the ex ante regression.

Ex post, developments which are company-specific are likely to be revealed both in stock returns and the underlying fundamentals. For the ex post regression the idiosyncratic component is likely to be captured by contemporaneous changes in fundamentals. In a similar way the common component is likely to be reflected in the average fundamental performance of the portfolio. Therefore, ex post the explanatory power of a regression which is based on portfolios should be of the same size as the explanatory power of a regression which is pursued on a stock by stock basis.

This is different for the *ex ante* approach. It is likely to be more difficult to forecast idiosyncratic components than to forecast the common component. The idiosyncratic component is subject to a lot of random noise. Therefore, it will be difficult to forecast this component. For portfolios the common component is more important. Shocks which hit different companies differently, should be diversified. In a stable economic environment it should be possible to forecast the common component to some extent.

Hypothesis VII (Portfolio Effects): *Aggregating stocks into portfolios increases the explanatory power of the ex ante regression. For the ex post regression it stays at the same level.*

The last hypothesis concerns the proposed linearity between stock returns and changes in profits for the ex post regression. Doubts can be raised whether this relationship should be linear. If fundamentals show a tendency to return to a normal level after extreme events this should be anticipated by the stock market. Then extreme events in fundamentals should lead to less than proportional reactions in returns. In addition, profits are not an objective measure of the fundamental performance of a company. They are a result of the interplay between the fundamental performance and the accounting policy. In particular the accounting policy induces some additional "behavioural" noise into the relationship which might also induce some nonlinearity in the regression equation. For the ex ante regression the question arises how changes in fundamentals affect stock returns one period ahead. Also here extreme events in fundamentals are likely to show up in a different way in future returns than normal changes. Therefore, I test for nonlinearities both in the ex ante and in the ex post regression.

Hypothesis VIII (Nonlinearity): *For the ex post and the ex ante regression the relationship between returns and changes in profits is nonlinear. For large positive and large negative changes in profits the reaction of returns is less than proportional.*

6.2.2
Estimation Results

In this section I run modified versions of the regression equations (35) and (37). I use mainly the same regressors as in these regressions. For the ex ante regression I only include past variables (past returns, size, dividends and profits). For the ex post regression I include past variables as well as contemporaneous variables (contemporaneous: dividends, profits, size, past returns, dividends, profits). Past returns, dividends, and profits are included in a slightly different way than in the previous analysis. There I included dividends and profits as differences and as cumulative values. The past return was included as return for the last five years. Here, I include the vector of lagged values of yearly returns, dividends and profits per year. I run the following regression equation

$$R_t = \alpha_0 + \beta_2' X + \beta_3' R(L) + \beta_4' D(L) + \beta_5' \Pi(L)$$

$R(L)$ is the vector of past yearly returns, $D(L)$ is the vector of past dividends, and $\Pi(L)$ is the vector of past profits. All these variables are included up to lag 5. X denotes the remaining variables. This regression is run in an ex ante specification and in an ex post specification. In the ex ante specification X includes only past variables, in the ex post specification it includes past and contemporaneous variables.

First, I test for time horizon effects. I run the regression on a stock by stock basis for different time horizons for R_t. Second, I test for portfolio effects for a time horizon of 5 years. Instead of using data on a stock by stock basis I run the regression for portfolios of different size. For the portfolio regressions I use portfolio means for both returns and regressors.

Time Horizon Effects
Based on a stock by stock regression results for different horizons are presented in table 34. The table presents the total sum of squares, the explained sum of squares, and the adjusted R^2 for both the ex post and the ex ante regression. The first column presents the sum of squares as a measure of variability. The second and third column present evidence for the ex post regression. They show the explained sum of squares and the adjusted R^2. The forth and fifth column present the explained sum of squares and the adjusted R^2 for the ex ante regression.

Table 34. Explanatory power: Time horizon effects for a stock by stock regression

Time Horizon	Sum of Squares	*Ex post* Regression			*Ex ante* Regression		
		Sum expl.	R^2	Adj. R^2	Sum expl.	R^2	Adj. R^2
1 year	84.3594	12.3175	14.60%	13.27%	8.3933	9.95%	8.81%
2 years	46.7223	10.7220	22.95%	21.74%	4.7225	10.11%	8.97%
3 years	31.0711	9.6636	31.10%	30.02%	3.6345	11.70%	10.58%
4 years	24.7345	8.4632	34.22%	33.18%	3.0511	12.34%	11.22%
5 years	19.3200	6.8922	35.67%	35.05%	1.6581	8.58%	7.98%

Three observations can be made from table 34. First, as I increase the time horizon the sum of squares diminishes from 84.359 to 19.320. This is due to intertemporal diversification. Second, the explained sum of squares (Sum expl.) is always larger for the ex post than for the ex ante regression. This is due to the effect that the ex post regression contains more information than the ex ante regression. Third, the explained sum of squares diminishes for the ex ante and for the ex post regression to a different extent. For the ex ante regression the total and the explained sum of squares diminish in a roughly proportional way. For a one year horizon to a four year horizon the adjusted R^2 increases only slightly from 8.81% to 11.22%. For a five year horizon an adjusted R^2 of 7.98% can be observed. For the ex post regression the explained sum of squares decreases in a less than proportional way. The adjusted R^2 increases from 13.27% for a one year horizon to 35.05% for a five year horizon.[45] With respect to hypothesis VI I find supportive evidence for the ex post regression. Contemporaneous fundamental variables can explain long run developments better than short run developments. Transitory components in returns are not fully explained by fundamentals. For the ex ante regression I have to reject hypothesis VI. It is as difficult to forecast the temporary component in the cross section of stock returns as the permanent component.

Portfolio Effects
Table 35 presents the effects of portfolio building for our benchmark time horizon of five years. Portfolios are built in the same way as in previous chapters according to past performance. I run the regression for 5, 10, 50 and 100 portfolios and include the case where no portfolios are built as a benchmark case. Results are presented in table 35. The last row is the same as in table 34. Three major findings arise. First, aggregating stocks into portfolios diminishes the total sum of squares. On a stock by stock level the total sum of squares is 19.32. If only 5 portfolios are investigated this sum diminishes by a factor of more than 100 to 0.15. The second main finding is that the explanatory power of the ex post regression remains con-

---

[45] The maximum value which I have reported in the previous section has been 26.72%. This implies that the model specification which is used here is more informative than the previous one. The time series structure during the past periods seem to have additional explanatory power.

stant for different levels of aggregation. This implies that contemporaneous variables can keep track of the idiosyncratic component in individual stock returns as well as of the common component in portfolio returns. The third main finding is that the explanatory power of the ex ante regression increases if stock returns are aggregated into portfolios. The explanatory power increases from a level of 7.98% for individual stocks to a level of 33.36% for the case of 5 portfolios. It is easier to forecast portfolio returns than to forecast returns of individual stocks. This implies supportive evidence for hypothesis VII both for the ex post and for the ex ante regression. For the ex post regression the explanatory power remains roughly at the same level. For the ex ante regression aggregating stocks into portfolios increases the explanatory power.

Table 35. Explanatory power: Portfolio Effects – Portfolios are built according to past performance for 5 year returns

# Portf.	Sum of Squares	Ex post Regression			Ex ante Regression		
		Sum expl.	R^2	Adj. R^2	Sum expl.	R^2	Adj. R^2
5	0.1533	0.0784	51.14%	33.52%	0.0699	45.60%	33.36%
10	0.3478	0.1445	41.55%	32.73%	0.1055	30.33%	23.28%
50	3.7254	1.3205	35.45%	33.72%	0.5162	13.86%	12.27%
100	13.6807	4.9648	36.29%	35.42%	1.2427	9.08%	8.23%
total	19.3200	6.8922	35.67%	35.05%	1.6581	8.58%	7.98%

Nonlinearities

To test for nonlinearities I use the same regression framework which I have used in the first section of this chapter (cf. equations (35) and (37)). I investigate 5 year stock returns on a stock by stock basis. The hypothesis of nonlinearity is investigated from an ex ante as well as from an ex post point of view.

First, I turn to the *ex post* regression. So far I have related stock returns to changes in profits in a linear way. In a short hand notation the ex post regression can be written as

$$R_t = \alpha_0 + \beta'X + d\Delta\Pi_t$$

where $\Delta\Pi_t$ denotes the difference between the first and the fifth year of the test period and X is the vector of the remaining variables. To test for nonlinearity in the relationship between stock returns and changes in profits I sort stocks according to changes in profits $\Delta\Pi_t$ into quintiles. I include a different coefficient for the differences in profits variable for the upper quintile, the lower quintile and the three middle quintiles. Conditioning on this information should not cause any problem from the point of view of econometric methodology as we condition on information on the right hand side of the regression equation. In our short hand notation the regression equation becomes

$$R_t = \alpha_0 + \beta'X + d_1 q_1 \Delta\Pi_t + d_2 q_2 \Delta\Pi_t + d_3 q_3 \Delta\Pi_t \tag{40}$$

where $\Delta\Pi_t$ is again the difference in profits during the return period. The q_i's are the dummy variables: For the lowest quintile of the $\Delta\Pi$ distribution: $q_1 = 1$, $q_2 = q_3 = 0$, for the middle quintiles $q_2 = 1$, $q_1 = q_3 = 0$, and for the highest quintile $q_3 = 1$, $q_1 = q_2 = 0$. This regression is tested by a maximum likelihood estimation of the Lagrangean function. From solving for the Lagrangean function the significance of the restriction can be tested by means of a t-test on the Lagrangean multiplier.[46]

Results for the ex post regression are presented in table 36. I investigate two specifications of the regression equation (40). In a first step I test for the claim that the relationship between stock returns and changes in fundamentals is nonlinear in a simplified framework. This first regression only includes changes in profits as an explanatory variable. Results for this most simple specification

$$R_t = \alpha_0 + d_1 q_1 \Delta\Pi_t + d_2 q_2 \Delta\Pi_t + d_3 q_3 \Delta\Pi_t \tag{41}$$

are presented on the left hand side of table 36. On the right hand side I present the full specification which maximizes the adjusted R^2. The table is organized as follows. At the top it presents the different coefficients for $\Delta\Pi$: d_1, d_2 and d_3. Then the remaining coefficients are presented. At the bottom I present the estimators for the Lagrangean multipliers. I test for the restriction $d_1 = d_2$ and $d_2 = d_3$.

The results for the simple specification are in line with my hypothesis. All of the coefficients are significant and show the hypothesized pattern: For the lower and for the upper quintile the slope is smaller than for the middle quintiles: 1.3721 for the lower quintile and 0.9971 for the upper quintile as compared to 10.6477 for the middle quintile. The differences between the slopes are also significant. Nevertheless, one has to be careful in interpreting these results. As one can see from the full specification of the model on the right hand side, the sparse model is misspecified: various other variables are also significant.

Table 36 is the nonlinear equivalent to table 31. The results which are obtained for the second specification are similar for the linear and the nonlinear analysis. In addition, all coefficients for the changes in profits turn out to be significant. In the regression analysis of table 31 the regression coefficient for $\Delta\Pi$ was insignificant. In the nonlinear case, all coefficients for $\Delta\Pi$ were significant. This finding presents strong evidence for the relationship between stock returns and fundamentals to be nonlinear.

---

[46] cf. Judge, Hill, Griffiths, Lütkepohl, and Lee (1988), p. 260, where λ denotes the squared Lagrangean multiplier. See also Greene (1997), p. 342.

Table 36. Nonlinearities: Ex post regression – 5 year returns are related to the entire set of explanatory variables both contemporaneous and from the previous 5 years

regressor	Specification 0[a]			Specification II[b]		
	coeff.	std.	sign.	coeff.	std.	sign.
Changes in Profits $[t]^c$						
1st quintile: d_1	1.3721	0.2675	***	−0.4890	0.2754	*
2nd - 4th quintile: d_2	10.6477	1.4769	***	5.4778	1.2872	***
5th quintile: d_3	0.9971	0.2886	***	0.8447	0.2877	***
intercept	0.7118	0.0315	***	0.0475	0.1875	
return $[t-1]^d$	n.a.	n.a.		−0.2300	0.0362	***
$\beta(R_M - R_F)[t]$	n.a.	n.a.		1.3354	0.1239	***
size $[t-1]$	n.a.	n.a.		0.0471	0.0140	***
Fundamentals $[t]$						
Dividends						
cum.[e]	n.a.	n.a.		−0.2844	0.1971	
diff.[f]	n.a.	n.a.		6.0112	0.6410	***
Profits						
cum.	n.a.	n.a.		0.9831	0.0924	***
Fundamentals $[t-1]$						
Dividends						
diff.	n.a.	n.a.		2.7565	0.6400	***
Profits						
diff.	n.a.	n.a.		0.6767	0.2569	**
adj. R^2		6.51%			34.02%	
# of obs.		1300			1300	
Restrictions[g]						
LM for $H_0 : d_1 = d_2$	−4.4042	0.7193	***	−2.6700	0.5828	***
LM for $H_0 : d_2 = d_3$	4.4636	0.7104	***	2.0273	0.5744	***

[a] Specification 0 includes only changes in profits during the return period. Variables which are not relevant for the specification are marked by "n.a" (not applicable)

[b] Specification II includes aggregate profits. All parameters which are reported are included in the final specification of the model. For variables which are excluded from the regression the entries are left blank

[c] index t: contemporaneous variables, e.g. changes in profits during the 5 years of the test period

[d] index $t-1$: variables from the previous 5 years, e.g. the returns for the 5 years prior to the test period

[e] cum. = cumulative: $\sum_{t=1}^{5} D_t$

[f] diff. = difference: $D_5 - D_0$

[g] Lagrangean Multiplier for the restrictions $d_1 = d_2$ and $d_2 = d_3$

The analysis for the ex ante regression is pursued in a similar way. Starting point is again the regression which has been pursued in the first part of this chapter

$$R_t = \alpha_0 + \beta'X + d\Delta\Pi_{t-1}$$

As explanatory variables this regression only includes variables prior to the five year return period. $\Delta\Pi_{t-1}$ denotes the changes in profits from the first to the fifth year of the formation period. X is the vector of the remaining variables. For the ex ante regression I sort stocks according to past changes in profits $\Delta\Pi_{t-1}$ into quintiles. Again I include a different coefficient for the differences in profits variable for the upper quintile, the lower quintile and the three middle quintiles. The equivalent short-hand notation to equation (40) is

$$R_t = \alpha_0 + \beta'X + d_1 q_1 \Delta\Pi_{t-1} + d_2 q_2 \Delta\Pi_{t-1} + d_3 q_3 \Delta\Pi_{t-1} \tag{42}$$

I test again for differences in the coefficients d_1, d_2 and d_3.

Table 37 presents the results for the ex ante regression. Here, I investigate the two specifications from the first section of this chapter. The first specification includes profit components, the second specification includes only aggregate profits. In both regressions differences in aggregate profits are included as $d_1 q_1 \Delta\Pi_{t-1} + d_2 q_2 \Delta\Pi_{t-1} + d_3 q_3 \Delta\Pi_{t-1}$. All other differences in profits and profit components are excluded. Table 37 is the nonlinear equivalent to table 32.

The results in tables 37 and 32 are very similar. Again specification I has more explanatory power than specification II (9.11% as compared to 6.16%). This is slightly more than in table 32 (7.96% as compared to 5.24%). In both regressions only for the three middle quintiles of the distribution the coefficient for $\Delta\Pi$, d_2, is significant. For the extreme quintiles we obtain smaller and insignificant values. The differences between these coefficients are highly significant in all cases. This indicates that the nonlinear specification fits the data better. With respect to all other regressors the results are similar. Only the coefficient for Jensen's α changes from 0.22 for specification I (5.95 for specification II) to large negative values: -8.26 for specification I (-6.25 for specification II).

For both the ex post and the ex ante regression I obtain supportive results for my hypotheses: The relationship between changes in profits and returns is nonlinear. Extreme events are reflected in returns in a less than proportional way. The question arises how much information we lose if we do not account for these nonlinearities. For the ex post regression the adjusted R^2 in the linear case was 32.76% which increases to a level of 34.02% as I account for nonlinearities. Similar improvements can be observed for the ex ante regression. The adjusted R^2 increases from 7.96% to 9.11% in the case of the profit decomposition. It increases from 5.24% to 6.16% in the case of aggregate profits. Hence, across all model specifications we obtain an increase of the adjusted R^2 of approximately one percentage point.

Table 37. Nonlinearities: Ex ante regression – 5 year returns are related to the entire set of explanatory variables from the previous 5 years

regressor	Specification I[a]			Specification II[b]		
	coeff.	std.	sign.[c]	coeff.	std.	sign.
Changes in Profits $[t-1]$						
1st quintile: d_1	0.2836	0.4099		0.5722	0.4142	
2nd - 4th quintile: d_2	1.3927	0.5091	***	1.5471	0.5180	***
5th quintile: d_3	−0.1773	0.3506		0.0108	0.3686	
intercept	0.1431	0.2195		0.2608	0.2210	
return $[t-1]$	−0.2835	0.0512	***	−0.2443	0.0519	***
Jensen's α $[t-1]$	−8.2660	3.5807	**	−6.2537	3.6540	*
β $[t-1]$	0.2056	0.0725	***	0.2184	0.0724	***
size $[t-1]$	0.0363	0.0178	**	0.0337	0.0179	*
Fundamentals $[t-1]$						
Dividends						
cum.[d]	−0.8466	0.1821	***	-0.4549	0.2123	**
diff.	1.5231	0.6569	**	1.2281	0.6642	*
Profits						
cum.	n.a.	n.a.		0.1663	0.1293	
Profit Components (all cum.)						
ordinary profits	0.2454	0.0572	***	n.a.	n.a.	
financial profits	0.4647	0.0732	***	n.a.	n.a.	
extraordinary profits	0.3397	0.0707	***	n.a.	n.a.	
adj. R^2	9.11%			6.16%		
Restrictions[e]						
$H_0 : d_1 = d_2$	−3.9025	0.6785	***	−2.5916	1.6818	
$H_0 : d_2 = d_3$	4.0412	0.6717	***	4.4712	1.7625	**

[a] Specification I includes profit components. All parameters which are reported are included in the final specification of the model. Variables which are not relevant for the specification are marked by "n.a." (not applicable)
[b] Specification II includes aggregate profits. The exact specification can be seen from the table
[c] level of significance for a t-test: *** (**, *) implies that the hypothesis of the regression coefficient to be equal to 0 can be rejected at a 1% (5%, 10%) significance level
[d] cum. = cumulative: $\sum_{t=1}^{5} D_t$
[e] Lagrangean Multiplier for the restrictions $d_1 = d_2$ and $d_2 = d_3$

6.2.3
Discussion

In this section I have tested for time horizon effects, portfolio effects, and for a nonlinearity in the relationship between stock returns and changes in fundamentals. The explanatory power of the ex post regression increases as I increase the time horizon. The explanatory power of the ex ante regression remains roughly constant. For aggregation into portfolios I observe the opposite pattern. As stocks are aggregated into portfolios, the explanatory power increases for the ex ante regression whereas the explanatory power of the ex post regression remains constant. In addition, the relationship between stock returns and changes in profits appears to be nonlinear.

First, I take a closer look at time horizon and portfolio effects. To be able to interpret these findings I rely on a result from partial regression analysis.[47] In the following I compare two residual sums of squares. For a regression of y on a matrix of explanatory variables X we obtain a residual sum of squares, $e'e$. If we add the explanatory variable z, the residual sum of squares is $u'u$. These two sums of squares are related by the following equation[48]

$$u'u = e'e\left[1-\rho_{yz[x]}^2\right] \tag{43}$$

where $\rho_{yz[x]}^2$ denotes the squared partial correlation coefficient between y and z. The squared partial correlation coefficient is defined as

$$\rho_{yz[x]}^2 = \frac{(z'_*y_*)^2}{(z'_*z_*)(y'_*y_*)}$$

z_* and y_* are the residuals of a regression of z and y on X. Therefore, the partial correlation coefficient denotes the correlation between y and z which controls for the influence of X. This is the econometric equivalent of the economic *ceteris paribus* considerations. This analysis can be related to the ex post and the ex ante regression. Assume that from the ex ante to the ex post regression only one explanatory variable is added. Then $\rho_{yz[x]}^2$ captures the additional explanatory power of this variable.

If more variables are added to the regression equation, this analysis can be repeated. Assume that two variables, z_1 and z_2 are included. $e'e$ is the residual sum of squares which we obtain from a regression of y on x. If we add the explanatory variable z_1 we obtain u'_1u_1, if we add z_1 and z_2 we obtain u'_2u_2.

$$u'_2u_2 = u'_1u_1\left[1-r_{yz_2[x,z_1]}^2\right]$$
$$u'_1u_1 = e'e\left[1-r_{yz_1[x]}^2\right]$$

$r_{yz_1[x]}^2$ is the partial correlation coefficient between y and z_1 which controls for the influence of x. $r_{yz_2[x,z_1]}^2$ is the partial correlation coefficient between y and z_2 which controls for the influence of x and z_1. From these two equations we obtain

$$u'_2u_2 = e'e\left[1-r_{yz_1[x]}^2\right]\left[1-r_{yz_2[x,z_1]}^2\right] \Leftrightarrow$$
$$e'e = u'_2u_2 + \left[r_{yz_1[x]}^2+r_{yz_2[x,z_1]}^2-r_{yz_1[x]}^2r_{yz_2[x,z_1]}^2\right]e'e$$

[47] cf. Greene (1997), pp. 245-254
[48] cf. Greene (1997), p. 254

Although this expression is more complicated than in the one variable case, the idea remains the same: By adding more explanatory variables to the regression the residual sum of squares can be reduced. The extent of the reduction is captured by the partial correlation coefficient. To keep the argument simple, in the following I argue for the case that only one explanatory variable is added from the ex ante to the ex post regression. From a conceptual point of view the argument does not change if more variables are added to the analysis.

It is common econometric practice to decompose the total sum of squares *(SST)* into an explained sum of squares *(SSE)* and a residual sum of squares *(SSR)* which remains unexplained.

$$SST = SSR + SSE$$

For the ex post and the ex ante regression I obtain

$$1 = \frac{u'u}{SST} + \frac{SSE[\text{ex post}]}{SST}$$

$$1 = \frac{e'e}{SST} + \frac{SSE[\text{ex ante}]}{SST}$$

From equation (43) we can substitute

$$1 = \frac{u'u}{SST} + \frac{e'e\rho_{yz[x]}^2}{SST} + \frac{SSE[\text{ex ante}]}{SST} \tag{44}$$

$u'u / SST$ is the R^2 for the ex post regression. $\rho_{yz[x]}^2$ captures the additional explanatory power of the ex post variables.

I have run my regression for different time horizons and different numbers of portfolios. Hence, all variables in equation (44) depend on the investment horizon T and the number of portfolios N. As I increase the time horizon T, I observe the following pattern

$$1 \quad = \quad \underset{\text{decreases}}{\frac{u'u}{SST}} \quad + \quad \underset{\text{increases}}{\frac{e'e\rho_{yz[x]}^2}{SST}} \quad + \quad \underset{\text{constant with T}}{\frac{SSE[\text{ex ante}]}{SST}}$$

The part of the total sum of squares which is explained by the ex ante regression remains constant for different investment horizons. The additional explanatory power of the ex post regression increases with the investment horizon. So one could argue that for longer investment horizons the ex post regression captures larger parts of the cross sectional variation in returns.

However, it is important to keep in mind that $e'e / SST$ captures the relative explanatory power as compared to the total sum of squares. If we investigate the difference between $u'u$ and $e'e$ directly it turns out that this difference does not change a lot. We obtain values of 3.925[= 12.318 − 8.393], 6.000, 6.029, 5.412, 5.234 for a 1, 2, . . . 5 year investment horizon. Hence, in absolute terms no additional explanatory power is gained for longer investment horizons. The increase in relative explanatory power is entirely due to the decrease in the total sum of squares. This might imply that there is considerable noise in one year return data. This noise is not captured by the additional ex post accounting variables. As this noise diminishes for longer investment horizons the relative explanatory power increases.

A different picture emerges as I aggregate stocks into portfolios. As I aggregate stocks into portfolios, the explanatory power of the ex ante regression increases. At the same time the additional information from the ex post variables diminishes. If we start from a high level of aggregation into portfolios, disaggregate the portfolios and thereby increase the number of portfolios N, we can state:

$$1 \quad = \quad \underbrace{\frac{u'u}{SST}}_{\text{constant}} \quad + \quad \underbrace{\frac{e'e\rho^2_{yz[x]}}{SST}}_{\text{increases}} \quad + \quad \underbrace{\frac{SSE\left[\text{ex ante}\right]}{SST}}_{\text{decreases with N}}$$

The explanatory power of the ex ante regression decreases as we disaggregate the portfolios. At the same time the additional explanatory power of the ex post variables increases. Hence, the ex post variables capture the cross-sectional variation. Common components are captured by the ex ante variables.[49]

My findings have practical applications as well as implications for further research. The implications for practitioners are twofold: First, if we want to obtain good forecasting results we have to look at portfolios instead of individual stocks. Second, if we want to explain stock returns ex post we should look at longer time horizons. Nonetheless, one has to be careful: following this advice I am able to increase the relative explanatory power of my regressions as it is measured by R^2. The absolute explanatory power as expressed by the explained sum of squares diminishes. Further research should investigate the derived diversification effects more closely both from an empirical and a theoretical point of view. From an empirical point of view one can investigate the diversification effect for different model specifications. In particular, it might be interesting to observe in which way fundamental variables keep track of the idiosyncratic movements in the ex post regression. So far the portfolio building has been based on past performance. It is reasonable to use other selection criteria as for example size and industry. The ex ante and the ex post regression might perform differently if portfolios are built according to these criteria. However, these investigations have to remain on an explorative level as long as we do not have a theoretical framework to address the relevant questions. Therefore the more important task is to derive a conceptual framework of asset pricing starting from cash flows which is able to capture the

---

[49] Unfortunately, in this case this discussion can only refer to the relative explanatory power. It does not make sense to look at the difference between $u'u - e'e$ for different numbers of portfolios as absolute numbers. These differences cannot be compared if the number of observations is different. The more stocks are aggregated into one portfolio, the less observations are available.

observed effects. A model which could serve as a theoretical benchmark should start from the underlying cash flows. Conditions should be derived under which the observed properties of the variance decomposition presented above occur.

Also the observed nonlinearity in the data has practical applications and implications for further research. Investors should react cautiously to extreme good or bad news in terms of fundamentals. In the long run these news show up in returns only in a less than proportional way. On the other hand for an explanation of the cross section of stock returns the importance of nonlinearities should not be over-emphasized. Although the coefficients which capture the nonlinearity are all significant, the adjusted R^2 increases only by about 1 percentage point. We do not lose much explanatory power if we neglect the nonlinearity. The interesting question from a theoretical point of view is which mechanisms are responsible for the nonlinearity. A possible explanation could be as follows. From time to time the management shows all accumulated losses or on the other hand wants to show a turn around by boosting profits. As the capital market knows already part of the truth in advance, the effect on prices and hence returns is less than proportional.

6.3
Summary and Outlook

This chapter investigates to which extent it is possible to explain the cross section of German stock returns by a regression of returns on two sets of explanatory variables, the CAPM β and size on the one hand and fundamentals on the other hand. Stock returns are mainly driven by contemporaneous information. I investigate stock returns both from an *ex ante* and from an *ex post* point of view. The *ex ante* analysis forecasts returns and therefore excludes this contemporaneous information. The *ex post* analysis explores returns after this information has become apparent. It includes the contemporaneous information as explanatory variable. In the first part I have investigated which variables explain returns best both from an ex ante as well as from an ex post point of view. The analysis has been based on 5 year returns on a stock by stock basis. In the second part I have tested for the model specification: I have explored the effect which the time horizon and portfolio building has for our results. Finally, I have investigated whether the relationship between changes in profits and returns is nonlinear.

In the first part I have tested for the explanatory power of the following two sets of variables: the CAPM β and size on the one hand and fundamental variables on the other hand. I have investigated this question both from an ex post as well as from an ex ante point of view. In the ex post regression 32.76% of the variation in returns can be explained. About one third of the explanation derives from the CAPM, about two thirds from fundamentals. From an ex ante point of view I have found that for a time horizon of 5 years up to 10% of future returns can be explained using the full set of explanatory variables. The lion's share of this explanation can be attributed to fundamental variables and time series properties. The explanatory power of the asset pricing variables is negligible. We can increase the explanatory power of our regression if we run the regression for returns of portfolios instead of single stocks.[50] For the ex ante regression the explanatory power stays roughly constant for different time horizons.

For the ex post regression the part of the total sum of squares which we can explain is larger than in the forecasting regression. This does not come as a surprise as we include more recent information in terms of fundamentals. For a time horizon of 5 years we can explain up to 30% of returns. Again the major part of the result is explained by fundamental variables. In this case the explanatory power of the regression depends on the time horizon. For shorter return periods the results deteriorate: For a return period of 1 year we obtain an explanatory power which is about 13%. The effect which leads to the increase in explanatory power for the long horizon is similar to the portfolio effect in the forecasting regression: with an increasing time horizon the total sum of squares diminishes faster than the explained sum of squares.[51] In addition, I have found that the relationship between changes in profits and stock returns is nonlinear. For large changes in profits the reaction of stock returns both in the ex ante and in the ex post regression is less than proportional as compared to small changes. The explanatory power of the regressions increases by 1 to 2 percentage points if one takes the nonlinearity into account.

To understand these results further research is needed. I see the major challenge of my results in the field of theoretical research. A firm theoretical understanding of the empirical findings can only be obtained in a theoretical framework where asset prices and hence returns are derived from the underlying cash flows. Both the ex ante and the ex post relationship between fundamentals and returns should be investigated in a unified framework. One possible outline of such a model has been presented in the previous chapter. There I have investigated long-term reversals in the cross section of stock returns. It should be explored whether this framework can be used for a more general analysis of the relationship between stock returns and fundamentals. In particular, one should investigate whether it is possible to derive testable implications from the model. Alternatively, the empirical properties can be used to restrict the theoretical model. From an empirical point of view the question arises whether we can improve our results by including more variables into our analysis. Two sets of variables are of particular interest. So far we have included dividends and profits which capture changes in the fundamental performance. In addition it might be interesting to include industry dummies which could be specified conditional on the business cycles. In this way

---

[50] By means of portfolio building the total sum of squares diminishes faster than the sum of squares which is explained. An alternative way to state this observation is that the part of the variation in stock returns which we do not understand diminishes faster than the part which we understand.

[51] An alternative way to state this is again that for longer time horizons the decrease of ignorance is faster than the decrease of that part of returns which we understand.

lead/lag effects of industries relative to the business cycles could be captured. Another set of variables are variables which do account for the capital structure or the asset structure of a company. This is the direction which is pursued in the next section. I turn again back to the intertemporal pattern of stock returns. I investigate whether we can explain the observed reversals in the cross section of stock returns by temporary problems of corporate control. I approximate problems of corporate control by the capital structure and other balance sheet characteristics.

Appendix: Granger Causality

In this section I have investigated the relationship between stock returns and other explanatory variables in a regression framework. In my analysis I have included contemporaneous and past variables. The aim of the analysis was to find out what drives the cross section of stock returns. In the literature on time series analysis similar questions have been investigated by means of vector autoregressions.

In a vector autoregression the time series pattern of several variables is investigated simultaneously. This is a substantial extension of the analysis which I have presented. In my analysis I have taken the fundamentals to be exogenous. The more general analysis is the vector autoregression approach.

In the most simple case that two variables and one lag are investigated a vector autoregression has the following structure[52]

$$\begin{bmatrix} B_{11} & B_{12} \\ B_{21} & B_{22} \end{bmatrix} \begin{bmatrix} y_t \\ z_t \end{bmatrix} = \begin{bmatrix} C_{11} & C_{12} \\ C_{21} & C_{22} \end{bmatrix} \begin{bmatrix} y_{t-1} \\ z_{t-1} \end{bmatrix} + \begin{bmatrix} u_{1t} \\ u_{2t} \end{bmatrix}$$

where y_t and z_t denote two time series. The covariance vector of the error term is

$$\mathrm{cov} \begin{bmatrix} u_{1t} \\ u_{2t} \end{bmatrix} = \begin{bmatrix} \Sigma_{11} & \Sigma_{12} \\ \Sigma_{21} & \Sigma_{22} \end{bmatrix}$$

One important question in a vector autoregressive analysis is to which extent the two processes for y_t and z_t influence each other.
Several concepts have been developed to answer this question. The most severe restriction is put on the model by the concept of *strong exogeneity*. In this case $B_{21} = C_{21} = \Sigma_{21} = 0$. In this case z_t is said to be strongly exogenous in the submodel for y_t. In this case the model can be written as

$$B_{11} y_t = -B_{12} z_t + C_{11} y_{t-1} + C_{12} z_{t-1} + u_{1t}$$
$$B_{22} z_t = C_{22} z_{t-1} + u_{2t}$$

The decisive implication of strong exogeneity is that there is no feedback from y_t to z_t. The process for z_t can be estimated on a stand alone basis.

---

[52] Davidson (1994).

Weak exogeneity allows for a non contemporaneous feedback. In this case $B_{21} = \sum_{21} = 0$, and hence,

$$B_{22}z_t = C_{21}y_{t-1} + C_{22}z_{t-1} + u_{2t}$$

Hence, weak exogeneity allows for a non-contemporaneous feedback. Lagged values of y_t enter the regression equation.

A concept which is closely related to the concept of strong exogeneity is the concept of *Granger causality*. If y_{t-1} can help to forecast z_t, it is said to Granger cause z_t. If we denote the forecasted value one period ahead as $\hat{z}_t$ we can write

$$z_t = B_{22}^{-1}C_{21}y_{t-1} + B_{22}^{-1}C_{22}z_{t-1}$$

y_{t-1} Granger-causes z_t if $C_{21} \neq 0$. From this analysis we obtain

strong exogeneity = weak exogeneity + Granger non-causality

The framework of my analysis does not allow for any feedback from returns to fundamentals. I implicitly assume that fundamentals are strongly exogenous. Already from this analysis we have obtained considerable insight into the way in which fundamental variables influence stock returns.

A vector autoregression can be seen as a complementary analysis to the analysis pursued in this chapter. Long-horizon regressions which I have presented in this chapter have the advantage that they investigate the relationship between returns and explanatory variables directly. The more complete picture which can be obtained from the vector autoregression does come at a cost. As more data is needed for the vector autoregression approach, this approach can only be pursued in the short run (Campbell, Lo, and MacKinlay (1997, p. 279f.)). Assuming that the time series behaviour is constant over time, the long run behaviour can be extrapolated from the short run behaviour. Nevertheless, the vector autoregression approach might provide additional useful insights.

III Explaining Cycles in Fundamentals

In the fifth chapter I have related stock returns to movements in fundamentals. The main finding has been that stock return and changes in fundamentals move in parallel. For the winner portfolio upswings during the formation period are followed by downswings during the test period. For the loser portfolio the reverse pattern can be observed. In this third section I investigate which might be the economic forces which determine the underlying cash flows.

Two different sources for the observed pattern can be proposed: market structure on the one hand and corporate control on the other hand. Changes in market structure may lead to long-term reversals in the following way. During the formation period winner firms earn profits in excess of the market. This lures new entrants into that market and diminishes profits subsequently. The incumbent winner firm is forced to participate in a costly price competition which leads to an underperformance during the test period. For the loser firms the opposite holds: They are engaged in a costly competition for a market during the holds: They are engaged in a costly competition for a market during the formation period. E.g., they invest particularly into advertising and are unprofitable in the short run. But in the long run these firms might be able to establish a brand and earn substantial extra profits on that brand. This leads to an overperformance during the test period. A different possible source for long-term reversals are problems of corporate control. If the management of a company has performed outstandingly in the past, it might be difficult for shareholders to exercise control and induce the management to show excellent performance in the period to come. The management will always refer to its former merits if shareholders try to put pressure on it. Instead the management may start to invest into thick carpets and nice cars at the cost of the company and hence push the performance of the company down. This is different for the loser firms. After poor management performance during the formation period shareholders will face less problems to induce the management to show excellent performance during the test period. They can always threaten to fire the management. The turnaround after the formation period might also be due to a new management in place. In the following I will refer to problems of corporate control as the driving force of cycles in cash flows.

7 Reversals in Stock Returns and Temporary Problems of Corporate Control

In this chapter I investigate whether cycles in stock returns are related to temporary problems in corporate control. This approach broadens the perspective of my analysis. Properties of returns and fundamentals are related to the theory of management control. The main hypothesis is that firms which show cycles in their performance suffer from temporary problems of corporate control. I pursue this hypothesis by an analysis of accounting data. Jensen (1986) has related problems of corporate control to the available free cash flow. An abundance of free cash flow loosens management control and as a consequence management performance deteriorates. From this idea I derive hypotheses with respect to different accounting variables. This section presents hypotheses, the empirical results and a discussion. In an appendix I deliver a more complete analysis of the payout decision.

The implicit assumption in the subsequent analysis is that the winner-loser effect is due to a surprise effect. Investors do not anticipate problems of corporate control for the winner portfolio during the test period. In the same way they do not anticipate the tightening of management control for the loser portfolio. As in the second part of this monograph where I have related stock returns to movements in fundamentals an alternative interpretation is that the winner-loser effect occurs within a framework of rational asset pricing. Then temporary problems of corporate control have to be related to the pricing kernel. In this chapter I only refer to the first interpretation that the winner-loser effect is due to a surprise effect.

7.1
Problems of Corporate Control: Hypotheses

The main hypothesis in this chapter is that winner and loser firms both suffer from a temporary lack of management control. For the winner firms the problem is supposed to be as follows: During the formation period their management shows excellent performance and as a consequence these firms outperform the market. However, during the next period shareholders will face problems in motivating strong performance of the management furtheron. The management can always refer to its former merits if shareholders try to enforce a better performance. Instead the management may start to invest into low value projects and hence slow down the performance of the company.

For the loser firms the problem is supposed to be the other way round: After a period of poor performance it might be easier for the shareholders to induce the management to show excellent performance with the threat to fire the management. The turnaround after the formation period might also be due to a new management in place. During the test period former winner firms turn out to be the new loser firms, former loser firms turn out to be the new winner firms. Hence problems reverse. Therefore, I state the main hypothesis of this chapter as follows:

Both winner and loser firms suffer from a temporary lack of corporate control. In the winner firms a period of tight management control is followed by a period where management control is loose. The reverse holds for the loser firms.

In this chapter I investigate whether problems of corporate control drive the winner-loser effect by analyzing accounting data. Accounting data are related to problems of corporate control only in an indirect way. Key variables of financial decision making like capital structure and dividends have been related to problems of corporate control. They are at the center of the hypotheses which I derive in the following. In addition I derive hypotheses with respect to three other variables.

First, I turn to the question how *capital structure* might be related to problems of corporate control.[53] The literature on corporate control has always favoured debt as a device of management control (Shleifer and Vishny (1997), p. 763). Debtholders have a claim on interest payments and repayment of the principal of their loans which they might enforce in court. The rights of equity holders are much weaker and more difficult to enforce. Unlike for debt contracts there is no final date when equity has to be paid back. If a company is mostly financed by debt the management is forced to ensure that the company creates a cash flow which is sufficient to satisfy the claims of the debtholders. Otherwise debtholders may force the company into insolvency. In the case of insolvency the management is likely to bear some personal cost as they lose firm specific human capital and therefore, the management has an incentive to avoid insolvency. The threat of an insolvency is much weaker if a company is mostly financed by equity. If the claims of the debtholders are fulfilled there is no further threat of insolvency. With respect to my hypothesis of a temporary lack of control within the winner and the loser firms this implies: Capital structure provides tight [loose] control for the winner firms during the formation [test] period. For the loser firms control is loose [tight] during the formation [test] period. Therefore I can state my first hypothesis.

Hypothesis 1: *As compared to middle firms winner firms rely less [more] on equity during the formation [test] period. Loser firms rely more [less] on equity during the formation [test] period.*

---

[53] Tremendous effort has been spent on the question how capital structure might be linked to problems of corporate control. Harris and Raviv (1991) and Shleifer and Vishny (1997) provide excellent surveys of this literature.

In addition debt may be more or less effective in controlling the management depending on its maturity. According to Berglof and von Thadden (1994) tight control is exercised by *short-term debt* holders: Short-term loans have to be renewed most frequently and hence during the procedure of recontracting short-term loans banks will evaluate the performance of the management during past periods. As this control is supposed to be temporarily insufficient in the case of winner and loser firms, we can hypothesize:

Hypothesis 2: *As compared to middle firms the amount of short-term bank debt is large for winner [loser] firms during the formation [test] period and small during the test [formation] period.*

A second variable which has attracted the attention of financial researchers for a long time are dividends or to be more precise the *payout ratio*, i.e. the part of profits which is distributed as dividends to shareholders. Problems of corporate control have been related to dividend policy by Rozeff (1982) and Easterbrook (1984). High payout ratios are advocated to make corporate control more effective. They diminish the free cash flow available to the management. Otherwise the management may abuse this free cash flow to build unprofitable empires or to invest in low value projects[54]. The payout of the free cash flow to shareholders tightens the management budget. In the case the management detects new profitable investment opportunities it has to raise new capital and hence money will be invested under close supervision of the investors. Therefore problems of corporate control are more likely to occur the more equity exists. Decisive for the control problem is the payout ratio at the beginning of a period. Low payout ratios at the beginning of a period indicate that there will be too much equity available during that period. High payout ratios indicate that the investment policy is under tight control. Therefore we can state the third hypothesis as follows.

Hypothesis 3: *As compared to the middle portfolio the payout ratio of the winner [loser] firms at the beginning of the formation period is high [low]. At the beginning of the test period it is low [high].*

Linking problems of corporate control to accounting data, the liabilities side of the balance sheet has been at the heart of theoretical reasoning for a long time. But also the *asset* side of the balance sheet might give a hint at the scope of agency problems as it reflects the investment policy of a company. The most prominent hypothesis on problems of corporate control and the investment policy of a company is due to Jensen (1986). Jensen argues that agency problems are severe if the management has many assets available which can be easily sold. In this case management can avoid the threat of bankruptcy: There will always be enough assets

---

[54] Anecdotal evidence for low value projects suggests "investments" for personal needs of the management at the cost of the company such as designer equipment, fancy cars, and company jets.

available which might be liquidated in the case of financial stress. Hence, agency problems should increase with the amount of money which is invested into assets which are highly liquid. According to this view periods of loose management control are characterized by an overinvestment into highly liquid assets which earn only a low rate of return. In periods of tight management control the investment into liquid assets is reduced in favour of investments into more profitable long-term investments. Based on this argument we can state the fourth hypothesis.

Hypothesis 4a: *During the formation period loser [winner] firms rely more [less] on liquid assets than the middle portfolio. During the test period loser [winner] firms rely less [more] on liquid assets than the middle portfolio.*

But the balance sheet does not only reflect the outcome of managerial discretion with respect to how much money is spent for liquid assets. It also reflects the competitive environment in which a company operates. The scope for managerial discretion will depend upon the degree of product market competition it faces. Agency problems are likely to be more severe in monopolistic markets which are uncontested. In a highly competitive environment agency problems are likely to be mitigated by product market competition. If the management of a company does not use its budget for investments in an adequate way it will get punished by competition in the product market. In industrial organization fixed assets are often seen as an obstacle to competition: Monopoly power may result from the amount which has to be spent to enter an industry. Industries will suffer from monopolistic structures if new potential entrants have to overcome high barriers to entry. Often high fixed costs imply high barriers to entry.[55] Problems of corporate control are likely to be less severe in industries where firms do not face high barriers to entry and which hence are more competitive. In these firms even temporary problems of corporate control are not likely to occur. According to my hypothesis of temporary problems of corporate control both winner and loser firms should be in less competitive industries with high barriers to entry. I approximate high barriers to entry by a large fraction of fixed assets.

Hypothesis 4b: *Winner and loser firms rely on fixed assets more heavily than middle firms.*

The next variable which I investigate is the *size* of a company. Agency problems are likely to be greater for large firms. The argument is that it is more difficult to exercise control in large firms: Management will have more space for discretion and cross subsidization. Temporary agency problems can be interpreted in a dynamic way as follows: In the case of the winner firms after a successful period managers will suffer from hubris and winner firms are likely to grow in size

---

[55] This perception of market structure has already been stated by Bain (1956). For a restatement of this argument in a two-stage game see Sutton (1991).

during the test period which signals that managers build unprofitable empires. The equivalent story in the case of the loser firms is a story of corporate reengineering after a period of poor performance. In that case firms concentrate on their core competences and are likely to shrink. Hence, with respect to size my hypothesis is:

Hypothesis 5: *Winner firms should grow during the test period. Loser firms should shrink during the test period.*

A final variable which I look at is the production structure or to be more precise the relative weight of capital and labour within the production process. I investigate *labour cost* as part of total cost. Firms which rely heavily on personnel will have to face the bargaining power of their employees. Their bargaining power is likely to encourage cyclical performance. After years of successful performance employees will try to obtain better payments. Therefore, they are likely to drive profits down in subsequent periods. On the other hand, if a company has shown a poor performance for a while, employees will be hesitant to insist on a large rise in wages. If they are supposed to behave adequately these companies are prone to show a better performance subsequently. On an institutional level one might object that labour contracts in Germany are the result of a bargaining process between the enterpreneurs and trade unions which takes place at a regional and sectoral level *(Flächentarifvertrag)* rather than at the level of the individual company. Hence, the performance of the individual firm will not influence the labour contract directly. However, even within this institutional setting there will be some scope for the employees to exercise power on the firm level, e.g. by bargaining about extra payments and boni. If cycles in the labour force are important for the cycles in fundamentals, both winner and loser firms should produce more labour-intensively than other firms. Therefore, I can state my last hypothesis as follows.

Hypothesis 6: *Both winner and loser firms produce labour-intensively. After the formation period labour costs should go up [down] for the winner [loser] firms.*

7.2
Estimation Results

In this section I present the results of my calculations. As the winner-loser effect is most pronounced for a period length of 60 months the empirical investigation is again based on this period length. Results are shown variable by variable and related to the hypotheses stated above. The broad picture which emerges from my results will be subject of the discussion in the following section.

Table 38 presents results for the *equity ratio* [i.e. equity as percentage of total capital]. Results are presented in the following way. The top row shows the median of the equity ratio of the total sample at three points in time: at the beginning of the formation period, at the end of the formation period and at the end of the test period. The 3 × 3 matrix below represents the differences between the median of the respective portfolio and the median of the total sample. First, I show the difference between the winner portfolio and the total sample, second the difference between the middle portfolio and the total sample, third the difference between the loser portfolio and the total sample. Again I present results for the beginning of the formation period, the end of the formation period and the end of the test period. E.g., the first number −0.387 in the winner row means that at the beginning of the formation period the median of the winner portfolio is −0.387 percentage points below the median of the total sample which is at 33.269%. In addition to presenting the medians and the median deviations I test for significance of the differences both in the cross section as well as intertemporally by means of a Wilcoxon rank sum test.[56]

Below the table results are presented in the following way: The first row WIN/MID presents the sign of the difference between the winner and the middle portfolio where the + sign means that the median of the winner portfolio is larger than the median in the middle portfolio. The second row LOS/MID presents the difference between the loser and the middle portfolio. A + sign means that the median of the loser portfolio is larger than the median of the middle portfolio. The last row WIN/LOS presents the difference between the winner and the loser portfolio. In addition p-values are stated below the sign if the difference between the two samples is significant at a level below 10%. E.g., the loser firms have less equity available than the middle portfolio at the beginning of the formation period, which is significant with a p-value of 9.56%.

On the right hand side of the table I summarize the intertemporal development: The first sign column presents the sign of the change from the beginning of the formation period to the end of the formation period for the respective portfolio. In the case of an increase during that period this will be denoted by a + sign. The

---

[56] As compared to a t-test the Wilcoxon rank sum test has the advantage that it is non parametric, i.e. it does not rely on a special distributional assumption. The methodology of the Wilcoxon rank sum test has been discussed in greater detail in the second chapter.

second sign column presents the sign of the change from the end of the formation period to the end of the test period. Again an increase during that period that will be denoted by a + sign. As for the cross section, in addition p-values are stated in the case that the change is significant at conventional levels of significance for a Wilcoxon rank sum test. E.g. the relative importance of equity financing during the formation period has increased for the winner firms which is significant at a level of 7.32%.

Table 38. Equity ratio (equity as percentage of total capital) The table is based on German data 1968-1986 from the Frankfurt stock exchange, assets come from the most liquid segment of this market [Amtlicher Handel], medians and differences are presented for overlapping samples; the average sample size is 150.7

	Median 0[a]	Median 5	Median 10	Diff. 0/5[b]		Diff. 5/10	
				sign	signific	sign	signific.
Total	33.268943	33.426589	34.903293				
Δ Winner[c]	−0.387517	0.878293	−0.086202	+	0.073158	−	
Δ Middle	0.533683	0.553689	0.266151				
Δ Loser	−1.570770	−2.032737	−0.895910	−		+	0.049165
Win/Mid[d]							
sign	−	+	−				
significance							
Los/Mid							
sign	−	−	−				
significance	0.09558	0.00713					
Win/Los							
sign	+	+	+				
significance		0.00768					

[a] Median 0: median of the distribution at the beginning of the formation period; Median 5: median of the distribution at the end of the formation period; Median 10: median of the distribution at the end of the test period

[b] Diff. 0/5 [5/10]: Difference between the distribution at the beginning of the formation [test] period and the end of the formation [test] period; p-values are given if the difference is significant

[c] Difference of the median of the Winner portfolio and the median of the total sample

[d] Win/Mid [Los/Mid; Win/Los]: Sign of the difference of the median of the Winner [Loser; Winner] portfolio and the median of the Middle [Middle; Loser] portfolio; p-values are stated below if the difference is significant

Which are the results for the *equity ratio* (cf. table 38)? The total picture which emerges is in line with my hypothesis: For the winner portfolio the equity ratio increases during the formation period and decreases again afterwards. The equity ratio starts at a level below the sample median, increases to a level above that median and drops below that level afterwards. This pattern is in line with my hypothesis. However, only the intertemporal movement during the formation period is significant. Contrary to my hypothesis for the loser portfolio there is less equity available at the beginning of the formation period than for the middle portfolio. However, the intertemporal development is in line with my hypothesis. During the formation period the equity decreases, it increases again during the test period. Hence, the development of the capital structure may reflect temporary agency problems.

Short-term debt is measured in percentage of total capital (cf. table 39). Although I have formulated my hypothesis for short-term bank debt, on the balance sheet I cannot distinguish between bank debt and debt which is issued in the market. Therefore, I have to rely on total short-term debt and have to assume that short-term bank debt is a constant proportion of total short-term debt. All differences for short-term debt between the extreme portfolios and the sample median are positive. They range between 0.54 and 2.70 percentage points. The difference between the extreme portfolios and the middle portfolio is significant at the beginning of the formation period and at the beginning of the test period.

Table 39. Short-term debt (Short-term debt as percentage of total capital) [Legend cf. table 38]

	Median 0[a]	Median 5	Median 10	Diff. 0/5[b]		Diff. 5/10	
				sign	signific.	sign	signific.
Total	36.055225	34.638039	32.743433				
Δ Winner[c]	2.113489	2.703753	0.589441	+		−	
Δ Middle	−0.911586	−1.245306	−0.639562				
Δ Loser	0.537733	1.661050	0.555744	+		−	0.067403
Win/Mid[d]							
sign	+	+	+				
significance	0.04593	0.03764					
Los/Mid							
sign	+	+	+				
significance	0.04100	0.07142					
Win/Los							
sign	+	+	+				
significance							

Intertemporally, the pattern for the loser portfolio is in line with my hypothesis. At the beginning of the test period the loser firms rely more heavily on short-term debt than at the beginning of the formation period. As the winner portfolio shows the same pattern intertemporally, I have to reject my hypothesis for the winner portfolio. According to my intertemporal hypothesis variables for winner and loser firms always move anticyclically. Hence, in the context of the winner-loser effect short-term debt can not play the role which it has been assigned in the literature.

I now turn to the *payout ratio* measured by dividends in percentage of total profits as the second variable which is central for my analysis (cf. table 40). For the payout ratio the question arises how to treat negative profits. I use the following convention. If profits are negative or equal to zero, the payout ratio is set equal to 0% if no dividends are paid. It is set equal to 100% if dividends are paid. For the winner portfolio I observe an increase in the payout ratio during the formation period from table 40. During the test period the payout ratio stays at a level of 2 percentage points above the total sample mean. For the loser portfolio a sharp decrease during the formation period leads to a payout ratio at the end of the formation period which is 17.3 percentage points below the total sample mean. During the test period a moderate increase can be observed. These results do not support the view that the dividend policy causes problems of corporate control. Payout ratios mirror the development of asset returns. Periods of overperformance are connected to increases in the payout ratio. Periods of underperformance are connected to a decrease in the payout ratio. However, my hypothesis stated that the payout ratio should behave anticyclically. Hence with respect to dividends the results do not support the hypothesis of temporary agency problems.

Table 40. Payout ratio (Dividends as percentage of profits) [Legend cf. table 38]

	Median 0[a]	Median 5	Median 10	Diff. 0/5[b]		Diff. 5/10	
				sign	signific.	sign	signific.
Total	30.545410	25.016406	24.780525				
Δ Winner[c]	−0.328451	2.863548	2.106153	+	0.003001	−	0.089522
Δ Middle	0.768839	0.428886	0.930740				
Δ Loser	−2.006578	17.300849	−7.161340	−	0.000493	+	
Win/Mid[d]							
sign	−	+	+				
significance		0.00092	0.08596				
Los/Mid							
sign	−	−	−				
significance		0.00000	0.00013				
Win/Los							
sign	+	+	+				
significance		0.00000	0.00081				

Turning to the asset side of the balance sheet, *fixed assets* are measured as a percentage of total assets (cf. table 41). During the formation period both winner and loser firms rely to a lesser extent on fixed assets than their companions in the middle portfolio. The loser portfolio has invested 6.5 percentage points (i.e. 4.7 + 1.8 percentage points) less into fixed assets than the middle portfolio. The difference for the winner portfolio is smaller (2.4%), albeit still significant. Intertemporally, during the formation period the amount invested into fixed assets increases for the loser firms whereas it decreases for the winner firms. During the test period it increases for both winner and loser firms. These findings are not in line with the hypothesis of Jensen (1986). According to Jensen periods of underperformance should occur if the amount of liquid assets is high. But also my industrial structure argument does not hold: Instead of more fixed assets I observe significantly less fixed assets for winner and loser firms. Again the empirical evidence with respect to fixed assets does not support my hypothesis of temporary problems of corporate control.

Table 41. Fixed assets (Fixed assets as percentage of total assets) [Legend cf. table 38]

	Median 0[a]	Median 5	Median 10	Diff. 0/5[b]		Diff. 5/10	
				sign	signific.	sign	signific.
Total	47.060505	45.236145	46.380481				
Δ Winner[c]	−0.626164	−0.812480	2.421452	−		+	0.056754
Δ Middle	1.791476	2.012577	1.049374				
Δ Loser	−4.693705	−4.102887	−3.278602	+	0.097179	+	
Win/Mid[d]							
sign	−	−	+				
significance	0.00093	0.00898					
Los/Mid							
sign	−	−	−				
significance	0.00006	0.00172	0.00445				
Win/Los							
sign	+	+	+				
significance			0.00075				

Size is measured by the sum of total assets (cf. table 42). I find a larger proportion of large companies in the winner portfolio and a larger proportion of small companies in the loser portfolio. This difference is particularly pronounced at the end of the test period and highly significant at the end of the formation period and at the end of the test period. The size of the winner firms increases from 82 billion to 237 billion DM relative to the sample median. With respect to the intertemporal development, I find support for the hypothesis of hubris and overinvestment for the winner firms during the test period. This is equally true for the hypothesis of successful reengineering in the loser firms during the test period. The size of the loser firms decreases from -47 billion to -89 billion DM relative to the sample median.

Labour intensity of production is measured by personnel expenses as a percentage of total expenses (cf. table 43). Both winner and loser firms rely more heavily on personnel, a finding which is significant at least for the winner portfolio. Intertemporally, periods of overperformance are related to a decrease in expenses for personnel and vice versa. Both results are consistent with my interpretation of the role of bargaining power of the employees in supporting cyclical performance. Labour costs play a greater role in both winner and loser firms. Employees may react to a good performance of a company with a demand for higher wages which leads to a subsequent underperformance. A poor performance may induce them to step down on their demand for wages which leads to a subsequent overperformance.

Table 42. Total assets (Total assets in million DM) [Legend cf. table 38]

	Median 0[a]	Median 5	Median 10	Diff. 0/5[b]		Diff. 5/10	
				sign	signific.	sign	signific.
Total	267827.50	347162.00	413600.00				
Δ Winner[c]	38376.00	82913.00	237044.00	+		+	
Δ Middle	−4388.50	6636.50	10401.00				
Δ Loser	−10406.50	−47027.00	−89718.00	−		−	
Win/Mid[d]							
sign	+	+	+				
significance							
Los/Mid							
sign	−	−	−				
significance		0.05171	0.01683				
Win/Los							
sign	+	+	+				
significance		0.06277	0.01644				

Table 43. Expenses for personnel (Labour costs as percentage of total costs) [Legend cf. Table 38]

	Median 0[a]	Median 5	Median 10	Diff. 0/5[b]		Diff. 5/10	
				sign	signific.	sign	signific.
Total	28.250213	28.502866	27.538894				
Δ Winner[c]	3.794064	0.260174	1.340597	−	0.020718	+	
Δ Middle	−0.966545	−0.647647	−1.033431				
Δ Loser	−0.008561	1.675428	2.098517	+		+	
Win/Mid[d]							
sign	+	+	+				
significance	0.00000	0.02962					
Los/Mid							
sign	+	+	+				
significance							
Win/Los							
sign	+	−	−				
significance	0.00046						

7.3
Discussion

My findings support the view that the winner-loser effect is due to changes in fundamentals. The evidence that these changes are due to temporary problems of corporate control is mixed. The results for capital structure, size, and labour intensity are in line with my hypotheses. To some extent both winner and loser firms appear to suffer from temporary problems of corporate control. Cycles in the available equity and anti-cycles in labour costs support this view. For both types of firms the problem of corporate control has not been solved sufficiently well. For the remaining variables of financial decision making the evidence is not so supportive. I first turn to the financial variables.

The *capital structure* as one of the key variables of financial decision making evolves in the way predicted by agency theory. It might indicate temporary problems of corporate control. However, this interpretation is subject to two qualifications. The first is to look at the relative size of intertemporal changes. Although some of the intertemporal changes in capital structure are significant it is not clear whether these changes are large enough to cause the management to change its behaviour. The second qualification is that the intertemporal development of the capital structure has to be linked to other variables such as profits and the payout ratio. Retained earnings lead to an increase of equity and hence these variables are not independent. On the other hand the company can also raise new capital by issuing new equity or debt. Hence, it might be interesting to investigate the relative importance of these different sources of capital for the investigated sample. It is a question to be investigated further whether we can observe changes in the capital structure which are not purely a result of the development of profits and the payout policy.

The interaction between financial variables is also important for a better understanding of the observed procyclical behaviour of the *payout ratio*. The increase in the payout ratio can be understood to signal improved business prospects to the shareholders. On the other hand a decrease in the payout ratio might indicate a deterioration of the business prospects. However, for my investigation this signal would have been misleading. It is surprising to find a procyclical movement of the payout ratio and profits. Dividend smoothing is the observation we would have expected. However, so far we have restricted our attention to the central moment of the payout distribution. A special feature of the payout decision is that profits may take negative values whereas dividends cannot. A more complete model of the payout decision as a censored linear model is presented in the appendix. In this model we do not find any evidence for an active role of the dividend policy. Dividends are paid neither pro- nor anticyclically.

In the context of the winner-loser effect *short-term debt* does not show the characteristics which have been assigned to it in the literature. An unresolved question is whether the maturity structure plays a role at all. To investigate this question further it might be reasonable to account for different maturities in a more detailed way. So far we have distinguished between short-term and long-term debt only in a very crude way.

Investment into *short-term assets* does not play the role which it has been assigned by Jensen (1986) nor does it relate to the industry structure in the proposed way. However, its intertemporal development still might give a hint on how weak or good performance of a company is reflected on its balance sheet. E.g., if loser firms increase the relative proportion invested into fixed assets during the formation period this may be due to a reduction of liquid assets which are used to pay back debt. Again the question whether this is true can only be resolved in a multivariate context. Therefore, not only the relative amount which is invested into fixed assets has to be investigated but also how these findings interact with the total size of the company.

Size and labour costs both support my hypothesis of temporary agency problems. With respect to *size* I find evidence for managerial empire building in the case of the winner firms. This finding relates to a current field of research which investigates whether the strategy of corporate diversification has proved to be successful (Berger and Ofek (1995), Servaes (1996)). According to these papers in most cases corporate diversification has turned out to be an unprofitable investment. Our finding can be interpreted as providing further evidence which hints into the same direction.

Finally, I turn to *labour intensity* of production: Together with the finding of a parallel movement of asset returns and profits the intertemporal development of labour expenses relate to an early model of the business cycles. In a robber prey model by Goodwin (1967) business cycles are interpreted in an analogy to a biological model. Trade unions are supposed to act as sharks chasing small fish. (i.e. profits). Once profits have grown up (i.e. profits have increased) sharks start devastating the fish population (trade unions take a tough stance and labour costs grow). Unfortunately, this behaviour endangers the very existence of the sharks themselves as only few fish survive this attack (profits go down). Due to a lack of nutrition sharks become too weak to catch the fish (trade unions are weak after periods of bad performance and hence labour costs decrease). As the number of sharks diminishes the population of small fish flourishes again (profits increase). My findings are consistent with this story.

7.4 Summary

Starting point of this chapter is the observation of long-term reversals in the cross section of stock returns. Former winner firms become loser firms subsequently, former loser firms turn out to be the later winners. The hypothesis of this chapter is that temporary problems of corporate control determine this outcome. According to this view periods of good performance are due to tight control whereas periods of poor performance are due to loose control. The following variables are at the centre of the investigation: equity/total capital, short-term debt/total capital, the payout ratio, fixed assets/total assets, total assets (size), and labour costs/total costs. I find evidence for cyclical behaviour of the capital structure: Changes in capital structure are small but significant. In addition I find evidence that winner firms might suffer from unprofitable empire building of their managers. After a profitable period managers seem to use profits to invest into unprofitable projects which increases companies and slows returns down. For the loser firms my findings can be interpreted as successful reengineering after periods of underperformance. After periods of poor performance loser firms shrink and at the same time show an overperformance in the stock market. Finally, I find that cycles in labour costs may contribute to an explanation of the winner-loser effect. By and large, I find substantial structure on the balance sheets of the winner and loser firms, especially intertemporally. This can be taken as further evidence that the winner-loser effect is due to movements in fundamentals. From the perspective of corporate control managerial hubris and cyclical labour costs are among the forces which determine circles in long run stock returns. Further research should investigate two types of questions: multivariate approaches and alternative explanations. So far the analysis was based on a variable by variable approach. An interesting question is in which way different variables interact. Therefore, it would be useful to apply a multivariate approach. A second question is to which extent other factors than temporary problems of corporate control contribute to the observed reversals in stock returns. These factors include lead-lag effects across industries and the rise and decline of monopolistic structures.

Appendix: The Payout Decision

This chapter has investigated variables of financial decision making in a variable by variable approach. In this appendix I take a closer look at the observed difference in dividends between portfolios. Already in the fifth chapter we could observe that winner firms pay larger dividends than middle and loser firms, $D_W > D_M > D_L$. The question arises what determines these differences. In this appendix I propose the following decomposition. Dividends are determined by a function of profits and other exogenous variables. Hence, two factors might drive differences in dividends. First, differences in dividends might be due to different payout policies. Then the function which relates dividends to the underlying profits differs between portfolios. Second, differences might be due to differences in profits and other exogenous variables. If differences in the payout policy are an important factor to explain the winner-loser effect these differences should account for major parts of the total difference in dividends.

Special attention in this appendix is given to the way in which dividends are modelled as a function of profits and other exogenous variables. So far I have investigated whether there are differences in the payout ratio across portfolios. The payout ratio is the most simple way in which dividends can be related to profits. In this appendix I model the payout decision in a more complex way. First, I relate dividends to additional exogenous variables as past dividends and past profits. In addition, I take into account that dividends cannot become negative. I apply a censored regression model.

The analysis proceeds in two steps. First, I present the methodological setting. Then I present the empirical results.

Methodology

Before I turn to the exact specification of my model I first explain the proposed decomposition. Starting point for the investigation in this appendix is the observed difference in dividends between portfolios. This difference can be split into two parts: one which is due to differences in the payout policy and one which is due to differences in profits and other exogenous variables. In the most simple case we can model dividends in period t, $D(t)$, as a function of profits in t, $\Pi(t)$:

$$E\big[D(t)\big] = E\big[f\big(\Pi(t)\big)\big]$$

Differences in dividends between portfolios might be due to two effects. First, the function f might differ across portfolios. Second, $\Pi(t)$ might differ.

To investigate which of these two factors is more important in determining the difference in $E[D(t)]$ across portfolios I rely on a methodology which has been introduced into the literature by Blinder (1973) and Oaxaca (1973). They were interested in wage discrimination: they investigated whether wage differentials were due to different endowments (like education or experience) or whether wage differentials were due to discrimination.[57] Applying their methodology to my problem, the difference between the dividends of the winner and the loser firm can be decomposed in the following way.

$$D_W(t) - D_L(t) = E\left[f_W\left(\Pi_W(t)\right)\right] - E\left[f_L\left(\Pi_L(t)\right)\right]$$
$$= \left[E\left[f_W\left(\Pi_W(t)\right)\right] - E\left[f_W\left(\Pi_L(t)\right)\right]\right]$$
$$+ \left[E\left[f_W\left(\Pi_L(t)\right)\right] - E\left[f_L\left(\Pi_L(t)\right)\right]\right]$$

The first difference $E\left[f_W\left(\Pi_W(t)\right)\right] - E\left[f_W\left(\Pi_L(t)\right)\right]$ is the difference which is due to differences in profits across portfolios, i.e. the difference between the expected value of the dividends of the winner portfolio and the expected value of the dividends if the winner firms had the lower profits of the loser firms. It is only the second difference which is due to differences in the payout policy: $E\left[f_W\left(\Pi_L(t)\right)\right] - E\left[f_L\left(\Pi_L(t)\right)\right]$. It is the difference between the expected dividends for the winner and the loser firms if both had the profits of the loser firms. If differences in the payout policy play a significant role for the winner-loser effect this second term should account for major parts of the total difference $D_W(t) - D_L(t)$.

Alternatively, also a second decomposition is available which has the same intuition:

$$D_W(t) - D_L(t) = E\left[f_W\left(\Pi_W(t)\right)\right] - E\left[f_L\left(\Pi_L(t)\right)\right]$$
$$= \left[E\left[f_L\left(\Pi_W(t)\right)\right] - E\left[f_L\left(\Pi_L(t)\right)\right]\right]$$
$$+ \left[E\left[f_W\left(\Pi_W(t)\right)\right] - E\left[f_L\left(\Pi_W(t)\right)\right]\right]$$

Again, also in this case the first difference captures the difference which is due to differences in profits across portfolios. The second difference is due to differences in the payout policy. This decomposition and the decomposition presented above are equally plausible. I therefore present results for both of them.

Dividends as a function of profits can be modelled in different ways. The most simple way to investigate the functional relationship between dividends and profits is to look at the payout ratio. This is the approach which has been pursued in the previous section. This simple approach is extended in this appendix in two ways. First, I do not only model dividends $D(t)$ as a function of profits of the same period, $\Pi(t)$. In addition, I also include dividends and profits from the previous period, $D(t-1)$ and $\Pi(t-1)$. Furthermore, it turns out to make a difference whether profits have increased from period $t-1$ to period t or not. Therefore, I include a dummy variable which takes a value of 1 if profits have increased and 0 otherwise.

---

[57] cf. For two recent applications of the Blinder-Oaxaca decomposition in labour economics compare Darity, Guilkey, and Winfrey (1995) and Fairlie (1999).

The second feature of my model is that it takes into account the cut-off point for dividends at a level of zero. I apply a censored regression model. The regression equation can be written as

$$D(t) = \max\left(\alpha + \beta_1 d + \beta_2 \Pi(t) + \beta_3 \Pi(t-1) + \beta_4 D(t-1) + \varepsilon, 0\right) \qquad (45)$$

where α is the intercept, d is dummy for the case that profits have increased from period $t-1$ to period t, $\Pi(t)$ are profits in period t, $\Pi(t-1)$ and $D(t-1)$ are profits and dividends in period $t - 1$. I estimate the above equation for the winner, the middle, and the loser portfolio separately by means of a maximum likelihood estimation. A logistic function turns out to fit the model best.

Alternatively, equation (45) can be written as an index function (cf. Greene (1997), p. 962)

$$D^* = \alpha + \beta_1 d + \beta_2 \Pi(t) + \beta_3 \Pi(t-1) + \beta_4 D(t-1) + \varepsilon$$
$$D = 0 \quad \text{if} \quad D^* \leq 0$$
$$D = D^* \quad \text{if} \quad D^* > 0$$

One has to be careful to distinguish between D and D^*. D is distributed such that no negative values occur. As D^* can take negative values, its mean is lower than the mean of D. If the latent variable D^* is normally distributed, the conditional expected dividend for an observation which is randomly drawn from the population can be calculated as follows (cf. Greene (1997), p. 963)

$$E\left[D_i \,\middle|\, \Pi_i\right] = \Phi\left(\frac{\beta'\Pi_i}{\sigma}\right)\left(\beta'\Pi_i + \sigma\lambda_i\right)$$

with

$$\lambda_i = \frac{\phi\left(\dfrac{\beta'\Pi_i}{\sigma}\right)}{\Phi\left(\dfrac{\beta'\Pi_i}{\sigma}\right)}$$

Table 44. Summary Statistics – Dividends per nominal equity

portfolio	# obs.	# D = 0	mean	median	std.	skew.	kurt.
all	15143	3333	5.180	5.466	4.465	3.057	26.264
winner	2981	402	6.682	6.220	5.955	3.750	24.364
middle	9149	1788	5.167	5.581	3.770	1.937	20.266
loser	3013	1143	3.735	3.477	4.203	2.560	16.024

$\beta\Pi$ is the short hand notation $\alpha + \beta_1 d_i + \beta_2\Pi(t)_i + \beta_3\Pi(t-1)_i + \beta_4 D(t-1)_i$, σ is the standard deviation of the latent variable D^*, $\phi(\cdot)$ is the standard normal density function and $\Phi(\cdot)$ is the cumulative distribution function.

In the following I apply the Blinder-Oaxaca decomposition to $E[D^*]$: These values can be obtained by multiplying the estimated values for $\alpha, \beta_1, \beta_2, \beta_3$ and β_4, with the values for the exogenous variables.[58] The analysis proceeds in two steps. First, I estimate the censored regression model for the entire dataset and then separately for the different portfolios. Second, I sub tute the exogenous variables for the different portfolios back into the estimated payout functions. Thereby, I determine the values for $E[D^*]$ conditional on two factors: first, the payout function of a portfolio, and second, the exogenous variables of a portfolio. These values provide the basis for the Blinder-Oaxaca decomposition. It shows to which extent differences in dividends are due to differences in the exogenous variables and to differences in the payout policy.

Empirical Results
The results of my empirical analysis are presented in three steps. First, I present summary statistics for the estimated sample. Second, I present evidence for the estimated coefficients. Finally, I turn to the Blinder-Oaxaca decomposition.

I use a sample of 15143 observation (cf. table (44)). For 3333 of these observations ($\approx$ 22% of all observations) D = 0, which shows that it is indeed necessary to rely on a censored regression. The means and the medians which are presented in third and fourth column corroborate our findings from the fifth chapter that $D_W > D_M > D_L$. The difference in means between the winner and the middle portfolio is of almost the same size as the difference between the middle and the

Table 45. Tobit Estimates for the Payout Policy

portf.	α	d^a	$\Pi(t)$	$\Pi(t-1)$	$D(t-1)$
all	−1.0375	0.9815	0.1759	0.0187	0.7721
winner	−0.6362	0.8438	0.1954	−0.0210	0.7543
middle	−0.8672	0.8243	0.1920	0.0202	0.7452
loser	−2.0540	1.7335	0.1332	0.0488	0.8476

[a] Dummy which is equal to 1 if $\Pi(t) > \Pi(t-1)$ and 0 otherwise

loser portfolio: $D_W - D_M$ = 1.5155 and $D_M - D_L$ = 1.4319. For the medians the results are similar. The distribution of dividends is skewed to the right for the total sample and for the subsamples. This is due to the censoring of the distribution at 0. Also all of the subsamples show an excess kurtosis of similar size.

---

[58] The calculation of the values for E[D], but on a qualitative level the results should be similar.

Table (45) shows the results for the estimated coefficients of the censored regression model. The top row shows the estimation results for the entire sample. Results for the portfolios are presented below. For the entire sample and the subsamples we observe positive coefficients for the dummy variable. A particularly large value of 1.7335 can be observed for the loser portfolio. If profits increase from period t to period $t-1$ this has a positive impact on dividends. A positive coefficient is also obtained for the coefficient on profits: values between 0.13 and 0.19 are obtained for the coefficients of $\Pi(t)$. The values for $\Pi(t-1)$ are substantially smaller. The negative value for $\Pi(t-1)$ for the winner portfolio might be due to interaction with other variables such as the dummy variable and $D(t-1)$. Values which are obtained for dividends are about 0.8 and similar across portfolios.

Comparing the coefficients for different portfolios shows in particular that there are not a lot of differences between the winner and the middle portfolio. The coefficients which are obtained for the payout policy of the loser portfolio however look slightly different. The coefficient on the dummy variable is larger and the coefficient on $\Pi(t)$ is smaller. Whether this difference in the payout policy accounts for a large part of the observed difference in dividends is subject of the Blinder-Oaxaca decomposition.

Table (46) presents the values of the Blinder-Oaxaca decomposition for the latent variable D^*. On the left hand side I present again the means for the observed variable D. Then the latent variable D^* is calculated for the payout policy of the three portfolios. The value 6.4302 in the $D^*[W]$ column and the first row is the value

Table 46. The Blinder-Oaxaca Decomposition for the latent variable for dividends D^*

	D^a	latent variable D^*		
		$D^*[W]\,[^b]$	$D^*[M]\,[^b]$	$D^*[L]\,[^b]$
Winner	6.6822	6.4302	6.4821	6.1480
Middle	5.1667	4.8786	4.8468	4.4127
Loser	3.7348	3.3163	3.1762	2.7206

[a] Mean of the dividend per nominal equity
[b] Mean of the latent variable D^*. As opposed to D, D^* can take negative values and cannot be observed directly. $D^*[W](D^*[M], D^*[L])$ applies the payout function of the winner portfolio (of the middle, the loser portfolio) to the exogenous variables of the winner, the middle, and the loser firms. Hence, the entry for *Winner* and $D^*[W]$ is the latent variable for the winner portfolio (here: 6.4302), whereas the entry for *Winner* and $D^*[M]$ applies the payout function of the middle portfolio to the exogenous variables of the winner portfolio (here: 6.4821)

D^* for the payout policy of the winner portfolio and the exogenous variables of the winner portfolio. The value in the $D^*[M]$ column is the value for the payout policy of the middle portfolio: given the exogenous values of the winner portfolio 6.48 is the value of the uncensored D^* distribution for the payout policy of the middle portfolio.

The values of D^* for the payout policy and the exogenous variables of the same portfolios are on the main diagonal. The differences between these values are to be explained by the Blinder-Oaxaca decomposition. As I have noted above the Blinder-Oaxaca decomposition can be pursued in two ways. Therefore, the results are presented in a matrix. E.g., the difference between D_M^* and D_L^* can be split into $4.8468 - 4.4120 = 0.4348$ (payout policy) and $4.4127 - 2.7206 = 1.6921$ (exogenous variables) or alternatively in $3.1762 - 2.7206 = 0.4556$ (payout policy) and $4.8468 - 3.1762 = 1.6706$ (exogenous variables). In both cases the major part of the difference is due to differences in the exogenous variables rather than the payout policies.

This holds also for the differences between D_W^* and D_M^* and between D_W^* and D_L^*. Differences in the payout policy are captured by differences which occur in a row. Differences in exogenous variables are captured by differences in a column. For the payout policy of the winner portfolio we obtain values of 6.43, 4.87 and 3.31 which capture almost the entire differences in D^*: The major part of the differences in D^* is due to differences in exogenous variables.

Summary
In this appendix I have taken a closer look at the payout decision. Starting from the observed difference in dividends between portfolios I have proposed a Blinder-Oaxaca decomposition: Part of the observed difference in dividends is due to differences in profits and other exogenous variables. Another part is due to differences in the payout policy. Estimating the payout function for the different portfolios, in particular the loser firms appear to pursue a different payout policy than the winner firms. However, the major part of the differences in dividends are due to differences in exogenous variables. Therefore, it is unlikely that the winner-loser effect is driven by differences in the payout policy.

Conclusion

Discovery commences with the awareness of anomaly, i.e., with the recognition that nature has somehow violated the paradigm-induced expectations that govern normal science. (Thomas Kuhn)[59]

The winner-loser effect is an anomaly in the stock market: Stocks which have underperformed the market (the "loser" stocks) outperform the market subsequently. Stocks which have outperformed the market (the "winner" stocks) underperform the market subsequently. Stock returns are predictable from past performance.

The ruling paradigm in financial economics is that stock markets are efficient and stock returns can be explained within a framework of rational asset pricing. The main question of this monograph is whether the winner-loser effect can be explained within this paradigm. An alternative explanation is that stock returns are due to irrational behaviour of market participants. The assumption of irrational behaviour is a potential candidate for a new paradigm.

Empirically, I relate the winner-loser effect to two sets of explanatory variables: the CAPM β and changes in fundamentals such as dividends and profits. The CAPM can explain only a small part of the winner-loser effect. Differences in β between the winner and the loser portfolio are too small to explain the differences in returns between the two portfolios. Alternatively, the winner-loser effect is related to changes in fundamentals.

For the winner-loser effect stock returns and changes in fundamentals move in parallel. This is the main discovery of this monograph. For the winner portfolio a period of increases in profits is followed by a period of decreases. For the loser portfolio a period of decreases is followed by a period of increases. Two interpretations of these findings are presented. According to the new paradigm of irrational behaviour of investors the winner-loser effect is due to an overreaction to positive news in the case of winner firms and of negative news in the case of loser firms. Investors are disappointed by subsequent negative news in the case of winner firms and are surprised by subsequent positive news in the case of loser firms.

An alternative interpretation of these findings arises from the old paradigm of market efficiency. Fundamentals might proxy for changes in the exposure with respect to systematic risk. For the loser portfolio an increase in profits might proxy for an increase in the exposure to systematic risk. For the winner portfolio a decrease in profits might proxy for a decrease in the exposure. Although the CAPM

---

[59] Kuhn (1970), pp. 52 f.

fails to explain the winner-loser effect, the winner-loser effect might still occur in a framework of rational asset pricing. The CAPM might approximate the exposure with respect to systematic risk only imperfectly.

Therefore, the main question of this monograph remains unresolved. Both the old and the new paradigm provide an explanation of the winner-loser effect. Nevertheless, the anomaly of the winner-loser effect has lead to a remarkable discovery: the comovement between stock returns and changes in fundamentals.

The findings of this monograph should be taken as a starting point for further research. A question which deserves further investigation is which are the factors which drive the movements in the underlying fundamentals. The explanation which is proposed in this monograph is that long-term reversals in stock returns are driven by temporary problems of corporate control. The winner firms accumulate equity during the formation period. The additional available free cash flow loosens management control. As a result management performance deteriorates during the test period. The evidence suggests that the management in the winner firms suffers from managerial hubris and builds unprofitable empires. Evidence for the loser firms can be interpreted that the management succeeds in successful reengineering. The increase in labour costs for the winner firms during the test period suggests that after periods of good performance the employees are able to enforce better payments at the cost of the shareholders. These findings provide first evidence that temporary problems in corporate control might contribute to reversals in long run returns.

More research is needed to link problems in corporate control to the performance in terms of stock returns. In particular we need a better theoretical understanding. The question whether agency problems deteriorate the performance of public corporations has already been discussed for a long time. Nevertheless, we still lack a theoretical framework which relates stock returns to agency problems. At first sight this is surprising as for the valuation of a company the influence of agency problems is straightforward. In a rational asset pricing model the value of a company is the sum of its future dividends discounted at an appropriate rate. Agency problems reduce the sum of future dividends. Hence, if the shareholders face difficulties to motivate the management the company should be valued at a discount. The influence of agency problems is more subtle if we turn to a company's performance in terms of stock returns. Agency problems should already be discounted in the actual value of the company. In an equilibrium framework stock returns are determined by their covariance with the pricing kernel. In which way this covariance is influenced by agency problems is far from obvious. As we have shown, if the management creates additional cash flows this might even lead to a decrease in returns as long as these cash flows bear no systematic risk. To understand the underlying pattern in cash flows further research is needed which investigates the interaction between corporate control and stock returns. This monograph has provided first steps.

Results

In the *first* chapter I present an overview of the literature on the winner-loser effect. At the heart of the discussion is the question whether the winner-loser effect occurs within an efficient capital market. Whether the observed pattern in stock returns implies an inefficiency of the capital market is a question which can only be answered conditional on that an asset pricing model holds. Market efficiency cannot be linked to the martingale property of stock prices directly. Under the true probabilities the martingale property would imply market efficiency only if investors were risk neutral. In the case of risk aversion stock prices follow a martingale only under the equivalent martingale measure. The transformation of the true probabilities to the martingale probabilities depends upon the asset pricing model. In the literature three approaches have been pursued to explain the winner-loser effect. The first approach is a purely empirical one. The effect is related to other market anomalies and to lead-lag effects across portfolios. An interaction with the January effect and the size effect can be observed. For shorter time horizons lead-lag effects across portfolios induce autocorrelation in index returns. With respect to market efficiency these findings have no clear implications. The other two approaches address the question of market efficiency directly. Part of the literature claims that the winner-loser effect can be explained by the CAPM. Most researchers reject this hypothesis and resort to models where market participants suffer from irrational behaviour.

In the *second* chapter I investigate the winner-loser effect for the German stock market from 1968-1986. The performance of stocks is analyzed conditional on past performance. Stocks are sorted into five equally weighted portfolios according to their past performance. Depending on the investment horizon, different strategies turn out to be profitable. A momentum strategy is profitable for a one year investment horizon. Former winner firms outperform former loser firms by 3.24% p.a. For an investment horizon of two years or longer I obtain the reverse result. Former loser firms outperform former winner firms. A maximum excess return of 3.27% p.a. is obtained for five years. The evidence is based on a sample where observations from different overlapping investment periods are pooled. Without pooling the evidence is considerably weaker, albeit still significant in many cases. Long-term reversals could be due to a survivorship bias: If former loser firms were more likely to drop out of the sample and were therefore left out of the investigation this would bias the result in favour of a reversal. For my sample I do not observe a survivorship bias: winner firms are more likely to drop out of the sample than loser firms. Hence, the reported evidence understates the winner-loser effect. In addition the observed reversal is mainly due to an underperformance of the winner portfolio as compared to the middle portfolio. In a complementary investigation I determine a transition matrix: I estimate the probabilities of stocks to switch from a portfolio during the first five years to a portfolio during the next five years. The pattern of transition probabilities also implies reversals in the cross section of stock returns. The probability to switch from an extreme portfolio to a middle portfolio and vice versa is larger than to remain in the same portfolio. The coefficients of a general linear model also hint into this direction.

In the *third* chapter I provide the theoretical framework for my analysis. First, I present the framework of rational asset pricing. Starting from a condition of no arbitrage I derive a general asset pricing model. Expected returns are determined by the relationship between stock returns and the pricing kernel. A special case of this general asset pricing model is the CAPM. In the CAPM stock returns are determined by their exposure to the market return. Afterwards I present two frameworks for the analysis of the relationship between stock returns and fundamentals. According to the first framework the winner-loser effect is due to a surprise effect. Unexpected changes in fundamentals lead to unexpected returns. According to the second framework the winner-loser effect occurs within a framework of rational asset pricing: Expected changes in fundamentals lead to expected returns. This idea is developed in a stylized setting. Stock returns are measured against the benchmark of the market return, which is modelled as a geometric random walk. Together with a pricing kernel which shows constant elasticity this implies myopia on the level of market returns. To model the cash flows of the individual stocks I also use a geometric structure. The stochastic increment consists out of an 'idiosyncratic' component and a 'market' component which is proportional to the market increment. It turns out that within this framework the driving force of the winner-loser effect must be the market component. Parallel reversals in stock returns and fundamentals might be due to a cyclical exposure with respect to the market cash flow.

In the *fourth* chapter I investigate to which extent the CAPM is able to explain the observed pattern in stock returns. If the observed long-term reversals occur in a framework of rational asset pricing they must be due to changes in the exposure with respect to systematic risk. In the CAPM this exposure is measured by β. For the winner portfolio I observe a decrease of β from the formation to the test period, for the loser portfolio I observe an increase. During the test period the β of the loser portfolio exceeds the β of the winner portfolio by 0.2045. These findings support the view that the winner-loser effect is driven by changes in systematic risk. However, the risk premium is not large enough to explain the observed excess return of 3.27% p.a., it explains only 0.82% p.a.

In the *fifth* chapter I relate the observed pattern in excess returns to changes in fundamentals such as dividends and profits. I investigate whether the time series pattern in stock returns is parallelled by changes in fundamentals. For long-term reversals the reported evidence is supportive. For the winner portfolio a significant increase in fundamentals during the formation period is followed by a significant decrease during the test period. For an investment horizon of 60 months profits per nominal equity increase from 17.09% to 23.45% and decrease to a level of 16.51% afterwards. The reverse pattern can be observed for the loser portfolio. For the same time horizon profits per nominal equity decrease from 17.19% to 9.71% and increase again to 13.91%. Similar patterns can be observed for other time horizons. No comovement can be observed for short-term persistence. In addition, I investigate the following profit decomposition. I split profits into an ordinary part which captures normal business activities, a financial part which captures profits from financial activities of the firm, and an extraordinary part. Upswings in returns are driven by changes in financial income, downswings are driven by changes in ordinary income. Extraordinary income shows contrarian movements as compared to total profits. This might indicate that the management uses its discretion with respect to extraordinary income to smooth total profits.

In a second empirical part I investigate whether one can use fundamental information to differentiate between the winner and the loser portfolio. Portfolios have been built conditional on past returns. If the driving force of returns are changes in fundamentals it should be possible to use changes in fundamentals to mimick this selection process. Relying on fundamentals almost 80% of the stocks were sorted into the correct portfolios for the formation period. The discriminatory power of fundamentals is considerably weaker during the test period: the correct matching decreases to a level of 63%. This finding hints towards an asymmetry between the formation and the subsequent test period. Due to the research design of the winner-loser effect for the formation period one investigates realized returns, whereas for the test period expected returns are investigated. The relationship between realized excess returns and realized cash flows is closer than for expected returns and expected cash flows.

In a third step I investigate whether changes in fundamentals capture changes in the exposure with respect to systematic risk. Within the framework of the CAPM I find supportive evidence for this claim. In a regression analysis I relate changes in fundamentals to the market return. During the test period the change in profits is negatively related to the market return for the winner portfolio. It is positively related for the loser portfolio. Hence, for the winner portfolio the decrease in fundamentals captures a decrease in the exposure with respect to systematic risk. For the loser portfolio the increase captures an increase in the exposure.

The *sixth* chapter compares the explanatory power of fundamentals and the CAPM β directly. The results from the fourth and the fifth chapter have indicated that changes in fundamentals might be better able to explain the cross section of stock returns than the CAPM. This hypothesis is investigated by means of a regression analysis in two ways. Stock returns are mainly determined by information which is revealed during the same period. In an *ex ante* approach this information is excluded from the regression analysis, in an *ex post* analysis I include this information. In both regressions fundamentals and changes in fundamentals have more explanatory power than the CAPM variables β. Almost no information is lost if β is left out from the ex ante regression. The explanatory power of the regressions is measured by R^2, which is the explained part of the variation in stock returns as a ratio of the total variation in stock returns. For the ex ante analysis I obtain an explanatory power of up to 7.96%. For the ex post analysis this power increases to a level of 32.76%. The explanatory power of the ex ante regression increases if one investigates portfolios instead of single stocks. For the ex post regression the explanatory power increases if one investigates longer investment horizons. In both cases, the total variation in returns reduces faster than the explained part of the variation.

In the *last* section I pursue the hypothesis that the observed pattern in stock returns is driven by temporary problems of corporate control. I find supportive evidence for this claim for equity, for size, and for labour costs. At the beginning of the test period loser firms have less equity available than winner firms. This might induce a tighter control of the management of the loser firms and a better performance during the test period. The development of the size of the companies suggests managerial hubris and empire building for the winner firms which continue to grow during the test period and successful reengineering for the loser firms which shrink and become more successful during the test period. Labour costs for the winner portfolio increase after the formation period. This might be due to an increase of the bargaining power of the employees after the companies' successful performance during the formation period. No supportive results are obtained for additional hypotheses which are formulated with respect to short-term debt, fixed assets, and the payout ratio. A Blinder Oaxaca decomposition for dividends hints into the same direction. Differences in dividends between portfolios are mainly due to differences in the underlying profit distributions rather than to differences in the payout policy.

A final Remark: Data snooping

"The reliance of economic science upon nonexperimental inference is, at once, one of the most challenging and most nettlesome aspects of the discipline." (Lo and MacKinlay (1999), p. 213). Recently a lot of attention has been drawn to problems of "data snooping".[60] Data snooping occurs if properties of the data are used to guide subsequent research (cf. Aldous (1989), p. 252). This problem can influence the reliability of test statistics severely. Therefore, one should avoid data snooping as far as possible, otherwise one has to correct for data snooping explicitly.

Also the analysis presented in this monograph might suffer from the problem of data snooping. The largest return on a winner-loser strategy has been observed for an investment horizon of 5 years. Chapter 4 and 6 and also the third part of my analysis (chapter 7) refer to this investment horizon. It is therefore an important question to which extent this selection biases the analysis.

One of the main questions of my analysis has been to which extent the observed pattern in stock returns is driven by movements in fundamentals. This question has been investigated in chapter 5. This analysis is pursued for all investment horizons and can therefore not be subject to the problem of data snooping. In that chapter the investment horizon of 5 years has not turned out to be special. This can be taken as a first hint that the choice of this investment horizon does not harm the analysis.

---

[60] For a comprehensive overview cf. Lo and MacKinlay (1999), chapter 8.

Although chapter 4 and 6 rely mainly on an investment horizon of 60 months both of them present additional evidence which might alleviate the problem of data snooping. In the analysis so far stock returns from different sample periods have been pooled. In chapter 4 the analysis is pursued on a yearly basis. This allows to investigate whether there is a lot of variation in excess returns from year to year. This analysis might help to find out whether the winner-loser effect is driven by single years which are special. Such a finding would hint to a data snooping bias. As such a pattern cannot be observed, such a bias is less likely. In the second part of chapter 6 time horizon effects are investigated explicitly. In this section the investment horizon of 5 years is only a starting point for the analysis. Again, this investment horizon does not turn out to be special.

The part of my analysis which is most likely to suffer from problems of data snooping is the third part which relates the winner-loser effect to problems of corporate governance. The analysis in this part is indeed subject to a qualification. More research is needed which also looks at other investment horizons. However, the main contribution of that part of my analysis is on a conceptual level. It is a first attempt to link the behaviour in the stock market to problems of corporate governance. Additional research and a multivariate approach is needed to obtain a better understanding of the underlying structure. My analysis has provided first steps.

References

Aldous, D. (1989): Probability Approximations via the Poisson Clumping Heuristic. Springer, New York

Alonso, A., Rubio, G. (1990): Overreaction in the Spanish Equity Market. Journal of Banking and Finance 14, 469-481

Bain, J. S. (1956): Barriers to New Competition. Harvard University Press, Cambridge (Massachusetts)

Ball, R., Kothari, S. P. (1989): Nonstationary expected returns: Implications for tests of market efficiency and serial correlation in returns. Journal of Financial Economics 25, 51-74

Banz, R. W. (1981): The Relationship between Return and Market Value of Common Stocks. Journal of Financial Economics 9, 3-18

Barberis, N., Shleifer, A., Vishny, R. (1998): A Model of Investor Sentiment. Journal of Financial Economics 49, 307-343

Beaver, W. H., Lambert, R. A., Morse, D. (1980): The information content of security prices. Journal of Accounting and Economics 2, 3-28

Beaver, W. H., Lambert, R. A., Ryan, S. G. (1987): The Information Content of Security Prices - A Second Look. Journal of Accounting and Economics 9, 139-157

Beaver, W. H., McAnally, M. L., Stinson, C. H. (1997): The information content of earnings and prices: A simultaneous equations approach. Journal of Accounting and Economics 23, 53-81

Berger, P., Ofek, E. (1995): Diversification's effect on firm value. Journal of Financial Economics 37, 39-65

Berglof, E., von Thadden, E.-L. (1994): Short-term versus long-term interests: Capital Structure with multiple investors. Quarterly Journal of Economics 109, 1055-1084

Bernard, V. L., Thomas, J. K. (1990): Evidence that stock prices do not fully reflect the implications of current earnings for future earnings. Journal of Accounting and Economics 13, 305-340

Bick, A. (1990): On Viable Diffusion Price Processes of the Market Portfolio. Journal of Finance 45, 259-275

Black, F., Scholes, M. (1973): The Pricing of Options and Corporate Liabilities. Journal of Political Economy 81, 637-654

Blinder, A. S. (1973): Wage Discrimination: Reduced Form and Structural Estimates. Journal of Human Resources 18(4), 436-455

Breeden, D. (1979): An intertemporal asset pricing model with stochastic consumption and investment opportunities. Journal of Financial Economics 7, 265-296

Büning, H., Trenkler, G. (1978): Nichtparametrische statistische Methoden. De Gruyter, Berlin

Campbell, J. Y. (1991): A Variance Decomposition for Stock Returns. Economic Journal 101, 157-179

Campbell, J. Y., Lo, A. W., MacKinlay, A. C. (1997): The Econometrics of Financial Markets. Princeton University Press, Princeton

Chan, K. C. (1988): On the Contrarian Investment Strategy. Journal of Business 61, 147-163.

Chopra, N., Lakonishok, J., Ritter, J. (1992): Measuring Abnormal Performance: Do Stocks Overreact? Journal of Financial Economics 9, 3-18

Daniel, K., Hirshleifer, D., Subrahmanyam, A. (1998): A Theory of Overconfidence, Self-Attribution, and Security Market Under- and Overreactions. Journal of Finance 53, 1839-1885

Darity, W., Guilkey, D., Winfrey, W. (1995): Ethnicity, Race, and Earnings. Economic Letters 47, 401-408

Davidson, J. (1994): Lecture Notes: Methods of Economic Investigation, Lent Term. London School of Economics

DeBondt, W. F. M., Thaler, R. H. (1985): Does the Stock Market overreact? Journal of Finance 40, 793-805

— (1987): Further Evidence on Investor Overreaction and Stock Market Seasonality. Journal of Finance 42, 557-581

DeLong, J., Shleifer, A., Summers, L., Waldmann, R. (1990): Positive Feedback Investment Strategies and Destabilizing Rational Speculation. Journal of Finance 45, 379-395

Dothan, M. U. (1990): Prices in Financial Markets. Oxford University Press, Oxford

Dressendörfer, M. (1998): Zyklische und antizyklische Handelsstrategien am Schweizer Aktienmarkt. Working paper, University of St. Gallen

Duffie, D. (1988): Security Markets - Stochastic Models. Academic Press, Boston

Easterbrook, F. (1984): Two agency cost explanations of dividends. American Economic Review 74, 650-659

Easton, P., Harris, T. (1991): Earnings as an Explanatory Variable for Returns. Journal of Accounting Research 29, 19-36

Easton, P. D., Harris, T. S., Ohlson, J. A. (1992): Aggregate accounting earnings can explain most of security returns. Journal of Accounting and Economics 15, 119-142

Elton, E. J., Gruber, M. J. (1995): Modern Portfolio Theory and Investment Analysis. John Wiley & Sons, New York, 5th edn.

Fairlie, R. W. (1999): The Absence of the African-American Owned Business: An Analysis of the Dynamics of Self-Employment. Journal of Labor Economics 17, 80-108

Fama, E. F. (1970): Efficient Capital Markets: A Review of Theory and Empirical Work. Journal of Finance 25, 383-417

— (1976): Foundations of Finance. Basic Books, New York

— (1991): Efficient Capital Markets: II. Journal of Finance 46, 1575-1617

Fama, E. F., French, K. R. (1988): Permanent and temporary components of stock prices. Journal of Political Economy 96, 246-273

— (1996): Multifactor Explanations of Asset Pricing Anomalies. Journal of Finance 51, 55-84

Fama, E. F., MacBeth, J. (1973): Risk, Return, and Equilibrium: Empirical Tests. Journal of Political Economy 71, 607-636

Ferson, W. E. (1995): Theory and Empirical Testing of Asset Pricing Models. In Finance (Handbook in Operations Research and Management Science), ed. by V. Maksimovic, Robert E. Jarrow, and W. Ziemba, pp. 145-200. North Holland, Amsterdam

Franke, G. (1984): Conditions for Myopic Valuation and Independence of the Market Excess Return in Discrete Time Models. Journal of Finance 39, 423-442

Franke, G., Hax, H. (1999): Finanzwirtschaft des Unternehmens und Kapitalmarkt. Springer, Berlin, 4th edn.

Franke, G., Stapleton, R. C., Subrahmanyam, M. G. (1998): Who Buys and Who Sells Options? The Role of Options in an Economy with Background Risk. Journal of Economic Theory 82, 89-109

— (1999): When are Options Overpriced? The Black-Scholes Model and Alternative Characterisations of the Pricing Kernel. To appear in: European Finance Review

Goodwin, R. M. (1967): A Growth Cycle. In Socialism, Capitalism and Economic Growth, ed. by C. H. Feinstein, pp. 54-58, Cambridge

Greene, W. H. (1997): Econometric Analysis. Prentice-Hall, New Jersey, 3rd edn.

Harris, M., Raviv, A. (1991): The Theory of Capital Structure. Journal of Finance 46, 297-355

Harris, T. S., Lang, M., Möller, H. P. (1994): The Value Relevance of German Accounting Measures: An Empirical Analysis. Journal of Accounting Research 32, 187-209

Harrisson, M., Kreps, D. (1979): Martingales and Arbitrage in Multiperiod Securities Markets. Journal of Economic Theory 20, 381-408

Hendry, D. F., Pagan, A. R., Sargan, J. D. (1984): Dynamic Specification. In Handbook of Econometrics, ed. by Z. Griliches, and M. D. Intriligator. Amsterdam, North Holland

Hollander, M., Wolfe, D. A. (1973): Nonparametric Statistical Methods. John Wiley & Sons, New York

Hong, H., Stein, J. C. (1997): A Unified Theory of Underreaction, Momentum Trading, and Overreaction in Asset Markets. Working paper, Stanford Business School and MIT Sloan School of Management

Hosmer, D. H., Lemeshow, S. (1989): Applied Logistic Regression. John Wiley & Sons, New York

Ippolito, R. A. (1989): Efficiency with costly information: A study of mutual fund performance, 1965-1984. Quarterly Journal of Economics 54, 1-23

Jegadeesh, N. (1990): Evidence of Predictable Behavior of Security Returns. Journal of Finance 45, 881-898

Jegadeesh, N., Titman, S. (1993): Returns to Buying Winners and Selling Losers: Implications for Stock Market Efficiency. Journal of Finance 46, 1427-1444

Jensen, M. (1986): Agency costs of free cash flow, corporate finance, and take-overs. American Economic Review 76, 323-329

Judge, G. G., Hill, R. C., Griffiths, W. E., Lütkepohl, H., Lee, T.-C. (1988): Intro-duction to the Theory and Practice of Econometrics. John Wiley & Sons, New York, 2nd edn.

Kahnemann, D., Tversky, A. (1982): Intuitive Prediction: Biases and Corrective Procedures. In Judgement under Uncertainty: Heuristics and Biases, ed. by D. Kahneman, P. Slovic, and A. Tversky, pp. 327-351

Kendall, M. G. (1962): Rank Correlation Methods. Griffin, London, 3rd edn.

Kreps, D. M., Porteus, E. L. (1978): Temporal resolution of uncertainty and dy-namic choice theory. Econometrica 46, 185-200

Kruschwitz, L. (1995): Finanzierung und Investition. Berlin

Kuhn, T. (1970): The Structure of Scientific Revolutions. Chicago University Press, Chicago

Lee, C. F. (1993): Statistics for Business and Financial Economics. D. C. Heath & Co., Lexington (Mass.)

LeRoy, S. F. (1973): Risk Aversion and the Martingale Property of Stock Prices. International Economic Review 14, 436-446

— (1989): Efficient Capital Markets and Martingales. Journal of Economic Literature 27, 1583-1621

Lev, B. (1980): On the usefulness of earnings: Lessons and directions from two decades of empirical research. Supplement of Journal of Accounting Research 27, 153-192

Litzenberger, R., Ramaswamy, K. (1979): The Effect of Personal Taxes and Dividends on Capital Asset Prices: Theory and Evidence. Journal of Financial Economics 7, 163-196

Lo, A. W., MacKinlay, A. C. (1990): When are contrarian profits due to stock market overreaction? Review of Financial Studies 3, 175-205

— (1999): A Non-Random Walk Down Wall Street. Princeton University Press, Princeton

Lucas, R. E. (1978): Asset Prices in an Exchange Economy. Econometrica 46, 1429-1445

MacKinlay, A. C., Richardson, M. (1991): Using Generalized Methods of Moments to Test Mean-Variance Efficiency. Journal of Finance 46, 511-527

McCullagh, P., Nelder, J. A. (1989): Generalized Linear Models. Chapman and Hill, London, 2nd edn.

Meyer, B. (1994): Der Overreaction-Effekt am deutschen Aktienmarkt - Einordnung und empirische Untersuchung der langfristigen Überreaktion, Schriftenreihe der SBZ-Bank, Vol. 8. Fritz Knapp Verlag, Frankfurt am Main

— (1999): Intertemporal Asset Pricing - Evidence from Germany. Springer

Miller, M. H. (1986): Behavioral Rationality in Finance: The Case of Dividends. Journal of Business 59, 451-468

Neftci, S. N. (1996): An Introduction to the Mathematics of Financial Derivatives. San Diego

Oaxaca, R. (1973): Male Female Wage Differentials in Urban Labor Markets. International Economic Review 14(3), 693-709

Ohlson, J. A. (1992): The theory of value and earnings, and an introduction to the Ball-Brown analysis. Contemporary Accounting Research 8, 1-19

Ohlson, J. A., Shroff, P. K. (1992): Changes versus Levels in Earnings as Explanatory Variables for Returns: Some Theoretical Considerations. Journal of Accounting Research 30, 210-226

Poterba, J. M., Summers, L. (1988): Mean Reversion in Stock Prices. Journal of Financial Economics 22, 27-59

Richardson, M., Smith, T. (1991): Test of Financial Models with the Presence of Overlapping Observations. Review of Financial Studies 4, 227-254

Richardson, M., Stock, J. H. (1989): Drawing Inferences from Statistics based on Multiyear Asset Returns. Journal of Financial Economics 25, 323-348

Roberts, H. V. (1967): Statistical versus Clinical Prediction of the Stock Market. Unpublished paper, University of Chicago

Roll, R. (1977): A critique of the asset pricing theory's tests - Part I: On past and potential testability of the theory. Journal of Financial Economics 4, 129-176.

— (1984): A Simple Implicit Measure of the Effective Bid-Ask Spread in an Efficient Market. Journal of Finance 39, 1127-1140

Ross, S. A. (1976): The arbitrage theory of capital asset pricing. Journal of Economic Theory 13, 341-360

Rozeff, M. (1982): Growth, beta and agency costs as determinants of dividend payout ratios. Journal of Financial Research 5, 249-259

Samuelson, P. A. (1965): Proof That Properly Anticipated Prices Fluctuate Randomly. Industrial Management Review 6, 41-49

Schiereck, D., Weber, M. (1995): Zyklische und antizyklische Handelsstrategien am deutschen Aktienmarkt. Zeitschrift für betriebswirtschaftliche Forschung 47, 3-24

Servaes, H. (1996): The value of Diversification during the conglomerate merger Wave. Journal of Finance 51, 1201-1225

Shanken, J. (1992): On the Estimation of Beta-Pricing Models. Review of Financial Studies 5, 1-34

Shleifer, A., Vishny, R. W. (1997): A Survey of Corporate Governance. Journal of Finance 52, 737-783

Stapleton, R. C., Subrahmanyam, M. G. (1978): A multiperiod equilibrium asset pricing model. Econometrica 46, 1077-1096

— (1990): Risk Aversion and the Intertemporal Behavior of Asset Prices. Review of Financial Studies 3, 677-693

Stock, D. (1990): Winner and Loser Anomalies in the German Stock Market. Journal of Institutional and Theoretical Economics 146, 518-529

Sutton, J. (1990): Explaining Everything, Explaining Nothing? Game Theoretic Models in Industrial Economics. European Economic Review 34, 505-512

— (1991): Sunk Costs and Market Structure - Price Competition, Advertising, and the Evolution of Concentration. MIT Press, Cambridge (Massachusetts)

Vermaelen, T., Verstringe, M. (1986): Do Belgians overreact? Working paper, Catholic University of Leuven

Zarowin, P. (1989): Does the stock market overreact to corporate earnings information? Journal of Finance 44, 1385-1400

Author Index

Index

Lecture Notes in Economics
and Mathematical Systems

For information about Vols. 1–320
please contact your bookseller or Springer-Verlag